Praise for *Temptation* by

"Given how reluctant we are to ask tough questions about our behavior, Mr. Akst's approach is a helpful one, inviting a wide audience to think hard about a difficult problem and offering some ideas for solving it." —*The Wall Street Journal*

"As Akst recognizes, arguments about the reality of personal autonomy have political resonances. . . . Willpower, Akst says, is like a muscle that can be strengthened but is susceptible to exhaustion."
—George F. Will, *The Washington Post*

"There is power in naming the problem, and this is part of what makes Akst's book good. He lays it all out—all the many ways in which the modern matrix acts upon our psyches to our physical and emotional detriment. But the book is also good because it is positive, dedicated to seeking solutions." —*The New Yorker Book Bench* blog

"As Americans have learned to embrace their desires and break away from stern Puritan traditions, 'the only thing left is to avoid killing ourselves with our newfound freedom.'" —Bloomberg Business Week

"In a book full of startling facts, this might be the most startling: of the 2.5 million deaths in the U.S. annually, 'something approaching half could be prevented . . . if people simply managed to lead healthier lives.' . . . It is this kind of willful self-destruction, Akst concludes, that's killing us in greater and greater numbers. A very thought-provoking and colorfully written book." —*Booklist*

"You wouldn't be able to stop yourself from reading this book! Daniel Akst is among the sharpest, most perceptive writers of his generation, and he is in fine form in *Temptation*."

—Gregg Easterbrook, author of *Sonic Boom*

"This book entertains even as it pokes at our most sensitive spots. Daniel Akst handles the touchiest heretical ideas with charm, humor, and painless scholarship. With no ax to grind, no cause to serve but reason he opens up the foregone conclusions by which we live and leaves a reader with new and alternate views of ourselves and others. Like the finest essayists Akst makes the deepest ideas fascinating and fun to read."

—Nicholas von Hoffman

"The more a society progresses, the bigger a problem self-control turns out to be. If you wish to be ahead of the curve for understanding America's problems, Dan Akst's excellent and informative book is the place to start."

—Tyler Cowen, professor of economics at George Mason University and cocreator of *The Marginal Revolution* blog

PENGUIN BOOKS

TEMPTATION

Daniel Akst has written for the *New York Times,* the *Wall Street Journal,* the *Los Angeles Times,* and many other publications. His previous books include *Wonder Boy,* which chronicled the wondrous financial fraud he had a hand in exposing, and the novels *St. Burl's Obituary* (a PEN/Faulkner finalist) and *The Webster Chronicle.* He lives with his wife and sons in New York's bucolic Hudson Valley, generally a good place to hide from temptation.

Temptation

FINDING SELF-CONTROL IN AN AGE OF EXCESS

Daniel Akst

PENGUIN BOOKS

Previously published as *We Have Met the Enemy*

PENGUIN BOOKS

Published by the Penguin Group

Penguin Group (USA) Inc., 375 Hudson Street, New York,

New York 10014, U.S.A • Penguin Group (Canada), 90 Eglinton Avenue East,

Suite 700, Toronto, Ontario, Canada M4P2Y3 (a division of Pearson Penguin Canada Inc.) •

Penguin Books Ltd, 80 Strand, London WC2R 0RL, England • Penguin Ireland, 25 St. Stephen's

Green, Dublin 2, Ireland (a division of Penguin Books Ltd) • Penguin Books Australia Ltd,

250 Camberwell Road, Camberwell, Victoria 3124, Australia (a division of Pearson Australia

Group Pty Ltd) • Penguin Books India Pvt Ltd, 11 Community Centre, Panchsheel Park,

New Delhi—110 017, India • Penguin Group (NZ), 67 Apollo Drive, Rosedale,

Auckland 0632, New Zealand (a division of Pearson New Zealand Ltd) •

Penguin Books (South Africa) (Pty) Ltd, 24 Sturdee Avenue, Rosebank,

Johannesburg 2196, South Africa

Penguin Books Ltd, Registered Offices: 80 Strand, London WC2R 0RL, England

First published in the United States of America as *We Have Met the Enemy* by The Penguin Press,
a member of Penguin Group (USA) Inc. 2011
Published in Penguin Books 2011

1 3 5 7 9 10 8 6 4 2

THE LIBRARY OF CONGRESS HAS CATALOGED THE HARDCOVER EDITION AS FOLLOWS:

Akst, Daniel.

We have met the enemy : self-control in an age of excess / Daniel Akst.

p. cm.

Includes bibliographical references and index.

ISBN 978-1-59420-281-0 (hc.)

ISBN 978-0-14-312080-3 (pbk.)

1. Self-control.   2. Moderation.   3. Supply and demand.   I. Title.

BF632.A35 2011

153.8—dc22

2010028525

Printed in the United States of America
DESIGNED BY AMANDA DEWEY

The life of every man is a diary in which he means to write one story, and writes another.

—J. M. Barrie

Contents

Preface   *xi*

1. A Democracy of Excess   *1*

2. Sickening Excess   *17*

3. On Having Yourself Committed   *32*

4. The Cost of Good Inventions   *45*

5. The Perils of Prosperity   *55*

6. Self-control and Social Change   *70*

7. The Greek Way   *81*

8. The Marshmallow Test   *96*

9. The Seesaw Struggle   *110*

10. Let My People Go   *121*

11. The Intimate Contest   *132*

12. The Mind-Body Problem   *146*

13. Self-control, Free Will, and Other Oxymorons   *161*

14. Odysseus and the Pigeons   *175*

15. Crimes of Passion   *192*

16. Addiction, Compulsion, and Choice   *203*

17. Tomorrow Is Another Day   *212*

18. Cutting Loose   *227*

19. Government and Self-government   *239*

20. Being Your Own Godfather   *251*

21. Carpe Diem   *261*

Acknowledgments   *277*
Notes   *279*
Index   *293*

Preface

For a writer in today's marketplace, moderation is an affliction. There's something to be said for bourgeois respectability, of course, but nobody wants to read memoirs about heroic retirement saving, the Sturm und Drang of predawn carpooling, or the epic compromises that, strung together over the decades, produce an enduring marriage. All writers know this.

"The tranquil current of domestic happiness affords no materials for narrative," Mary Brunton concluded two centuries ago in a didactic novel called *Self-Control*. "The joys that spring from chastened affection, tempered desires, useful employment, and devout meditation, must be felt—they cannot be described." This is a truth universally acknowledged, which may be why Brunton has her heroine flee an evil boyfriend by tying herself to a birch-bark canoe and plunging over a Canadian waterfall. People made fun of that ending, but it sold books.

The same sort of thing sells nowadays, too, except it's the writer's hair-raising escape from his own demons that rings up the registers. A book about self-control today ought rightly to be about the author's struggles (however embroidered) to conquer some fiendish addiction.

The problem is that, despite my best efforts, nobody could lead a more humdrum life than I do. Although I check my e-mail a little too often, I am not addicted to anything. I do not even struggle with my weight, except—and this is embarrassing—for when it gets too low. I've had my excesses over the years, but the sad fact is that I never quite manage to take them to excess. Nor does religious fervor move me to ecstasy or wrath. In general I am deaf to spirituality; the main thing I do religiously is maintain our cars. I will admit that in Las Vegas once, on assignment, I developed a gambling problem. The problem was that I lost $10 on the Penn-Dartmouth football game, the sting of which is with me still. Some years after this youthful binge I married my dentist, compared to whom I am the long-lost twin of Amy Winehouse raised by wolves.

Yet even I have self-control problems. Do you have any idea how long it took me to buckle down to work on the paragraphs you just read? First, of course, I had to explore the vast discography of the pianist Paul Bley via the Internet, that accursed underminer of all our best intentions. In doing so I naturally worked up quite an appetite, which meant time out for food, followed by a restorative nap. While "working" on this same section I also found time to add to my remarkable e-mail oeuvre, dispatching messages of unparalleled artistry and wit to correspondents the world over. (As it is for most writers these days, e-mail is by far the form in which I am most prolific.) I did some laundry, went to the gym, and took measurements for various household repairs that I'm still putting off. I even kept a close eye on techbargains.com for—well, for some great tech bargains, the nature of which I haven't yet imagined.

Now, during all this frantic self-distraction, I knew somewhere deep inside that sooner or later I really would *have* to write this preface—and that the longer it took the less money and self-regard I would have. As time went by I grew anxious, and finally even furious. After a while I was practically desperate to get going. Yet somehow, for days on end, I failed to yoke my actions to what I could have sworn all along was my will, leaving the necessary work undone. The question is, how can such a thing possibly happen? Why, in other words, is self-control so difficult?

And why does it seem to be so much harder for some people than for others? Is it a matter of circumstances? Or maybe it's a matter of just a single circumstance—the circumstance of birth, in which our ancestors perform the function of the Fates, investing our DNA with our destiny. What if even your garden-variety, mild-mannered, house-maintaining dad is programmed to someday run amok like the Manchurian Candidate or the Malaysian *pengamoks* who gave us the term?

This book is the result of my attempt to find some answers. In searching for them, I discovered all sorts of interesting things—including the extent to which procrastination has been an enduring occupational hazard for writers. Victor Hugo, to cite a single example, supposedly ordered his valet to confiscate his clothes so he wouldn't go off and waste time doing something—anything!—other than writing. Even the prolific Irving Wallace, who cranked out commercial fiction the way Ben Bernanke cranks out greenbacks in a crisis, had to face this problem, which he addressed in an academic paper called "Self-Control Techniques of Famous Novelists."

What a relief to learn that, despite my boring rectitude, I share at least one of the characteristic failings of my scribbling brethren, for an excess of propriety is troubling in a writer. As a novelist familiar with the erratic history of my tribe, I'm all too aware of how often the lives of writers appear to be out of control, and after wallowing in the subject for a while, I came away afflicted with a worrisomely Calvinist perspective on my own feeble career. Think of Coleridge's opium habit or Faulkner's drinking. Alcoholism, debauchery, and other such excesses might not assure greatness, but what if they are God's signs of literary grace—precious markers suggesting that you are, after so much doubt, really among the elect? And what if, despite filling in "writer" year after year on your tax returns, you had none of these markers whatsoever?

I console myself that obscurity likely beckons regardless of my excesses or any lack thereof. Meanwhile, we scribes without addictions can at least claim to be sensibly following Flaubert, who urged us to "be regular and orderly in your life . . . so that you may be violent and original in your work."

The pages that follow are as violent and original as I could make them. Book buyers, take note.

Temptation

1

A Democracy of Excess

Liberty is dangerous.

—ALBERT CAMUS

Large, amiable Greg Kilgore clearly retains a sense of wonder about what he does. A friend, he reports, has told him of an 800-pound man whose death posed a problem for the local morgue: they were unable to jam his massive corpse into the freezer. Kilgore hears such stories because he sells motorized toilets for fat people. Very fat people. The LiftSeat 600 is so named because it will smoothly raise a person of 600 pounds to a standing position. A person of that weight should be as rare as he is enormous, but the number and size of such superobese Americans is growing fast, and LiftSeat Corp. is eager to keep up with a changing marketplace. So on its next model, Kilgore discloses, "We're looking to go to 750."

I encountered Kilgore at the twenty-sixth annual meeting of the American Society for Metabolic and Bariatric Surgery, held at a resort outside of Dallas, where I discovered that products for people weighing even 750 pounds aren't necessarily sufficient these days. Other vendors were showcasing electronic scales that could weigh someone of 1,000 pounds to within 100 grams of accuracy (wirelessly transmitting the results to a computer), and operating tables four feet wide instead of the usual three. A clever inflatable mattress for elevating the obese without endangering caregivers (or requiring a team of stevedores) was rated for 1,700 pounds—not so very far short of a ton. Surreally, most of the vendors had bowls of candy on their tables, as if determined to drum up more weight-reduction surgeries even among players in the weight-reduction industry.

The rise of bariatric surgery, which limits caloric intake by walling off parts of the stomach or removing some intestine, speaks volumes about the dilemma that is the subject of this book: the challenge of moderation in the face of freedom and affluence. A generation ago, when obesity was still relatively rare, restricting calories by brute surgical force was virtually unheard of. Today, with two-thirds of American adults overweight and nearly half of those qualifying as obese, weight-loss surgery is so common that a whole industry has sprung up around it. We now have medical centers that do nothing but bariatric operations, finance companies to help patients pay for them, and Web sites to help doctors, in the words of one vendor, "take away the roadblocks for getting patients to the table." While American manufacturers of cars and other such standbys have been in decline for years, business is booming for domestic producers of industrial-strength gurneys and extra-long laparoscopic devices (the better to penetrate all those layers of fat). Nowadays, a remarkable 220,000 weight-loss surgeries are performed in this country annually.

Those operations are a sign of just how hard it can be to control ourselves in a world that appeals ever more effectively to our desires—even if these happen to be desires we'd prefer not to indulge. Self-control is by its nature a conundrum; why, after all, if nobody is holding a gun to my head and my wishes do not violate the laws of physics, shouldn't I be able to carry out my own will as easily as I might take a step or dial a telephone? But it's a conundrum that is especially urgent today, when our surroundings so insistently beckon us to excess. In 2006, for example, the most recent full year unsullied by financial panic, lenders sent Americans nearly 8 billion direct-mail credit card solicitations, each one an invitation to financial trouble. No doubt some of the resulting new plastic was used to grab a fattening bite to eat, since the number of fast food outlets per capita grew more than fivefold from 1970 to 2004.

Or how about gambling? In 1970 casinos were legal only in Nevada, while New Hampshire, New Jersey, and New York were the only states with lotteries. Today the picture is almost entirely reversed, with every state but Utah and Hawaii having legalized casinos or lotteries or both. And if near-ubiquity isn't convenient enough, the Internet entices at all hours with offshore "virtual" casinos accessible from the comfort and privacy of home.

These kinds of changes make daily life, for many of us, an ongoing test of self-control. It's not that we have less willpower than we used to, but rather that modern life immerses us daily in a set of temptations far more evolved than we are. The ideology of temptation has changed, too, so that it's guilt now, rather than indulgence, that has a bad name. By now we've learned to exalt the passions, forget our longstanding obsession with the afterlife, and shake off the dour Puritan traditions to which we still imagine ourselves beholden; the only thing left is to avoid killing ourselves with our newfound freedom. For in our fair land the weapons of mass consumption—McDonald's, credit cards, the Internet—are everywhere.

Yet while temptations have multiplied like fast food outlets in suburbia, the superstructure of external restraint that once helped check our impulses has been weakened by loosening social constraints, the inexorable march of technology, and the same powerfully subversive force—capitalism—that has given us the wherewithal to indulge. We have spent something like one hundred years now in flight from the selective suffocation of Victorian life, with what David Marquand called its "vast eiderdown of conformity, pressing down, ever so gently, but to deadly effect, on the individuals who made it up." In this project, for the most part, we have succeeded. In the Western world tradition, ideology, and religion have loosened their grip. People are freer now to live, love, and express themselves than ever before, so that, in Western cultures at least, the theme of man against society—a staple of drama going back to Sophocles—has lost some of its potency.

That we have the chance to get ourselves into so much trouble—with food, drink, money, and one another—is actually a testament to human progress, for what we're talking about here is nothing less than the democratization of temptation. It came about as the result of a great expansion of human freedom that has been gathering steam since the Industrial Revolution, and which accelerated around the turn of the twentieth century. In Western societies we've mostly been liberated from backbreaking labor, prefabricated sex roles, and taboos against physical pleasure. This unshackling of more and more of the world's citizens from the bonds of ignorance, poverty, and convention may be civilization's greatest achievement. But the price of this achievement is ever more pressure on the *self* in *self-control*, which can no longer rely as much on tradition, community, or the sheer brutality of stigma to keep excess at bay.

Self-mastery will always be a problem, of course, because each of us has conflicting desires—desires that swell and ebb depending on the gravitational pull of temptation, which varies with proximity. People have wrestled with their appetites since Adam and Eve were expelled from the Garden of Eden in a self-regulatory lapse of truly Biblical proportions. The ancient Greeks were all over the subject, which was connected with their ideas about virtue, politics, and even the soul. Plato took up the issue more than once, and for the most part held that people may judge badly what is best but can't really act against their own will. Aristotle, on the other hand, knew that weakness of will was all too real, and he delineated the problem with such obsessive precision that his anatomy of it speaks to us to this day.

But the Greeks were far from the last to puzzle over it. On the contrary, this business of self-control has obsessed not just garden-variety dieters, procrastinators, and philanderers but philosophers, theologians, psychologists, economists, and just about every other flavor of thinker from time immemorial. Saint Paul lamented the alien-seeming impulses—"the sin that lives in me"—which drove him to vice despite his longing for virtue. Medieval Christians worried about the seven deadly sins, five of which (all but pride and envy) were classically shortcomings of self-control. David Hume considered our myopic preference for short-term rewards over long-term goals an immutable fact of human nature, with vast political implications. And Freud, the somewhat unwitting architect of modern attitudes on the suppression of desire, was never quite able to suppress his own insatiable desire for cigars, puffing right through sixteen agonizing years of oral cancer and surgery until finally his inability—or was it his unwillingness?—to resist this particular temptation killed him.

Societies, moreover, tend to oscillate between indulgence and restraint; in the early nineteenth century, for example, Americans drank so much it's a miracle our country's symbol isn't a pink elephant instead of a bald eagle. A national backlash got us to clean up our act, and boozing plummeted. Crime, teenage pregnancy, and other signs of disorder have similarly ebbed and flowed, and the scandals of Eliot Spitzer, John Edwards, and Tiger Woods have ample historical analogs. As the sociologist Gary Alan Fine reminds us, "Belief in a golden age is misleading. Perhaps in bygone days actresses did not flaunt their absence of undergarments quite so publicly, but the censure that comedian Michael Richards and shock jock Don Imus received after their racist remarks reminds us that, Cole Porter notwithstanding, we do not believe that 'anything goes.'"

If America has a characteristic literary form it is the jeremiad, often borne of the near-religious conviction, present in every generation at all times in human history, that the world is going to hell. But the world is not going to hell, and I could never muster the kind of frothing hysteria it would take to write such a screed. Life expectancy rises every year, violent crime is at thirty-year lows, and the boss can no longer chase his—or her!—secretary around the desk. The spending of Americans, for all our profligacy, has lifted hundreds of millions of Asians out of poverty. No moral panic here, people. The problems of freedom and affluence—of managing desire in a landscape rich with temptation— are just the kind all of us should want to have.

Yet they are problems nonetheless—ones so large that they represent the biggest and most enduring challenge individuals in a free society are likely to face. These problems go beyond any state of grace we might hope to achieve from moderation, for what's at stake is not our souls but our lives. Dangerous habits like smoking, eating the wrong things, drinking too much, and having risky sex account for more than a million fatalities annually in this country, or close to half of all U.S. deaths. Most of these behaviors are undertaken by people who know that what they're doing is risky and in many cases—as with cigarettes—would prefer to act differently, despite a conflicting desire for one more smoke or cupcake or line of coke. To put those million early deaths in perspective: no armed conflict, present or past, accounts for as much carnage as our losing war with ourselves—not even World War II, in which there were all of 400,000 U.S. deaths. With our helmets and lawsuits and regulations, modern-day Americans appear to be obsessed with safety. But as a people, we're embarked on a campaign of slow-motion suicide.

A little self-mastery can improve the quality of your life as well as the quantity. If you are a man, it can preserve your marriage, since a strong predictor of marital stability is the husband's ability to control his impulses. And if you're a student, it can lead to higher lifelong earnings, since you are likely to do better—and go further—in school. Studies of teenagers have found that self-discipline is a much better predictor of academic performance than IQ—and may account for the superior grades of girls, who display more of it. Self-control is associated with more education, less violence, lower alcohol and drug abuse, higher earnings, and an optimistic outlook—but only moderate optimism. One study of 997 Catholic Church personnel found that a high score on a test of conscientiousness—defined as "a tendency to control impulses and be goal-directed"—predicted an 89 percent lower risk of Alzheimer's disease than the risk among low scorers, even after allowing for age, gender, and education level.

Yet for all its importance, this business of self-mastery remains essentially mysterious. I began investigating the problem of self-control in earnest for this book, but the deeper I delved, the more puzzling it became. Question soon piled upon question. Is willpower something you inherit, or can it be taught? Do people with anorexia or obsessive-compulsive disorder have too little self-control or too much? Is the suppression of instinct really, as Freud suggested, the price of civilization? After a while the very notion of self-control came to seem oxymoronic, or perhaps tautological; who else besides me could possibly be in charge of myself, after all? And if I fail to control myself, then to whom or what have I abdicated the job? Is it really possible that we're all mere robots, guided by mysterious impulses we can't begin to understand? And if so, how can we be held responsible for our own lapses?

Nowhere is the dilemma of self-control more plainly visible than here in America, where the democratization of temptation has reached something like an apotheosis. Until the recent recession, at least, life in this country had come to resemble a giant all-you-can-eat buffet, one that offers more calories, credit, sex, intoxicants, and just about anything else we can take to excess than at any time in history. We may vow, as we load up our plates, to start on a diet tomorrow, but tomorrow the buffet is still here. And when tomorrow comes, we're still hungry.

Maybe this is one reason disorders of the will are so much more common than they used to be. Anorexia nervosa and obsessive-compulsive disorder, both still relatively rare, are nonetheless much more common today than they were fifty years ago, not to mention the explosive growth of attention deficit disorder and addictions of all kinds. Some of this boom is just more frequent diagnosis, but it also reflects changing circumstances. That it's now possible to be addicted to cocaine, shopping, or sex is evidence of how far we've moved beyond the constraints of budget, custom, and embarrassment. There aren't many compulsive eaters, video game addicts, or—God knows—anorexics—in sub-Saharan Africa, but in the West men and women can be consumed with almost anything, including not eating, because here you can get or do almost anything. Opportunities for obsession abound.

Americans do tend to pioneer in all areas of self-gratification, but as in so much else, the rest of the world is catching up. Scarcity is falling away for many people in China and India as it did long ago in North

America and Europe, places where bounty has led companies to exquisite refinements in the art and science of selling—in exploiting taste, color, sound, and even smell to overcome consumer resistance. (No one cares more about how you make choices than the people trying to sell you something.) Obesity is surging all over the world, including in places where only recently the main dietary problem was getting enough to eat. South Korea, Turkey, and other countries have run into trouble with credit cards. License, it seems, can be contagious. As one banker put it, "One of the things the United States exported overseas was a debt culture."

The financial crisis of 2007–09 is perhaps the most vivid example yet of the self-control challenges posed by modern life. The crisis had many causes—cheap money from Washington and China, inadequate government oversight, reckless executives, and the divorce of loan-making from risk-bearing—but at bottom it was a colossal failure of regulation, including, especially, self-regulation. Lenders and consumers by the millions tacitly agreed to ransack the future by means of loans that people simply couldn't afford to repay. Consumer indebtedness reached epic proportions while the national savings rate fell to zero. Bankers exploited a skewed reward system to pad their personal fortunes by taking undue risks.

We've had crashes before, but this one was different. This was the people's crash, and with our swollen homes and credit card balances, our $4 coffees and gas-guzzling SUVs on lease, nearly all of us took part. Reckless overspending, once limited to the rich, was now a course open to practically every American, just like reckless investing. Suddenly we were all Emma Bovary, bored, entitled, and aghast when the piper at last demanded to be paid. "It is because she feels that society is fettering her imagination, her body, her dreams, her appetites," Mario Vargas Llosa writes in *The Perpetual Orgy*, "that Emma suffers, commits adultery, lies, steals, and in the end kills herself."

Our attitude toward our appetites has evolved as the space for indulging them has expanded. In recent years science has cast doubt on the whole idea that we control our actions, with far-reaching legal and ethical implications. Countless experiments have demonstrated that we often don't know why we do things, and that our ability to regulate our behavior is influenced by a bevy of factors outside our conscious control, including our genes, our lunch, and our peers. Behaviorism suggests that we are merely creaking robots responding to environmental inputs. Genetics threatens to substitute heredity, making the robot that much harder to reprogram. Skepticism about free will has flourished in this environment, undercutting faith in personal responsibility. More and more behavior over the years has come to be seen as involuntary, and a disease model of transgression has taken hold. Cee-Lo Green of Gnarls Barkley might have been speaking for all of us when he sang, "You really think you're in control? Well, I think you're crazy."

At the same time, self-restraint has lost some of its traditional stature, at least compared with self-actualization. There are some good reasons for this; in the past people have been urged by someone or other to suppress every conceivable impulse and indulgence, no matter how innocent (hugging one's children was at one time censured, and masturbation was said to induce blindness and lunacy), until finally the suppression of instinct itself fell into disfavor. At venues like the bariatric meeting I attended, no one speaks of gluttony anymore. Other behaviors once seen as issues of character—drug abuse, excessive playing of video games—have been medicalized as well, subtly absolving us of responsibility and thereby denying our power over an ever broader range of human action. At one point a top associate of New York's governor (the governor whose predecessor quit in a prostitution scandal) found himself in hot water for not paying five years of income taxes. His lawyer said the man was suffering from "non-filer syndrome."

This shift in thinking, humanely inspired though it might have been, has paradoxically undermined the thing that makes us most distinctly human, which is our ability to disobey our impulses in favor of some larger purpose. At the heart of our difficulties is the confusion over which of our behaviors are voluntary. We increasingly operate on the notion, pioneered by Plato, that self-destructive behavior can't be in this category—that when we harm ourselves by our deeds we must act out of ignorance, illness, or the malign effects of genes or circumstances, for who could otherwise do evil to himself?

But on such matters we should be following not Plato but Aristotle, who understood that self-destructive behavior often occurs because of recklessness or weakness. In neither case was an action to be regarded as "compulsive," or beyond a person's choice, for at the very least there is a kind of negligent acquiescence at work. A goal of this book, in fact, is to reinflate the narrowed arena of the elective, reclaiming most excessive behaviors from the realm of disease. The range of actions—and therefore outcomes—that are subject to volition is much larger than we have been led to believe. If we hold ourselves responsible for our behavior—none of which is *entirely* voluntary—we are more likely to consciously direct our actions rather than succumbing to impulse. The magnificent result might be for more of us, even in some small way, to take charge of our own destiny. Doing this requires a kind of faith, but only in our own power to choose. It requires imagination, so that we can visualize the future that our sacrifices might produce. And it requires cleverness, for creating methods to promote the kind of deeds we prefer. In the absence of these three things we too easily become our own worst enemy.

I saw this firsthand one morning at the conference near Dallas, during a starchy breakfast at a motel where I encountered a bariatric nurse who was perturbed by the implications of a book about the problem of self-control. This nurse was extremely fat despite having had bariatric surgery herself, and she contended that self-control was not the issue: people's weight problems are genetic, or the result of high-fructose corn syrup, or fast food, or ignorance of healthy eating, or advertising, or their inability to access or afford fruits and vegetables. And while this prosperous, well-educated health care professional made these arguments—all of which have some plausible basis in fact—she ate not one but two Styrofoam plates full of waffles, smeared heavily with cream cheese.

The good news in all this is that, in much of the world, the problem of survival has been swapped for the more manageable one of self-control.

The bad news is that self-control in modern life is so hard—which is a shame, because it turns out to be so damned important. I say this with some trepidation, because usually such observations come only from the kind of moralizing gasbags and hypocritical scolds typically found, in their off-duty hours, playing craps, visiting prostitutes, or soliciting anonymous sex. Such characters have a long and ignoble history in this country; the speakeasies were probably full of them during Prohibition. William Bennett made himself ubiquitous on the subject of values— and even published *The Book of Virtues*—until we learned what a high roller he was at Las Vegas casinos. Horatio Alger, whose name became synonymous with hortatory fictions about plucky young men, was run out of Massachusetts for being just a little too fond of boys. (Did I mention that he was also a minister?) The subject of self-mastery is always fraught, and anyone who makes too much of it may eventually wish he had heeded John Dewey's caution that "it is the part of a gentleman not to obtrude virtues noticeably upon others."

The moral dimensions of self-control inevitably lead us to political questions. If you believe your life is largely the result of your own discipline and decisions, you're going to feel very differently about taxes, regulations, and redistribution than if you believe your life is largely the sum of your genes and your environment—factors irretrievably beyond your control. In general, conservatives seem to believe in people's ability to control themselves more strongly than liberals do, except when the behavior is bad for women, minorities, or the planet, in which case the two sides trade places. Either way, the troubles many of us have with willpower raise big questions about how far government should go to try to save us from ourselves. Both sides claim to advocate lots of freedom, yet both support government intervention to keep people from exercising it, whether by limiting divorce or abortion (those conservative bête noires) or piling on taxes and regulations (the perennial choices of liberals).

But before we can decide whether self-control is a moral issue, or even whether it exists at all, we had better decide first just what the heck we mean by it. When the actor David Duchovny entered treatment for "sex addiction" in 2008, we recognized a self-control problem of some kind, even if it was shrouded in the exonerating terminology of disease. Yet there are many ways in which the term "self-control" is casually used, and any self-respecting taxonomy of the subject ought to provide a clearer sense of what it is.

"Control of one's emotions, desires, or actions by one's own will," the definition offered by *The American Heritage Dictionary*, is hardly adequate, and it raises more questions than it answers. If you break your diet in an orgy of pizza and chips during the Super Bowl, by whose will did these things find their way into your mouth if not your own? Did Tiger Woods have a self-control problem during his years as a one-man make-work project for America's cocktail waitresses, or was he acting precisely in accord with his own will, which was to get his hands on as many babes as he possibly could?

To get a better handle on this problem, let's think for a moment about desires. Like people, they fall fairly easily into two broad categories: those that we like and those that we don't. What I mean by self-control is deciding which of your desires you really want to espouse and then upholding them against the challenges of the competing desires that you like less. This distinction—between any old desire that we may have and the desires we actually want for ourselves—is crucial. We'll call the former first-order desires, to describe the grab bag of appetites and longings that seem to beset us without conscious intervention. The others—those essential desires that you actually prefer—we'll call second-order desires.

To the philosopher Harry Frankfurt, who enjoyed a short-lived celebrity outside the world of academic philosophy when his brief book *On Bullshit* climbed the best-seller lists, those second-order desires are the things that make you a person. Frankfurt's notion is that while lots of creatures can deliberate, what sets *Homo sapiens* apart is the "structure" of our will—the way we can select or even cause our own motivation, or *will* our own will. Your humanity, in a sense, derives from having preferred preferences, and you are free to the extent that you are able to make your actions conform to the desires you want for yourself. Self-control, in other words, is what makes you a mensch.

Now imagine a person who doesn't have second-order preferences— say, a drug addict who simply doesn't care about his harmful cravings. If he wants drugs, he takes drugs, but he doesn't trouble himself to consider whether he *wants* to want drugs or should struggle against his desire for them. In Frankfurt's view, this individual doesn't care about his own will, and in this respect is "no different from an animal." To Frankfurt, he is not a person but a *wanton.*(Frankfurt, by the way, was not the first to locate our humanity in our responses to our own desires—or in their origins. John Stuart Mill defined character in much the same way: "A person whose desires and impulses are his own—are the expression of his own nature, as it has been developed and modified by his own culture—is said to have a character. One whose desires and impulses are not his own, has no character.")

So self-control, we might say, consists simply in honoring and adhering to one's second-order preferences, whatever they may be—and this is something we mostly can do. It just requires forming some intentions for yourself and finding ways to stick to them, a process that makes us not just happy and healthy, but free. "We have a power," John Locke wrote, "to suspend the prosecution of this or that desire; as everyone may daily experiment in himself. This seems to me the source of all liberty."

Now, these desires that you prefer don't always have to involve temperance, chastity, or some other traditional virtue. You may have a considered preference for more indulgence and less prudence, or even to cheat on your spouse, and it may take enormous self-control to carry out this desire. As you can see, a certain agnosticism about values is built in here, and, in fact, people sometimes struggle with some truly terrible second-order preferences. Huck Finn beat himself up for failing to blow the whistle on Jim, the runaway slave who accompanied him on that Mississippi River raft. In *Crime and Punishment,* Raskolnikov dreaded taking a life but forced himself to live up to some perverse second-order preference that led him to murder the pawnbroker. There are reports of Nazi functionaries steeling themselves against their reluctance to murder Jews; these men had a second-order preference to uphold the grotesque dictates of the Reich, and in order to do so some of them had to overcome a natural first-order preference not to pull the trigger.

The challenge, then, is exalting our second-order preferences without ignoring the instincts—like Huck's compassion for Jim—that are as important to our humanity as our conscious choices about how to live and who to be. Not all instincts are base, and most of them at least enjoy seniority.

What self-control doesn't mean, in my book, is mindless self-sacrifice or knee-jerk self-denial. On the contrary, it represents an affirmation of self, for it requires not the negation of instinct but its integration into a more complete form of character—one that takes account of more than just immediate pleasures and pains. The self-control I'm talking about means acting in keeping with your highest level of reflection.

And it's not easy. One of the most important things I learned in the course of this book is that while we can do better, we can't do it alone. Willpower by itself won't get the job done without the help of institutions—a sensible legal framework and strong social connections. The desire to master our impulses will have to be matched with the means to commit to our desired courses of action, so that when strength of will falters (as it inevitably must) we don't find it as easy to succumb. Reason can't reliably overpower passion by force, and so will have to use its wiles.

Besides, what matters, when it comes to self-control, isn't so much willpower as vision—the ability to see the future, so that the long-run consequences of our short-run choices are vividly clear. In that sense, our shortcomings in this arena are really failures of imagination; we are like Felix Carbury, Trollope's debt-ridden wastrel, who "lacked sufficient imagination to realize future misery" as long as his troubles didn't compromise "the outward comforts of the moment." But self-control is all about seeing beyond the moment—about deferring gratification if necessary because we have some larger ongoing wishes that we prefer not to subvert. It would be great to have another drink for the road just now, but it would be better not to wake up in the drunk tank tomorrow.

Unfortunately, immediate rewards, with their great visibility, are always more seductive than those far off in the misty future somewhere (which is why foolish actions are so often called "shortsighted"). This is something modern neuroscientists have demonstrated again and again, yet they might have saved themselves the trouble just by asking Socrates. "Be so good as to answer me a question," he begs slyly of Protagoras, in the dialogue of the same name. "Do not the same magnitudes appear larger to your sight when near, and smaller when at a distance?"

The history of our never-ending struggle with self-regulation is interesting for many reasons, not least because, from the ancient Greeks to the travails of modern life, the same themes occur again and again, as ever present as temptation itself. They include the debate over whether self-command is freedom or slavery, the nature of compulsion, the role of government in protecting us from ourselves, the place of the individual in his social context, the ways in which commerce is subversive or inhibiting, the sense that each of us is divided in some way (between body and soul, animal and god, passion and reason, ego and id), the extent to which we should live for today or plan for tomorrow, and finally the use of commitment devices by means of which one of our selves can bind the other(s) against temptations to come.

Modern science has managed to shed some light on these unchanging features of our Sisyphean self-regulatory landscape, with ambiguous results. Science can help with technologies and techniques designed to give mastery to the part of ourselves we most wish to obey. On the other hand, science may have made things harder by suggesting that we have quite a bit less self-control than we might like, to the point that defense lawyers in murder trials are now busily chipping away at the edifice of personal responsibility with the hammer and chisel of neuroscience. We may know at last where our self-regulatory functions are located—and in some very rudimentary way, how to manipulate them—but with this knowledge comes a nagging doubt about just who—or what—is really in charge.

The issue is no longer just personal. Our appetite for illegal narcotics has had political and economic ramifications from Latin America to Afghanistan, and while legalizing drugs would surely mitigate some of these effects, it might do so at the price of even more self-control problems here at home. And what else is global warming but the failure of each of us to restrain our use of fossil fuels? Given the evidence that human activity is causing potentially catastrophic climate change, the fate of the earth may hinge on our collective ability to resist our impulses and give up some ease, some wealth, and some pleasure in exchange for the more enduring satisfaction of a hospitable and harmoniously functioning planet. At the very least, the recent near-meltdown of the global banking system can plausibly be traced to a yawning self-control deficit among American borrowers and lenders—which is pretty much all of us, come to think.

Ultimately, the problem of self-control is the problem of the human condition, of whether we have free will, whether we're rational, whether evolution has left us ill-suited for modern life. We have no idea, most of us, that our prefrontal cortex is the site of such "executive" functions as forgoing the sweet-looking cheesecake on the counter (or the sweet-looking new hire in accounting). We forget that once upon a time self-control was an unalloyed good, only later to be tarred as repression and fingered as a cause of disease. We don't think about the limbic system, the role of evolution, the authenticity of Ben Franklin's public persona, the influence of glucose, the films of Billy Wilder, or the future-minded genius of Odysseus—but all have something to do with not just your desire for the cheesecake, but your response to your desire. To succumb or not to succumb? That is the question.

2

Sickening Excess

The true aim of medicine is not to make men virtuous; it is to safeguard and rescue them from the consequences of their vices.

—H. L. MENCKEN

It gives me no pleasure to say it—I swear!—but the consequences of our vices can be pretty dire. Consider tobacco; if we could get every American to stop smoking, we'd save an estimated 467,000 lives annually. Ending high blood pressure (much of it arising from unhealthy lifestyles) would save 395,000. And if we could get everyone to slim down to an appropriate body weight, we'd save 216,000.

These numbers come from a groundbreaking study, *The Preventable Causes of Death in the United States: Comparative Risk Assessment of Dietary, Lifestyle, and Metabolic Risk Factors*, which was prepared by leading scientists in the effort to measure the impact of various ailments on public health. The study looked at twelve behavioral risk factors, including smoking, drinking, being overweight, having high blood pressure, and being physically inactive. Because of some serious overlap, you can't just tote up all the lives that could be saved from each; obesity, for instance, causes a lot of hypertension. But Dr. Majid Ezzati, a Harvard School of Public Health professor who coauthored the report, told me that if you net out the double counting, more than a million people die annually from the dirty-dozen behaviors, which include the obvious (immoderate alcohol consumption) and the less so (eating too little fish, which is needed for omega-3 fatty acids).

Put more starkly: of the 2.5 million deaths that occur annually in America, something approaching half could be prevented—delayed, really, but by many years—if people simply managed to lead healthier lives. This is a total that dwarfs the number claimed by any other factor, including environmental pollutants and lack of medical care. Universal health insurance would surely help, and Dr. Ezzati is in favor of it, as am I. But as the authors of the study acknowledge, targeting a handful of big risk factors could save many more lives in this country than just providing insurance for all. The latest estimate, from a study also done at Harvard, is that medical coverage for all might save 45,000 lives annually—a drop in the bucket by comparison.

The problem is not medical but behavioral—it's about an environment rich with unhealthy temptations and the weakness of will with which we confront them. The pleasure offered by those temptations is certain and immediate, while the consequences of a single indulgence are almost nil. The problem, in other words, is self-control.

Failures of self-regulation are implicated in most of the United States' top ten killers. Take heart disease, at the top of the list year after year, despite medical advances that sharply reduced coronary deaths between 1980 and 2000. Major risk factors include obesity, smoking, poor diet, and lack of exercise—all things we do to ourselves, often knowing (and wishing) better.

Or how about cancer? The American Cancer Society says roughly a third of all cancers are related to smoking, while another third are related to overweight, poor eating habits, and a sedentary lifestyle. Stroke? Risk factors include obesity and smoking. Diabetes? It's strongly associated with eating too much of the wrong things, as is its frequent outgrowth, kidney failure. In fact, roughly one-third of all U.S. deaths are attributable to just three behaviors: smoking, inactivity, and a lousy diet.

Most of our health problems can be attributed to substance abuse, even though the substance is often something as innocuous-seeming as a cheeseburger. But we are susceptible to more straightforward methods of self-harm as well. The largest dependency survey we have, from 2001–02, found that a remarkable 30 percent of U.S. adults have a history of alcohol abuse or dependence, while 10 percent have a history of drug abuse or dependence. (There is, of course, some overlap.)

The devastation that we Americans inflict on ourselves is awful— but not unique. Among the world's high-income countries generally, lung cancer (largely from smoking) is the third leading cause of death. AIDS, another preventable disease, is the fourth leading killer among low- and middle-income countries. In Europe, the World Health Organization reports, largely preventable chronic diseases cause 86 percent of deaths.

This is to say nothing of homicide and suicide, both of which claim thousands each year. Most of us, though, do ourselves in more slowly and prosaically, jumping to a premature death in a sea of batter-fried shrimp, booze, and bad television, which we watch instead of exercising. Instead of a single overwhelming impulse to rub ourselves out, we succumb to thousands of impulses, each relatively harmless in itself but cumulatively fatal.

But can we be sure this is a self-control problem? What if people are happy with the trade-off between the risks and rewards of their actions? Or what if they don't understand the risks well enough to make an informed choice? Perhaps the problem is simple ignorance.

The evidence refutes these suggestions. People know the risks, roughly speaking, and they would very much like to act differently. Many do in fact change. But as is so often the case when self-control is involved, people with unhealthy habits seem divided against themselves. For a smoking gun of sorts, consider the problem of tobacco.

Evil Weed

Each year, smoking accounts for an astonishing one in five deaths in this country. The bulk of this carnage is self-inflicted, but fully 38,000 of these lost lives—about as many as occur each year on the nation's roads—are from secondhand smoke and therefore might be considered, if not murder, a form of negligent homicide at least. In fact, second-hand smoke is our *biggest* homicide problem; less than half as many Americans—around 17,000 annually—are murdered using guns, knives, or other more conventional means. And for every person killed by tobacco, many more come down with a serious illness such as emphysema. Smoking by pregnant women is a major contributor to premature births and infant mortality. Scientists lately have even raised alarms about *thirdhand* smoke, the chemicals left behind when secondhand smoke has dissipated.

These terrible facts about tobacco use do not automatically qualify smoking as a self-control problem. Based on their behavior, after all, many people seem to like smoking, so maybe we should conclude that they're only acting on their preferences. Many economists would reach just such a conclusion. The young Paul Samuelson, who would later win the Nobel Prize in economics, codified this notion of "revealed preference" in 1947 with the publication of his influential *Foundations of Economic Analysis*. You may claim to prefer reading Proust and writing in your journal, and you may even devoutly believe that these are your preferences. But if you spend all your free time watching mud wrestling and the Home Shopping Network on TV, to Samuelson your true preferences would be obvious. Bernard de Mandeville, whose satirical *Fable of the Bees* defended vices for their alleged public benefits, summed up this view nicely more than three hundred years ago:

> I don't call things Pleasures which Men say are best, but such
> as they seem to be most pleased with; how can I believe that a
> Man's chief Delight is in the Embellishments of the Mind, when
> I see him ever employ'd about and daily pursue the Pleasures
> that are contrary to them?

But there is a second school of thought about all this, also quite old and in its way equally hard-headed, which says that on some occasions we simply fail to adhere to our own true desires for ourselves.

Self-control lapses, in this view, are a kind of tragedy that seriously diminishes our well-being. Locke, for instance, believed we should take a free person at his word; if his actions are at variance with his expressed wishes, he presumably does not like the desires that prompt them.

So which is it with smokers? At first blush, it looks like Mandeville is on to something. The 45 million U.S. smokers put up with quite a bit of disapproval and expense in order to maintain their deadly habit. Surely they love smoking so much that they consider disease, early death, and the endangerment of loved ones to be costs worth bearing. And there are benefits: in addition to the bliss of smoke-filled lungs and the dopamine rush that appears to flow from nicotine inhalation, smoking actually promotes self-control in other areas. It suppresses the appetite for food, for example, which means smokers have an easier time controlling their weight, and it promotes concentration, which makes it easier to focus on work.

Then again, it's also possible smokers are just misinformed about the risks of smoking, or the extent to which they will value additional years of life once they are in the grip of a fatal cancer. They may be unfit to make a judgment on the subject at all because of tobacco's biochemical effects on the brain. Or maybe they're just taking one day at a time; they know that no one cigarette will make much difference to a smoker's long-term health, so if smoking is a pleasure, at each decision point it makes sense to light up. This myopic way of choosing is sometimes called melioration; it's approximately what procrastinators do ("What's a few more minutes surfing the Internet?"), and I can tell you from experience that it is the devil's own snare.

In fact, though, most smokers do *not* want to succumb to their own powerful desires for tobacco. What makes smoking the definitive self-control problem is the wish of most American smokers not to smoke.

This is not mere speculation. In a government telephone survey, for example, 70 percent of smokers said they wanted to quit. People lie about these things, but there is evidence these folks weren't just blowing smoke: in 2006 a survey found that fully 44 percent of American smokers had actually tried to quit by stopping for at least a day during the

preceding twelve months. (The best predictor of success? Education.)
Julia Hansen, after smoking for years, wanted so badly to quit that she
had herself locked up. In her memoir *A Life in Smoke*, she describes
enlisting her husband, John, to chain her to the dining room radiator for
a weeklong attempt to give up cigarettes. Hansen also wisely binds herself in the fetters of her own public promises. "Failure is not an option,"
she writes. "I've told too many people about Lockdown—my family,
John's family. Made a huge stink that this was it . . . Now, trapped in the
web of my bluster, I'll have to white-knuckle it."

Even people who make no effort to stop—or whose feeble efforts
fall short of chains and public humiliation—probably wish they didn't
have the habit; it's hard to believe that most smokers, if offered the
chance to have a wizard pass a magic wand and painlessly abolish any
taste for tobacco, wouldn't jump at it. Smoking has its pleasures, but
for experienced smokers the main joy of the next cigarette may well be
simply staving off the unpleasant cravings of cessation.

So smoking is a major self-control problem. How major? Well, the
World Health Organization has estimated that global warming claims
150,000 lives annually, a toll that could double by 2030. The very same
agency estimates that, by the very same year, tobacco will kill 8 million
annually around the world, *or roughly twenty-seven times the number of
deaths attributable to climate change.* The comparison raises a provoca-
tive question: Which is a bigger public health challenge, global warming or self-control?

Our Weighty Problem

For years after the discovery of vast oil and gas reserves in Qatar, once a
sleepy Persian Gulf backwater, its people were insulated from the resulting wealth by a ruler who kept much of the money out of circulation.
But when a younger emir ascended to the throne, things changed, the
economy boomed, and now native Qataris are among the richest people
in the world. They are also among the fattest, although the competition

is getting stiff. Nowadays more and more people in China, Brazil, and a great many other places are also overweight. Like the Internet or the game of basketball, the global obesity epidemic started in America, but the rest of the world seems determined to catch up.

Probably nothing better captures the essence of our self-control predicament than humanity's worldwide struggle with its weight. A generation ago, after all, the world's great food problem was hunger, and to this day, in many places, people still starve. But for hundreds of millions of the newly affluent, along with the hundreds of millions who've been growing more affluent, fat is what can only be called a growing public health problem.

This is especially the case in the United States, where our great girth has become a living symbol of excess—and where obesity has been called "the new tobacco" as a public health threat. Americans have been seriously gaining weight for roughly thirty years now, and in round numbers, if you'll forgive the expression, about a third of adults are obese and another third merely overweight. The causes of this remarkable development are the usual suspects implicated in self-control problems: technology, social change, and affluence. All of them are captured in the startling fact that, while we've been getting fat, the inflation-adjusted price of calories has fallen to perhaps the lowest level since the Garden of Eden. In 1919, for example, the average American had to work 158 minutes to buy a three-pound chicken, but now the figure is closer to 15 minutes—no plucking required. The cost of soda, frozen meals, fast food, and other such comestibles has also dropped. Consider the potato; before World War II Americans ate lots of these, but rarely as French fries because making them this way was too labor intensive. Now, though, advances in food science have made frozen French fries cheaply and readily available for deep-frying at McDonald's or even microwaving at home. Predictably, potato consumption in this country has soared, mainly in the form of fries. But these changes have not been matched by any evolutionary adaptation to the new environment of plenty, with the result that the great bulk of Americans— sorry about that—weigh more than they should.

There has been some controversy about just how dangerous it is to be overweight, but without wading too deeply into the competing studies, I think it's fair to say that the answer is: pretty dangerous, especially for those who are obese. Unfortunately, about half of overweight Americans fall into this category, and the government says the prevalence of obesity in the United States has more than doubled in the past thirty years.

What do we mean by "obese"? Our standard means of relating height to weight these days is the body mass index (BMI), and while imperfect, it offers a pretty good rule of thumb. The formula is:

$$\text{weight in pounds} \div (\text{height in inches})^2 \times 703$$

You can easily determine your BMI by using one of the BMI calculators that abound in the Internet. The government says a normal BMI is between 18.5 and 24.9. If yours is 30 or more, you're obese. To put this in perspective, a person five feet nine inches tall would have to weigh at least 203 pounds to qualify. And obese Americans are the fastest-growing weight category. When Rand Corp. health economist Roland Sturm analyzed data from telephone surveys conducted by the Centers for Disease Control and Prevention, he found that the number of "morbidly obese" Americans—those whose BMI is 40 or more—*quadrupled* between 1986 and 2000, to about 4 million. The number of superobese—those with BMIs topping 50—*quintupled*, to 500,000. (The numbers are undoubtedly worse today.) The typical man in the latter group, at five feet ten inches tall, weighed 373 pounds. Simple obesity—a BMI of 30 or more—doubled during the period. Bear in mind that people in phone interviews often add a little to their height or subtract a little from their weight. If the data were adjusted for these tendencies, the number of people qualifying as obese would be larger.

How did we get here? America's weight problem is a relatively recent phenomenon. For most of our history, superior nutrition made us taller than other people and fueled national productivity. At the turn of the twentieth century, only the rich were fat; the bellies of the era's plutocrats feature prominently in photographs and novels of the period, and at the Mission Inn in Riverside, California, you can still see an extra-wide chair made in 1909 to accommodate our enormous president at the time, William Howard Taft. (A century later, after the democratization of calories, the elites distinguish themselves by being thin, and Taft's counterpart is the whippet-like Barack Hussein Obama.) From 1960 to 1980, the proportion of American adults who were obese remained stable at 15 percent or less. But then it started climbing rapidly, reaching 33 percent in 2004.

What changed during this time? Surely not our genes, although immigration did change the nation's gene pool in that period. But in evolutionary terms, we remain the same scarcity-driven creatures we have always been. No, what changed was how we live. Americans really started to get fat around 1980, roughly when the microwave oven—that ultimate emblem of our bariatric predicament, if not our civilization— achieved ubiquity. The microwave is more symbol than culprit, but it's an apt metaphor for the real story, which is the plummeting effort and coordination required per calorie ingested. Families—and family meals—splintered. Driving increased, along with other calorie-sparing technologies (like the remote control you point at your TV when you're bored). Business perfected the art of offering tempting and highly caloric meals at little cost in time and money, until it was easy, almost everywhere, to obtain such dubious cuisine without ever getting out of the car.

Not surprisingly, we seem to be eating more. Waste-adjusted "food availability" data from the U.S. Department of Agriculture (USDA), a pretty good proxy for per capita intake, shows that in 1980 we got by on 2,196 calories a day. But by 2008 that number had risen to 2,674—an increase of 22 percent. And there is evidence we are eating less well, as is clear from our evolving beverage choices. "Between 1947 and 2001," the USDA reports, "per capita consumption of carbonated soft drinks more than tripled while beverage milk consumption declined by almost one-half. In 1947, Americans consumed on average 11 gallons of carbonated soft drinks and 40 gallons of beverage milk. In 2001, per capita milk consumption had dropped to 22 gallons, while soft drink consumption soared to 49 gallons." Condemned as "liquid candy" by critics, sweetened soft drinks now account for 10 percent of the calories in our diet.

Our sorry diet is causing biological changes aside from obesity. Lots of sugary foods can reduce insulin sensitivity over time, leading to diabetes. Rats exposed to very high-fat meals lose sensitivity to the hormones that normally signal satiation—and so they keep eating. Supercaloric diets (and the extra estrogen produced by the resulting additional fat cells) appear to be the main culprits in driving the average age of female puberty in this country down to eleven years old, with many reaching that stage even younger. Our high-carbohydrate, high-calorie diet has also been implicated in delaying brain maturity by a year or two. Full brain maturity may now take until age nineteen or twenty because too many calories lowers brain-derived neurotrophic factor, a protein important for the brain's development. (And delaying brain maturity means postponing the day when we achieve our fullest capacity for self-control.)

We've reached the point where most insured Americans regularly take at least one prescription medication, according to a study by Medco Health Solutions, Inc., the prescription benefits firm. The most widely used drugs are those aimed at hypertension and cholesterol. "Honestly, a lot of it is related to obesity," said Dr. Robert Epstein, chief medical officer at Medco. "We've become a couch potato culture [and] it's a lot easier to pop a pill" than to diet or exercise.

If every era has a characteristic disease, metabolic syndrome is surely ours. Metabolism is the set of crucial chemical processes that balance the energy coming in and going out. These processes normally are exquisitely calibrated, so that they require little conscious effort beyond finding food when hungry. In people with metabolic syndrome, these processes seem to go seriously out of whack, usually as a result of calorie- and technology-rich modern life. Definitions vary, but the National Heart, Lung and Blood Institute says it means having several particular problems—high blood pressure, high blood sugar, a big waistline, etc.—that together pose a substantially increased risk for heart attack, stroke, diabetes, and other health problems.

Age and heredity are big factors in metabolic syndrome, but it's also strongly associated with eating too much and moving around too little, which is why the number of people with the syndrome has grown so large. An astonishing 47 million Americans—about one in four adults—have metabolic syndrome, and given rising obesity rates, there is every reason to believe it is growing more common. In a study in *Diabetes Care* published in 2004, Dr. Earl S. Ford and his colleagues wrote, "The increased prevalence of the metabolic syndrome is likely to lead to future increases in diabetes and cardiovascular disease."

Type 2 diabetes is already reaching alarming proportions. Type 2, which represents more than 90 percent of all diabetes cases, is usually found in overweight adults—and it's booming. There were 5.6 million Americans with diabetes in 1980. By 2007 the figure had more than quadrupled to nearly 24 million, with another 57 million believed to be prediabetic. Eleven percent of adult Americans have the disease, which has grown right along with our body weight, but in this arena, too, the Chinese are proving competitive. Thanks to increasing affluence, China now leads the world in diabetics, with 92 million. Its adult rate of one in ten comes perilously close to ours.

The salient feature of this tragic story is people's inability to keep their weight within the range that nature intended and they would prefer. Hardly anyone wants to be fat; Americans expend vast sums of money and energy trying to lose weight, in part because being heavy carries considerable social, medical, and financial penalties. Yet eating does not seem to vary very reliably as a function of its consequences— our definition of voluntary behavior. We do not desire the desires we have with respect to food, but we seem unable to overcome them in favor of our more enduring wishes for a normal body weight.

Perhaps the new world in which we live just won't let us. A failure of will on this scale—two-thirds of all adults!—has to make you wonder if Americans are gorging themselves voluntarily, or whether technology, affluence, and social change, in riding roughshod over our desire to be svelte, have made being fat almost compulsory. The plain fact is that while most drug addicts manage to quit, most fat people (thanks in part to the body's diabolical resistance to weight loss) stay fat.

For many people, eating is a form of slow-motion suicide. But we shouldn't overlook the fast version, either, for it too has much to say about the problem of self-mastery.

The Future Is Now

Every year something like a million people around the world take their own lives, while many more try. Alarmingly, the global suicide rate is up about 60 percent over the past half century, although it's been falling in rich countries for about twenty years. In the United States, where suicide is down somewhat since 1950, the annual toll nonetheless exceeds 32,000, making it the eleventh leading cause of death (and plac-ing it far ahead of homicide). In America, four times more men than women commit suicide, but women try twice as often. The difference in outcomes is not a matter of competence but means; accounting for half of all suicide deaths, guns are the male method of choice and by far the most lethal one available.

"Suicide," B. F. Skinner contended, "is another form of self-control." There is, after all, no more effective technique for ending, as Ham-let says, "the heartache, and the thousand natural shocks that flesh is heir to." I suppose it's not unreasonable to form a second-order desire to shuffle off this mortal coil. Yet such decisions are not usually well considered; on the contrary, they are impulsive. Hamlet himself com-plained that the "native hue of resolution"—his impulse—in this department was "sicklied o'er with the pale cast of thought."

What we know about guns and suicide bears this out. In America, states with the highest rates of gun ownership have higher rates of sui-cide, even after you take account of poverty and other factors—yet there is no correlation between guns and suicide by other means. Guns, in other words, make it awfully easy to gratify the impulse to do away with oneself—suggesting that suicide isn't so much the result of self-control as the lack of it. Guns that are secured, even by despondent owners who have the key, or ammunition inconveniently stored in a different room from the weapon, can provide a crucial break for would-be suicides to calm down and give up on the whole idea.

Suicide prevention is probably one of the best arguments for gun control—and a good example of how people sometimes need to be protected from themselves. That guns speak to people about self-erasure has been well known for a long time. Nearly a hundred years ago, at a meeting of the Vienna Psychoanalytic Society, David Oppenheim said, "A loaded pistol positively urges the idea of suicide on its owner." Taking guns out of people's hands has an effect similar to installing higher railings and other impediments along bridges, which was demonstrated most dramatically in Washington, D.C., where a couple of bridges stand in clear view of one another spanning Rock Creek, 125 feet below. Like the Golden Gate in San Francisco, Washington's Duke Ellington Bridge had become the span of choice for local jumpers, and in the 1980s a suicide barrier was proposed. Opponents argued that the barrier would needlessly mar the historic span, merely sending the despondent jumping off the nearby Taft Bridge instead. But the barrier was installed, and suicides on the Ellington subsequently went to zero. Suicides on the Taft remained unchanged.

Perhaps the very best evidence that suicide is impulsive—that it's a self-control problem—comes from the United Kingdom, in the convenient natural experiment offered by the nation's shift to heating with natural gas. England for years had relied on cheap and plentiful coal gas, which is rich in carbon monoxide and thus can asphyxiate an unlucky householder in minutes if the doors and windows are closed. By the late 1950s, it accounted for nearly half of U.K. suicides. In 1963, the poet Sylvia Plath killed herself in her London home just this way—by turning on the gas and sticking her head in the oven. But by the early 1970s, when the changeover to natural gas was virtually complete, the English suicide rate had dropped by nearly a third and has stayed down ever since, indicating that people didn't simply turn to other means of doing themselves in. The coal gas evidently was too convenient, and unhappy people with a passing fancy to end it all could do the deed impulsively, without going anywhere or buying anything. In matters of self-control, as we shall see again and again, speed kills. But a little friction really can save lives.

There is also biochemical evidence that suicide is impulsive, and that evidence has to do with serotonin. You've heard of serotonin, perhaps in connection with selective serotonin reuptake inhibitors (SSRIs) such as Prozac, which act as antidepressants, presumably by increasing the availability of serotonin to those who seem to need more of it. Serotonin, like dopamine (the other biochemical star of this story) is a neurotransmitter important for mood and behavior regulation—and the connection between suicidal behavior and serotonergic dysfunction is well established. A low flow of serotonin to the prefrontal cortex—the section of the brain most important for self-control—seems to increase impulsivity, break down inhibition, and raise the odds that you'll take your own life. Mice who had a key serotonin receptor knocked out were more impulsively aggressive and consumed more cocaine and alcohol. SSRIs, on the other hand, seem to reduce impulsivity when administered to pigeons. Low serotonin in humans has been associated with all kinds of impulsively destructive behaviors in addition to suicide, including self-mutilation, pathological gambling, and kleptomania.

Yet suicide is not always impulsive. There are times when suicide is a rational self-control tactic, as when a captured secret agent, knowing he might spill the beans under inevitable torture, bites down on a cyanide capsule to prevent himself from divulging secret information. By taking his own life, he deprives himself of an undesired option. Terminally ill patients might be doing something tragically analogous by depriving themselves of the choice to withstand further pain. When Sigmund Freud, who for a while espoused the bizarre notion that people have a "death instinct," reached the end of his rope after years battling cancer, he prevailed upon his physician to end his suffering—and the physician did so with a lethal injection.

Freud died earlier than he needed to because of his smoking. All in all he might have been satisfied with the bargain he had struck for himself—trading a few years of life for the rewards of all those cigars—but too many of us will follow him unwillingly to an early grave, led there by habits we despise.

3

On Having Yourself Committed

If we chose always to be wise we should rarely need to be virtuous.

—Jean-Jacques Rousseau, *The Confessions*

Here's a burning question. Do SpongeBob SquarePants and Samuel Taylor Coleridge really have anything in common? Besides multisyllabic names, a Romantic sensibility, and some strong aquatic associations, there may well be collegiate English departments where both are equally esteemed. But even these amazing connections—practically spooky, aren't they?—don't tell the whole story.

Start with Coleridge. Opium was a huge albatross for the poet who gave us *The Rime of the Ancient Mariner*; for a while he even tried paying strong men to keep him away from the stuff. The problem was that later, when he was determined to get high, his flunkies had to figure out how to comply with the wishes of the prudent Coleridge without getting themselves fired by the one who was dying for some drugs. In Thomas De Quincey's telling, one of the men gently reminded his drug-addicted employer that, just the day before, Coleridge had insisted on being barred from the druggist's at all costs. "Pooh, pooh!" the poet replied. "Yesterday is a long time ago. Are you aware, my man, that people are known to have dropped down dead for timely want of opium?"

If abstinence could kill, clean-living SpongeBob would have croaked long ago, yet here too there is more in common with Coleridge than meets the eye, for the squarest cartoon character around once found himself in the same situation as the poet's hired men and suffered the same sort of confusion. It happened when SpongeBob's cheapskate boss, Mr. Krabs, fell in love and spent a fortune lavishing gifts on the object of his affections, one Mrs. Puff. Horrified by his lack of self-control, Mr. Krabs enlisted trustworthy SpongeBob to take charge of his money and keep him from spending any more. Predictably, when the time came, Krabs begged and railed for his boxy yellow trustee to go against his orders. SpongeBob thus was cast into the same unfortunate position as the porters and coachmen who depended on Coleridge for five shillings a day to stand between him and his high.

Now, if you think this sort of thing is just ancient history or cartoon fantasy, you aren't keeping up with the tabloids, which tell us that celebrities no longer need rely on mere porters and coachmen. Professional sobriety minders, often former alcohol or drug abusers themselves, charge considerably more than five shillings nowadays to keep well-heeled addicts away from their favorite high. A firm called Hired Power, run by a certified drug and alcohol counselor, reportedly employs nearly a hundred minders in nineteen states, and a competitor, Sober Champion, has branches in New York, Los Angeles, and London. The adventures of one real-life minder, however embellished, even became the basis of a TV show, *The Cleaner*.

We all know what it's like to ask someone else to keep us from doing something. Sometimes the stakes are modest, like when, on the way to a restaurant, you ask your spouse not to let you order a second or third drink later in the evening. And sometimes they're a matter of life and death, like when the writer Andrew Solomon, battling depression, buys himself a gun—and then gives it to someone else lest he turn it on himself. "Isn't that ridiculous?" he writes. "To be afraid you'll end up using your own gun yourself? To have to put it someplace else and instruct someone not to give it back to you?"

The best-known example of such behavior is from one of the greatest stories ever told, and like so much in our inquiry into the problem of self-control, it comes to us from the Greeks, who were obsessed with the subject. Wily Odysseus, on his way home by ship from the protracted nightmare of the Trojan War, orders his men to tie him to the mast and stop up their ears so he can hear the seductively lethal song of the Sirens without quite literally going overboard. Thus did our hero inoculate himself against his own predictable (and potentially fatal) desires—and thereby demonstrate his wiliness, for a person with less self-awareness might have trusted willpower alone. Odysseus knew that no one is immune to temptation, which is why he's a crucial figure in the history of self-regulation. His encounter with the Sirens could not be more momentous because the technique he used remains the foremost weapon in the human arsenal against temptation.

Advancing on the Enemy

These Odyssean techniques for constraining our own behavior—paying men to keep us out of opium dens, giving away the guns we fear we'll turn on ourselves—are known in the self-control racket as forms of *precommitment*, because we use them to constrain ourselves in advance against the foreseeable strength of some later desires. Precommitment is about limiting our own choices while we're safely distant from the temptations we suspect we can't otherwise handle.

Why should we need any of this clanking self-control paraphernalia, with which the future haunts the present like some rattling ghost afflicting Scrooge? The answer is in the bedeviling problem known to self-control cognoscenti as *time inconsistency*, which describes the frustrating way our preferences change along with our state of desire. Think of Coleridge's conflicting views of opium: When the poet was clean and calm, he hired men to keep him that way, on the basis of a strong preference for sobriety. But when he had a hankering, he demanded that the men stand clear, because, crucially, his preferences had reversed.

It happens to all of us. How often do we awaken with the best of intentions in favor of work, diet, exercise, temperance, fidelity, or some other such virtue, only to succumb later on, when temptation is immediately at hand? John Cheever struggled daily with these competing priorities, as he made plain in his journal. Cheever's tenacious alcoholism vied with his desire to be a good husband and a productive writer. On many mornings he resolved not to take a drink until some reasonable hour later in the day. Yet day after day he broke down and, in some sense against his own will, hit the bottle before noon. "There is a path through the woods that I can take this rainy morning," he writes. "But instead I will take the path to the pantry and mix a Martini. Look, look, then, here is a weak man, a man without character."

If Cheever had really wanted to stop himself from drinking, he might have taken some steps to put the bottle out of reach—enlisting his wife, for example, or checking himself into a rehab center. Most of us have done the same sort of thing, in our own mundane way. We make like Odysseus, even if a tad less heroically, whenever we decide not to buy any potato chips (lest we fail to eat just one), or have the name Joan tattooed on a biceps (lest we take up instead with Barbara). Joining a gym might get you in shape; joining the marines certainly will. Cutting up your credit cards, getting married (and wearing a hard-to-remove ring), depositing money in an IRA (which penalizes early withdrawals)—these are all examples of precommitment in everyday life.

It's what Gene Wilder does in *Young Frankenstein*. Wilder plays Dr. Frederick Frankenstein, who at one point asks to be locked in a room with the monster.

> **Frankenstein:** Love is the only thing that can save this poor creature, and I am going to convince him that he is loved even at the cost of my own life. No matter what you hear in there, no matter how cruelly I beg you, no matter how terribly I may scream, do

not open this door or you will undo everything I have worked for. Do you understand? Do not open this door.

Inga: Yes, Doctor.

Igor: Nice working with ya.

Frankenstein, *after entering room with monster*: Let me out. Let me out of here. Get me the hell out of here. What's the matter with you people? I was joking! Don't you know a joke when you hear one? HA-HA-HA-HA. Jesus Christ, get me out of here!

Addiction problems practically cry out for precommitment devices, which is why Coleridge and his celebrity descendants hired sobriety minders. But there are simpler techniques. Alcohol abusers, for example, can take prescription drugs such as disulfiram (brand name Antabuse), naltrexone (ReVia), and acamprosate (Campral) to combat their addiction. Antabuse is the most interesting from a precommitment standpoint because it interferes with the way alcohol is metabolized in the human body so that you'll be miserably sick if you drink even a little. (Antabuse-induced symptoms that result from drinking include nausea, vomiting, sweating, and palpitations.) Antabuse is effective—if you take it. But you have to take it every day, which means a new act of will is required every twenty-four hours—and which is why Antabuse implants were invented. (They are used mainly in Europe.) One quick procedure and you're covered for a year.

Drinking presents a number of subsidiary self-control problems. Some people, for example, have a tendency to make regrettable phone calls when drunk—sometimes sobering up to realize they aren't even sure what they said to a boss or a former girlfriend when under the influence. "To alleviate the drinking-and-dialing problem," the economist Tyler Cowen reports, "a phone company in Australia started offering customers blocked 'blacklist' numbers, which they select before going out to drink. In Japan they sell a mobile phone with a breathalyzer, to see if you are really fit to drive home or, for that matter, to make a phone call. If a bus driver fails the test, his location is sent immediately to his boss by GPS."

More prosaic examples of precommitment are easy to find. One of my favorites is on display in the world's most sophisticated treatise on temptation—*The Seven Year Itch*. In this Billy Wilder classic, Tom Ewell plays a mild-mannered publishing executive who tries to control his smoking by locking the cigarettes away and putting the key out of reach on a high shelf—even though, when his beautiful upstairs neighbor (Marilyn Monroe) appears, he easily retrieves it with a stepladder.

The socialite Anne Bass played a similar game with herself. When thugs invaded her Connecticut home in 2007 and forced her to open the safe, they found that it contained a few valuables—and a bunch of chocolate. She kept her chocolate in the safe because she really, really loved the stuff and wanted to keep herself from eating it too fast. But of course, she knew the combination all along.

Frog and Toad, endearingly lugubrious characters from Arnold Lobel's children's stories, learn just how flimsy self-commitment arrangements can be. In the story "Cookies," Frog and Toad can't stop themselves from eating a mass of freshly baked cookies, so Frog tries putting them in a box, tying it with string, even using a ladder to place the box out of reach. But each time, Toad points out, they have the ability to undo these weak forms of precommitment—just as Tom Ewell did when confronted with Marilyn Monroe. Finally, Frog takes the cookies outside and gives them to the birds, who eat every last crumb.

The moral of the story is that, ideally, a precommitment should be *binding*. If it's going to work, it has to be genuinely coercive—but the coercion is one that we impose upon ourselves. Ludwig Wittgenstein understood this when, after his terrible combat experience in the Austrian Army during the Great War, he determined not to allow himself to slip back into a life of comfort and ease. The philosopher's industrialist father had put all his money into American bonds before the war, an act of extraordinary foresight that made his son one of the richest men in Europe—and would have spared him the privations suffered by other affluent Viennese, including Freud. But Wittgenstein was determined to be rid of all this money and insisted on legal arrangements to transfer it irrevocably to his siblings, despite their objections. "A hundred times," his sister Hermine wrote, "he wanted to assure himself that there was no possibility of any money still belonging to him in any shape or form."

Modern law takes account of such desires. You can set up an irrevocable trust, for example, which is just what its name implies. Or you can go for a spendthrift trust, specifically designed to keep capital out of the hands of an untrustworthy heir. (A spendthrift trust forces the beneficiary to live on only what the trustee doles out.) The travel writer Rudy Maxa tells of a wealthy friend who was so irresponsible with money— and so chastened by the experience of blowing through at least one fortune—that he set up a version of a spendthrift trust with his remaining wealth to keep the bulk of his assets out of his own hands. Instead of carrying an ATM card, which he might abuse, the man would call his mother and have her wire him a small sum so he could go to dinner. It was costly and inconvenient, but that was the point.

The psychologist Dan Ariely has collected precommitment anecdotes, among them the story of one person who placed her credit card in a container of water in the freezer, thereby requiring a cooling-off—er, that is, warming-up—period before use, and the story of another who, before a date with a guy she knew she shouldn't sleep with, wore her "granniest" underwear—presumably to make her feel less attractive and deter herself from disrobing. In this she was unwittingly following the advice of Saint Jerome, who argued that the determined virgin "by a deliberate squalor . . . makes haste to spoil her natural good looks." Jerome's friend Paula, who ran a convent near his monastery in Bethlehem, evidently took the same view of cleanliness and chastity, warning that "a clean body and a clean dress means an unclean soul."

Historically, emigrants precommitted to their new lives when they embarked for some new land without enough money for a return ticket. Immigration is different today; it's easier to go home and easier still to stay in touch with home. This may or may not help; some evidence suggests that people are happier with choices that are irrevocable, perhaps because such finality slams the door on regret. ("Maximizers," as

Herbert Simon called those who are always shopping for a better deal, are a notoriously unhappy breed.)

People are often warned about burning their bridges, but sometimes armies destroy their ships after landing on some foreign shore, as Cortez did in conquering the Aztecs, or otherwise arrange things so that, as Ed Harris proclaimed in *Apollo 13*, "failure is not an option." The economist and Nobel laureate Thomas Schelling, who has written of his own self-control problems with tobacco, recalls just such a case from the ancient world: "When Xenophon, pursued by Persians, halted against an almost impassable ravine, one of his generals expressed alarm that they would have no escape. Xenophon . . . reassured him: 'As for the argument that . . . we are putting a difficult ravine in our rear just when we are going to fight, is not this really something that we ought to jump at? I should like the enemy to think it easy going in every direction for him to retreat; but we ought to learn from the very position in which we are placed that there is no safety for us except in victory.'"

As Schelling pointed out during the Cold War, when deterrence was a hot topic, whole countries can engage in precommitment—and can make themselves more credible to their enemies by doing so. An example: say your enemy knows that a nuclear attack on your soil will automatically launch massive retaliation *that you have no power to halt*. Nations also engage in much less ominous forms of precommitment, even if, on reflection, they might not be altogether democratic. The fledgling United States did just that more than two hundred years ago in making it difficult for subsequent politicians (and the nation's vastly more numerous subsequent voters) to change the Constitution.

The Social Security system is a form of precommitment against geriatric destitution whereby Americans force themselves to turn over a portion of their earnings to the government in return for a pension. Could we do better saving and investing on our own? Maybe, but the voters support Social Security, perhaps because they have a healthy skepticism about how much financial discipline they could muster if left to their own devices. (In precommitment circles, this makes them "sophisticated" compared to people who assume they have vast willpower—and are therefore "naïve." Humans have a predisposition toward overconfidence and so tend to be naïve about their willpower. In one interesting study, the psychologist Loran Nordgren found that, among a group of people trying to quit smoking, the ones who gave especially high ratings to their own willpower were most likely to fail.)

Once upon a time, greenbacks could be exchanged for a fixed amount of gold, which was an effective precommitment device. But after a while, maintaining a fixed exchange rate proved untenable, and soon it took more and more dollars to buy the same quantity of precious metal. Nowadays other countries that can't trust themselves with money will peg their currency to the U.S. dollar so they don't have the option of printing too much money. Some nations have even adopted the dollar as their legal tender, since you can't debase a currency that you don't issue.

Nations can also precommit by adopting the gold standard, scrapping weapons (to head off future battles), or, if engaged in a nuclear standoff, building a doomsday system to blow up their enemies— absent human intervention—when the bombs start falling. A doomsday arrangement is a species of "poison pill," familiar in politics from the tactic of attaching a distasteful amendment to some unwanted legislation so that even proponents can't vote for it. Similar tactics are used in business to ward off unwanted takeovers; corporate directors might decree that the acquisition by any outsider of more than a certain percentage of the firm's shares will trigger some massive stock issue or other event that would be hugely disadvantageous to the would-be acquirer.

On Manhattan's Lower East Side, the famous Eldridge Street Synagogue (which opened in 1887) used a poison pill of sorts to assure congregants who ponied up that it would remain pure. "When you bought a seat to pray at Eldridge, the contract promised that if the congregation ever allowed organ music, or men and women singing together in the choir, you'd get double your money back," says the synagogue's historian, Annie Pollard. "It was a strong anti-Reform statement."

. . .

Like a banana republic that can't trust itself with its own money, sophisticated precommitters enlist the help of others. In George Eliot's *Middlemarch*, the profligate Fred Vincy gives his mother £80 in a fleeting outbreak of self-awareness, solely to prevent himself from gambling the money away. And in *The Fountain Overflows,* Rebecca West's masterpiece, Claire Aubrey rejoices at the chance to pay her rent in advance: "It was a delight for her to snatch this money from the mysterious force that acted on all money in our family, annulling it as if it had never been; it was such an indulgence as she had not enjoyed for years to make a payment and prevent it from being even for a moment a debt."

Committing to Print

It's fitting that literature abounds with these episodes, because if people never did these things in real life, there might not be any literature, given the preference that most writers seem to have for doing almost anything besides writing. Georges-Louis Leclerc, better known as the Comte de Buffon, was a furiously productive eighteenth-century writer and naturalist who nonetheless liked to sleep in. "He had to order an elderly servant named Joseph to wake him at dawn," Richard Coniff reports in the *New York Times,* "promising payment if he succeeded in rousting him out of bed. One morning, other measures having failed, Joseph dumped a bowl of cold water in Buffon's face and duly collected his fee. 'I owe 10 to 12 volumes of my works to poor Joseph,' Buffon wrote."

And then there was Fyodor Dostoyevsky, who turned his own self-control problems (with gambling) into art by writing a novel on that very subject. How this work came to be is itself a classic tale of precommitment and, to my mind, a better story than the one he actually wrote. Always desperate for money, Dostoyevsky's contract for this book, with the publisher Stellovski, contained a draconian failure provision: the writer would get some money up front, but if he didn't deliver by the due date, Stellovski would get the right to publish all the author's works for nine years without paying him anything. Human nature being what it is, Dostoyevsky somehow allowed himself to slide toward the drop-dead date—November 1, 1866—without getting the book done. With less than a month to spare, he hired the young stenographer Anna Grigorievna Snitkina, to whom he dictated *The Gambler*—and got it in just under the wire. Better yet, he married his amanuensis a few months later.

Deadlines seem to benefit everyone. Dan Ariely has tried letting his students write short papers over the course of a semester with no deadlines (beyond term end), with deadlines of their choosing, or with deadlines that he imposed. Ariely found that students got better grades when given hard and fast deadlines spaced out across the semester. Students with no deadlines, who presumably had the most time and flexibility to work on all their papers, actually performed worst, while the performance of students who were allowed to set their own deadlines was only middling. The problem was that some students in the self-imposed deadline group underestimated their tendency to procrastinate—sound familiar?—and so set deadlines that weren't well spaced, leading to rushed, poorly written papers.

Seen in this light, perhaps Stellovski performed a service to literature. Onerous as Dostoyevsky's publishing contract was, it also served as a useful form of tough love—one that the author embraced in full knowledge of its terms. The critic John Leonard might have been speaking for all of us when he said of himself, "Deadlines are my spine."

Written on the Body

Since the human body is the battlefield of our conflicting desires, it shouldn't be surprising that it has also been the locus of any number of precommitment techniques. Tattooing is probably among the oldest forms of body alteration for precommitment, a function it fulfills by its very nature. The permanence of body art, after all, commits the many future selves who might inhabit your skin to live with your choice of decor for their home—and it is their home, even if it is not one they can escape. But often tattoos represent a more specific kind of individual precommitment. Young men who get Maori face tattoos in modern New Zealand are doing their best to prevent themselves from assimilating into white society.

Or consider the Hong Kong physician Tao Chi'en, in Isabel Allende's *Daughter of Fortune*, who loses all his money playing fan-tan and promptly has the word NO tattooed on his right hand—his betting hand—as a form of precommitment against gambling. Modern Americans who find themselves in similar straits can, in some states, enroll in a registry barring themselves for a specified period from that state's casinos. Of course, you can go out of state and gamble all you want.

Having the name of a significant other tattooed onto your body is a particularly romantic act of precommitment, but one that unfortunately often goes awry. Such a tattoo may make you stick it out a little longer when the relationship hits a rough patch, yet there are an awful lot of cases in which it was far from sufficient to keep things going. For Hollywood celebrities, in fact, tattoos are about as binding a form of precommitment as marriage. Geena Davis, for example, is said to have had the name of one of her husbands tattooed onto her ankle; after their divorce, she reportedly had it turned into the Denny's logo. Pamela Anderson changed the Tommy tattoo on her ring finger into MOMMY after a breakup. Johnny Depp's WINO FOREVER tattoo originally had to do with Winona Ryder, evidently, but was later edited.

In an example of the way technology can undercut precommitment, tattoos can be erased by a series of laser treatments, although they hurt. (New ink technologies may permit tattoos that can be removed in a single laser session, further weakening the binding force and signaling power of a name written in the flesh.) There is so much demand for undoing tattoos that at least one chain of tattoo-removal centers has sprung up. It's called Dr. Tattoff, and most of the clients are young women like Kelly Brannigan, a model who had her boyfriend's name inscribed on her wrist. (He did likewise with her name.) A year later, after the relationship ended, she had the tattoo removed at the Dr. Tattoff outlet in Beverly Hills, which charges $39 per square inch. Erasing a tattoo is painful and time-consuming, yet by one estimate (admittedly that of a laser manufacturer) Americans have 100,000 of them removed annually.

4

The Cost of Good Inventions

Times have changed. No longer must the fidelity-challenged make do with lying on mainstream dating services; now, at last, they have a Web site of their own: AshleyMadison.com, which bills itself as the place to go if you're married but want to get something going on the side. Prospective cheaters, in fact, have more than one choice online these days, and in addition to places like adult-friendfinder.com, which for a while was sending me regular e-mail alerts about potential partners nearby, individuals of any marital status can find a hookup on Craigslist, PlentyofFish, and other sites. Writing a book always entails sacrifices, and one of mine was having to explain to my wife that I was only exploring these places in the cause of advancing human knowledge. Just like Galileo or Madame Curie.

Ashley Madison is a tawdry place, but aside from its frank appeal to philanderers the most interesting thing about it is its motto—"Life is short. Have an affair."—which for all its simplicity could hardly say more about the challenges of modern living. Take the first part, "Life is short." The reality is that life has never been longer (life expectancy rises every year), yet this insistence on its brevity—as an excuse for infidelity, if nothing else—is characteristic and ubiquitous. It's a notion that tends to collapse time and devalue the future, which is of uncertain duration and possibly even—you never know—brief enough to be ignored. Ashley Madison's exhortation to have an affair, meanwhile, appeals to our most basic urges: not just for sex but also for novelty, admiration, and excitement. By offering such thrills beneath the cloak of anonymity, Ashley Madison positively exemplifies one of the most liberating—or perhaps just disinhibiting—developments of the Internet age. As the famous *New Yorker* cartoon put it, on the Internet nobody knows you're a dog.

Why is self-control so difficult? We might as well start by looking at our own devices, which have made everything cheaper, faster, and easier. Someday somebody will invent technologies that can help us exercise more self-control. In that golden tomorrow, we'll no doubt have new learning tools, commitment techniques, and even drugs that will promote the conquest of temptation and the living of a life more in keeping with the desires we desire. Meanwhile, unfortunately, technology is not the answer. Technology is the problem.

Cheaper

Technology spells trouble on the self-control front because it drives down the cost of nearly everything, stoking temptation by bombarding us with affordable novelty and enticement—in the process, democratizing consumption. That's a wonderful thing. "The capitalist achievement," as the economist Joseph Schumpeter reminds us, "does not typically consist in providing more silk stockings for queens, but in bringing them within the reach of factory girls in return for steadily decreasing amounts of effort."

But technology also democratizes overconsumption. Advances in farming, food science, transportation, refrigeration, and the like have made food in this country wondrously cheap, as we have seen. (A single datapoint illustrates the change: from 1970 to 2005, the proportion of after-tax income Americans spent on food fell from 14 percent to just 10 percent—and forty cents of every food dollar went for eating out, the USDA says.) One result is that we are mostly better fed than we used to be. Another is that we are mostly fat.

Making things cheaper and more widely available can have enormous social consequences. Take something small—as small as a transistor. In the early days of radio, people listened to broadcasts through hulking receivers that cost a lot and required a lot of space. So most families had a single radio to which they listened as a group, in the living room. The family-oriented programming of the times reflected the way people consumed it as well as the values that the grown-ups wanted to share. But the rise of transistors changed all that. Soon everyone could have a personal radio—and listen to something different. It wasn't long before youth-oriented programming began pouring from all those little radios—especially youth-oriented music, most of it sexy and subversive. Sales of this music, so irksome to parents, exploded because young listeners now had the power to choose it—and to listen out of earshot of Mom and Dad. The historically unprecedented youth culture that arose in mid-century was enabled by technology.

Faster

When it comes to self-control, speed kills, and technology undermines restraint by making everything happen faster. Counting to ten is a classic way to defuse anger, and governments sometimes impose waiting periods—for gun purchases or abortions—when a matter is considered grave enough that deliberation should be required.

But technology has accelerated our lives irrevocably, and while it's nice to be able to fly across the Atlantic in a few hours or get news of the latest findings in microbiology in a few seconds, this acceleration is bad news on the self-mastery front. The collapse of delay between impulse and action, between offer and decision, inevitably privileges impulse over reflection and now over later. By undermining deliberation, speed weakens the habit of deferring gratification and leaves no chance for second thoughts. Fast times make urges easy to gratify; the lack of temporal distance between the craving for fried chicken and a piping hot bucket, however caloric, means we can't be deterred anymore by the prospect of plucking, batter-dipping, deep-frying, and cleaning up— or acquiesce in the interim to second thoughts about the effect on our waistlines and arteries.

Want to buy something? Chances are that nearby stores are open (many Walmarts virtually never close), and with plastic in your pocket, you've got the wherewithal. A cop I once knew told me that crime is opportunity, and we are all more likely to succumb if the opportunity is present and the cost seems low. Picture what you eat for lunch on a typical day—not the occasional salad, but the burgers and fries, the meatball sub, whatever really is typical. Now imagine if you could decide a week in advance what you could eat—you'd make your choices in writing, and once made, no other food would be available. Would your lunches be healthier? Sure.

The all-around acceleration of life has also made us less willing to invest in such time-consuming (but subsequently rewarding) tasks as learning a foreign language or studying engineering or walking when we might drive. Technology and ever more efficient markets discourage this kind of thing by providing easy alternatives and rewarding extreme specialization. When cheap, immediate pleasures (like TV) are readily at hand, longer-term satisfactions requiring patience and diligence become comparatively more expensive—and more likely to be shunned.

It almost goes without saying that television is an inducer of self-control problems—particularly with respect to watching TV. Despite the Internet, Americans still average around five hours of TV daily, and there are good reasons for wanting to cut down. People who watch more TV tend to be less happy, for example, even after taking account of differences in income, education, and the like. Perhaps this is because the heavy TV watchers, research has shown, feel less safe, trust others less, are more materialistic, and less satisfied with their lives. They are also more likely to be fat. Many of these people, in fact, wish they watched less, meaning they have a self-control problem, and many of them know it. In Gallup polls during the 1990s, 40 percent of adults and 70 percent of teens said they spent too much time watching, while other surveys found that about 10 percent of adults considered themselves addicted to TV.

"TV doesn't really seem to satisfy people over the long haul the way that social involvement or reading a newspaper does," says University of Maryland sociologist John P. Robinson, who is known for his studies of how people use their time. "It's more passive and may provide escape—especially when the news is as depressing as the economy itself. The data suggest to us that the TV habit may offer short-run pleasure at the expense of long-term malaise."

The automobile was just as transformative a technology as television, and probably played a bigger role in the acceleration of daily life. At first, cars were only for the rich, but by 1930 there were 23 million on the road in the United States. By 1960, the number had rocketed to 62 million.

Every one of them was a getaway car. The automobile overthrew age-old community arrangements and the social ties that went with them, inventing a new, spread-out and more anonymous society in place of the village life that previously constrained the desires of so many Americans. Cars meant freedom and privacy, and when young people got behind the wheel, they would help transform courtship. (Think of Meat Loaf's operatic "Paradise by the Dashboard Light," in which former New York Yankees announcer Phil Rizzuto narrates the circuit of a sweaty automotive lothario around the sexual bases.)

One big change for which we can thank the automobile is that the eyes of our neighbors are no longer upon us. Despite a good deal of hand-wringing over electronic data security and the like, most of us in America enjoy an unprecedented degree of personal physical privacy, and the car helped make that happen. Universal driving led to freestanding houses in sprawling suburbs where, for the most part, nobody has any idea when you come and go, what your destination is, or what you do when you get there. If you could earn a scarlet letter today, it would have to go on your license plate.

It was the car that gave Americans something like a magic carpet, waiting at their beck and call to whisk them instantly (and invisibly) almost anywhere. Having a car meant getting places and doing things almost as soon as you thought of them. And with a car you could buy a lot more stuff and still get it home. Americans found ways to afford cars—though they were expensive, they seemed cheap to drive, especially to motorists who never thought about depreciation—which took the walking out of everyday life for people of all ages, reducing their calorie needs though not their intake of food. And the car created the fast food nation so familiar along Hamburger Alleys from coast to coast.

Easier

If life in America resembles a giant all-you-can-eat buffet, we might have invented the Internet to supply home delivery. It's a major force in driving down the price of practically everything, and it eradicates the kind of frictional costs that might otherwise constrain us. Pornography, for instance, can be consumed without a humiliating and time-consuming trip to some sleazy store, where porn would cost you money as well as embarrassment. For students, the temptation to cheat is surely greater; the Internet excels at bringing together buyers and sellers, after all, and nowadays it's easy for someone in need of a term paper to find someone else who will write it. The same is true of sex, available now almost literally on demand, at least for gay men trolling Craigslist, where an assignation can be had on something like a moment's notice.

Internet gambling, despite attempts to crack down in this country, stubbornly persists offshore, beckoning to risk takers worldwide even in their pajamas. Internet shopping is of course well established as a killer of both time and budgets. No more diabolical means of procrastination than the Internet has ever been created, since its delights and distractions come to us through the same machine we use for work.

It's thanks to the Internet that temptation has carried its war on rectitude right into the office, where nowadays life's riot is just a mouse click away at Web sites specializing in shopping, baseball, sex, and every other delicious sort of distraction. Mainly because of the Internet, Americans on the job waste two working hours every day, according to a survey conducted in 2005 by Salary.com and AOL. Although the survey doesn't sound very scientific (respondents in effect chose themselves, which means the most diligent of us might simply have been too busy), the amazing thing is that two hours is all people owned up to.

For Internet users ready to admit they're in the grip of a higher power, there is Covenant Eyes, a little piece of software that will keep track of all the Web sites you visit—and e-mail this potentially incriminating list to an "accountability partner" of your choosing. That could be your boss, your spouse, your pastor, perhaps even your mother. Covenant Eyes rates Web sites on a kind of taboo scale, so that your chosen overseer can tell at a glance whether you've been poring over market research online or taking in a peepshow. The interesting thing about Covenant Eyes is that you install it yourself and designate your own accountability partner (who is notified if you turn it off). The purpose, of course, is not to shock some third party with the tawdry record of your online time wasting and depravity. The purpose is to give you a fearsome weapon you can use against yourself in the battle for self-control. (Consider the force of a Post-it on your monitor with the reminder, "What would Mom think?")

Covenant Eyes is a classic precommitment device, and a binding one. For someone who needs only a little help, there are programs like Freedom for Mac, which will keep you off the Internet until you reboot (not hard to do, but perhaps just enough of a hurdle), so you can't waste half your day surfing celebrity gossip sites. There are also programs to limit access to certain specified sites or to restrict access during a given period of time or for a specified duration. The Firefox browser plug-in SelfControl, a free download, will warn you when you go on a time-wasting jag. It also lets you toggle the warnings off if you're really determined not to work. These programs (especially the more restrictive ones) function like the parental control software we use to limit our kids on the Internet, except the parent controlling you would be—you.

In the future, more of us may need this sort of thing, because technology increasingly forces us to use a single device for everything we do, making concentration on any one thing that much more difficult. Once upon a time, before telephones and e-mail and whatnot could vie for our attention, it was relatively easy to lose yourself in a book. But in the near future, you are likely to read that book on an electronic device, like the Apple iPad, which will also be a computer, a telephone, a stereo, a game player, a movie screen, and a TV. That's all great, but it will be a lot harder to focus on some boring metallurgical textbook in the face of such frantic yoo-hooing from all those other functions.

Technology also makes things easier by hiding their true costs. Spending money with a credit card is much less painful—or even noticeable—than reaching into your pocket for cash, with the result that some people overspend. All kinds of burgeoning payment technologies will have a similar effect. For example, thanks to the E-ZPass mounted on the windshield of my car, I can zoom relatively painlessly across the George Washington Bridge. But while I always used to know just what the toll was, I no longer do. The same is true for subway rides; now that I have a self-replenishing MetroCard for the New York City system, I no longer know what the fare is.

Spent

It was technology that nearly drove us over the edge in the recent financial crisis.

All the frenzied lending that led up to the crisis was facilitated by the rapid expansion of computing power since the 1960s. Panics have been a fact of financial life for centuries, of course. But disruptive technologies often play a role. This time around, one of the chief culprits was the digital revolution. In fact, the financial crisis is a superb demonstration of the way technology often gives us the illusion of control even as it magnifies risk.

First, ever more powerful computers have radically improved the efficiency of all sorts of financial operations, which is in itself a problem. Take mortgages. As interest rates commenced their long downward slide in the late 1990s, banks launched aggressive advertising campaigns to get consumers to refinance their home loans. Refinancings accordingly rose from a mere $14 billion in 1995 to nearly a quarter trillion dollars a decade later, and in most cases homeowners also took out some cash—all of which worked wonders in stimulating the economy.

This refinancing boom never could have reached such a massive scale were it not for automated credit scoring, computerized loan processing, and elaborately adjustable new loan products—a form of innovation in themselves—that required computers to calculate and track them. The digital revolution made it possible for customers to get thousands of dollars of credit in just seconds from a complete stranger at the local Home Depot—or drain equity out of a house with the help of a lender on the other side of the country, who was financed by capital from the other side of the world.

When lenders ran out of good borrowers, they started shoveling money at bad ones (subprime lending rose from $145 billion in 2001 to $625 billion in 2005), and technology made these excesses possible, too. Networked computers enabled the wholesale securitization of loans, which were packaged and then sliced and diced into a bewildering array of mystery-meat investments with opaque risk profiles. Computers also made it possible for lenders to sell these securities to investors worldwide, replenish their capital, and keep pushing loans out the door. Risk was supposedly under control; the big debt-rating agencies used sophisticated models to estimate the default risk on pools of complex commercial mortgages, and of course part of the point of all the packaging and slicing and dicing was to distribute (and presumably reduce) risk.

As it turned out, the innovations we relied on to reduce risk actually amplified it. Consider the rise of credit-default swaps—contracts whereby one big player (such as a bank) earns a fee by agreeing to insure the loans held by another. The sum covered by these swaps rose from $1 trillion in 2001 to $45 trillion in 2007. In theory, these things were great, allowing all sorts of diversification, risk reduction, and profit making. In reality, these derivatives were, as Warren Buffett said, "weapons of mass destruction," for they multiplied risk, suffused the system with it, and hid it from view.

Financial engineering is strong stuff. These derivatives represented capitalism's well-known powers of abstraction carried to a level beyond the comprehension of mere flesh and blood. The Greeks understood something about liquidity that we didn't. They were wary of wealth in forms that could easily be spent because they had noticed that when estates became liquid, they tended to vanish—not just in the sense that they could no longer be seen (money, unlike olive trees, is kept hidden) but in that, having been made consumable, they were subject to squandering. Liquids, after all, evaporate.

5

The Perils of Prosperity

Religion begot prosperity, and the daughter devoured the mother.

—Cotton Mather

The Amish communities of rural northern Indiana are just a couple of hours east of Chicago if you push it on the interstate, but they might as well be a world away. They mostly eschew the trappings of modernity; people get around in horse-drawn carriages and make or grow much of what they need. Materialism isn't normally one of their biggest problems.

But by 2007 the Amish were changing. Their part of Indiana is home to some recreational vehicle and modular-home factories, which pay well. And the Amish are good workers. More than half the men in communities like Shipshewana and Topeka had taken full-time jobs and by one estimate were averaging $30 an hour. Mervin Lehman, an Amish father of four, told the *Wall Street Journal* "he was making more than $50-an-hour and working up to 60 hours a week as an RV plant supervisor before he was laid off" in November 2008.

With money like that rolling in, Amish customs came under pressure. The traditional refusal to use the telephone began to weaken, and some Amish entrepreneurs adopted fax machines. Amish carriages were sometimes given velvet linings or were attached to pricey Dutch harness horses (the equivalent of trading in your Camry for a Lexus). Weddings got bigger and costlier. Some Amish began taking taxies on shopping trips, and using hired hands for help instead of neighbors to avoid incurring any obligation to reciprocate. Some even bought second homes in Florida. About spending, at least, the Amish were starting to act like everyone else.

The transformation, never complete, came to a halt in 2008 when the RV industry started laying off workers. That in turn slashed deposits to the Tri-County Land Trust, a local Amish-operated lending cooperative of the kind that exist in many Amish areas. It's only open to the Amish, doesn't carry federal deposit insurance, and doesn't run credit checks on potential borrowers. But it does follow the ultraconservative financial practices once common among thrift institutions, including keeping large cash reserves and making sure mortgage payments don't exceed a third of a homeowner's income. Tri-County symbolized the Amish traditions of trust, mutual support, and financial prudence—all of which were undermined by the local boom. Soon after the RV downturn, rumors spread that Tri-County was in trouble, culminating in a six-week bank run. Panicked depositors, distrustful of their own institution, wanted their money back.

Nobody knows better than the Amish that affluence can lead to excess—and nobody could be less typically American than "the plain people," as they are traditionally known. But the Amish experience of sudden wealth in this story is emblematic of America's larger struggle with prosperity, particularly the bubble prosperity that was fueled by debt and artificially inflated asset prices. In Indiana, easy money undermined values that had stood the Amish in good stead for a long, long time, including self-control and the community ties that bolster it.

The same thing happened to the rest of us, and in this we Americans were not alone, for until the recent troubles the entire world was awash in cheap money. Easy money changed the culture of Iceland until the recklessness of its bloated banks effectively bankrupted the whole country. Easy money inflated housing bubbles in Australia, Ireland, Spain, the United Kingdom, and elsewhere. And then there are the Greeks—the moderns, not the ancients—who hid the true size of their deficits from everyone, including themselves, until public spending and private tax evasion brought their country to the brink.

When money is cheap, borrowing is easy and nobody is terribly interested in deferring gratification. Credit in itself is not evil; on the contrary, it is the lifeblood of civilization, which it underwrites by fueling innovation and prosperity. The term *credit* comes from the Latin *credo*, meaning "I believe," and it implies a faith in tomorrow on the part of borrower and lender alike. But when credit is used to fund consumption rather than investment, we are taking from the future rather than investing in it, and for a while doing so became a near-universal practice. Since the turn of the twenty-first century, for example, credit card issuance had exploded practically everywhere, and by 2008, more than two thirds of the world's 3.67 billion payment cards were circulating outside the United States. In South Korea, at one point, 148 million cards were issued—in a country of 49 million people—until default rates reached 28 percent and the industry imploded. Credit card debt in Turkey grew to $18 billion in 2007, a sixfold increase in just five years.

A Double-Edged Sword

No invention did more for the human ability to defer gratification than money. Before money, saving was hard; you might dry some fish, or squirrel away some nuts, but money's unique properties as a store of value and an easily calculated medium of exchange made it especially effective at encouraging forethought and calculation. But money also renders wealth easier to spend, literally melting it down so that it can flow like water if you're not careful.

Just as money can be a double-edged sword, so too can capitalism, which Adam Smith praised for giving each of us strong incentives to moderate our behavior in socially productive ways—the better to assure our success in the marketplace. Capitalism really has been a powerful force on behalf of responsibility and temperance, inculcating such bourgeois habits as study and nonviolence, as well as legal and social structures that support these virtues. "A man is seldom so innocently employed," Samuel Johnson observed, "as when he is getting money."

In keeping with this tradition, the workplace is for the most part a citadel of moderation and restraint. In the modern office we're called upon to put forth more self-control than ever—particularly now that we mostly work in jobs interacting with people instead of animals or machines. In our work lives—and more of us work outside the home than ever—we're expected to regulate our comportment, our attitudes, and our outbursts, smile at visitors, refrain from off-color remarks, remain awake despite every postprandial impulse to the contrary, and in general keep all corporeal aspects of ourselves strictly under wraps. If we face customers all day we have to check the impulse to laugh at those who look ridiculous, to slap the rude ones silly, or, if they're attractive, to suggest that they strip. It's only after we knock off for the day that the system begins its hysterical whispering in our innermost ear. "Cut loose!" it says. "Buy. Eat. Screw."

And that's where the trouble starts, for in our lives as consumers, capitalism does everything it can to seduce our more indulgent selves— sometimes urging us to indulge so unrestrainedly that the system itself is endangered, as it was recently by a global debt orgy. Karl Marx saw the destabilizing nature of the system quite clearly, observing that capitalism, "wherever it has got the upper hand, has put an end to all feudal, patriarchal, idyllic relations. It has pitilessly torn asunder the motley feudal ties that bound man to his 'natural superiors,' and has left remaining no other nexus between man and man than naked self-interest, than callous 'cash payment.'"

This is precisely its glory, for anyone who prefers not to live in feudal peonage just because it is time-honored and picturesque. But capitalism cannot thrive without *some* moral and cultural framework to contain or at least channel its gales, for the essential contradiction of the system is that it's bent on producing self-controlled workers yet disinhibited shoppers—and thus undermines the self-mastery it inculcates. Adam Smith understood this, and regarded self-control as crucial. He also predicted the need for a larger state, which a capitalist society could well afford thanks to the great wealth it produces.

Unfortunately, capitalism tends to undermine the restraints we impose on it for its own good. Lobbyists oppose controls and people are clever at getting around them. Capitalism appears to suffer from a kind of bipolar disorder; during manias, it's buoyed by euphoria and blind to its own shortcomings. *Out of the way*, it proclaims confidently, blinkered by its amazing powers. At such times you can almost see the breakdown coming. Sure enough, things soon get out of hand, and the arrogant colossus turns into a pathetically gibbering hulk, its grand schemes in tatters.

In fairness, prosperity is often a plus on the self-control front. In general, the affluent are better at deferring gratification; people's talents in this arena may even be the cause of their affluence rather than its consequence. Perhaps that's why well-to-do Americans, for whom food is relatively cheapest, are paradoxically least likely to be overweight. But sudden access to a lot of money makes for problems, as we've seen from the many lottery winners who've run off the rails over the years. The difficulty seems to occur when affluence outstrips culture, as it can when credit expands much faster than custom or cultivation can contain it. That's why indebtedness can be such a problem—because it instantly bestows wealth beyond our accustomed capacity to manage it. The explosion of credit we've seen during the past thirty years was especially likely to lead to trouble, since it lifted a constraint on people's spending without giving them any more income. Basically, we put a blank check into everybody's pocket, along with a pen to fill in the amount. It's possible that a person's income is a broadly reasonable indicator of his self-regulatory resources, which means that magnifying people's earnings with enormous borrowing power is just begging for trouble.

Americans and Their Money

Our willingness to cash that blank check—to take on debt—is a function of our changing attitudes toward money. When did profligacy replace thrift? The short answer is: right around the time when we could afford it. The process got going in earnest somewhere between the 1880s and 1920s, when the country transformed itself from a nation of want into one of, well, wants. Unbridled economic growth undermined the Protestant ethos of self-denial and reticence, while the rising merchant class did its best to change the country's long-ingrained aversion to luxury. Consumer credit became more widely available, and religious denominations laid off the hellfire and brimstone in favor of a therapeutic approach to happiness in the present. Vast new big-city department stores leveled the full force of their merchandising grandeur at women, who understandably preferred to purchase items they once had laboriously to make.

America had changed, and Americans were changing, too. Pleasure was no longer quite so readily suspect. We were becoming "a society preoccupied with consumption, with comfort and bodily well-being, with luxury, spending, and acquisition, with more goods this year than last," in the words of historian William Leach, who quotes the merchant Herbert Duce summing up the new culture in 1912: "It speaks to us only of ourselves, our pleasures, our life. It does not say, 'Pray, obey, sacrifice thyself, respect the King, fear thy master.' It whispers, 'Amuse thyself, take care of yourself.' Is not this the natural and logical effect of an age of individualism?"

Catalyzed by mass communications (which made possible the stimulation of mass desire through advertising) and the rise of an urbanized middle class, consumerism exploded. From just 1890 to 1904, annual piano sales (to pick a single emblematic example of the growing democratization of affluence) rose from 32,000 to 374,000. "History," Charles R. Morris avers, "had never seen an explosion of new products like that in the America of the 1880s and 1890s."

All this shopping caught the attention of two important social theorists, one of them famous and the other largely forgotten. It's yet another irony in the saga of America's love-hate relationship with thrift that we live by the precepts of the thinker whose name hardly anyone remembers.

First, the one you know about. Thorstein Veblen, the peripatetic Norwegian American economist (he died in 1929, shortly before the great crash that might have brought him grim satisfaction), is best known today for his theory of conspicuous consumption, which argued that a lot of spending is just a wasteful attempt to impress. Veblen explained consumerism in terms of status and display, bringing evolutionary ideas to bear on economics and consumer behavior, to powerful effect. Reading Veblen is a little like reading Freud or Darwin, albeit on a smaller scale; do so and you'll never look at the world in quite the same way again.

The iconoclastic Veblen took a dim view of all the conspicuous consumption around him, regarding it as a species of giant potlatch in which competitive waste had run amok. You might call Veblen's the voice of thrift, and it is still heard today from leftist intellectuals who, from their tenured pulpits and arts and crafts homes, reliably denounce the spending of others (mostly the bourgeoisie; it's up to conservatives to denounce the spending of the poor). The truth is that nobody listens to these people, except to submit to their periodic floggings as a kind of penance for sins we have no intention of not committing.

But there was another voice heard back when thrift was in its death throes—that of Simon Patten, who was, like Veblen, a maladjusted economist with strong ideas about spending. Patten can seem naïve and even crass to us today, for he used his pulpit at the University of Pennsylvania's Wharton School to advocate the very thing that Marx feared: that business and consumer spending should sweep away all the old arrangements and remake the world according to the doctrine of plenty. Affluence, in Patten's view, would breed self-restraint by lightening the burden of monotonous and backbreaking labor, leaving human virtue to flourish amid plenty. But he recognized that abundance must be accompanied by education and external constraint if it was to leave us truly better off. Schools could educate the young about the implications of affluence, while colleges and universities could inculcate self-control and other good habits. Government had a role to play as well, both in adopting legal constraints such as limits on consumer credit and financial speculation (he even advocated Prohibition) and in creating something like a classless society through taxes and redistribution. More than once, Patten warned that unfettered getting and spending "could create a society dedicated to gluttony and vice."

Yet the fact remains that, unlike Veblen, Patten came on the scene not to praise thrift but to bury it. The old values that "inculcated a spirit of resignation" and "emphasized the repression of wants" must be abandoned, Patten argued. "Restraint, denial and negation" were old hat. "The principle of sacrifice continues to be exalted by moralists at the very time when the social structure is being changed by the slow submergence of the primeval world, and the appearance of a land of unmeasured resources with a hoard of mobilized wealth."

Patten was hugely influential in his time, especially in helping liberals to see that something like Adam Smith's "universal opulence" should be a goal and not a cause for shame. His particular genius was in recognizing capitalism's potential to realize something like a modern Cockaigne, the mythical land of plenty that beguiled the suffering masses in the Middle Ages. His thinking opened the door to such later fulfillment-oriented intellectuals as Abraham Maslow and Herbert Marcuse, who implicitly (or explicitly) disparaged the idea of deferring gratification—a notion that would come to seem as pointlessly self-sacrificial as postponing happiness until the afterlife.

The embrace of affluence—and especially expenditure—was also promoted by advocates of organized labor and the eight-hour workday. George Gunton, for example, started from the premise that greater consumption was better for labor; more leisure for workers would give them more time for consumption, and this increased demand would translate into more demand for labor, higher wages, and a higher standard of living for all. Gunton regarded affluence as an unalloyed good and didn't fret much about constraint. This stance put him on a slippery slope that eventually led him to justify all kinds of consumption, until finally he was extolling the 1895 opening of Biltmore, George Vanderbilt's surreally vast North Carolina monument to conspicuous consumption, whose 125,000 acres and 250 rooms included forty-three bathrooms, sixty-five fireplaces, an indoor pool, and a bowling alley.

The eight-hour workday gradually caught on (and was enshrined in federal law in 1916), but Gunton never had as much status or influence as Patten or Veblen. Both of the latter were right about consumerism, in important ways, but of the two, Patten was the true radical, and beside his starry-eyed utopianism, Veblen's sour conservatism is plain to see. As things turned out, it's Patten's world we live in, even if we use the language of Veblen to understand it.

Patten and Veblen both died in the 1920s, during which affluence, technology, and changing social mores joined forces to drive a stake through the heart of pecuniary restraint. When the Great Depression came along, yet another economist, this one more important than either, would provide the intellectual justification for banishing frugality once and for all. If Patten considered affluence to justify the abandonment of thrift, John Maynard Keynes used the lack of affluence to reach the very same conclusion.

To Keynes, thrift was the enemy, for it was consumption that spurred growth. Saving was all well and good, but the paradox—the now-famous "paradox of thrift"—was that if people saved too much, everyone would be poorer, because a lack of spending can kill the economy. Economic health rested on consumption, and Keynes's prescription for the Great Depression was to increase government spending to spur increased private spending. If necessary, he said, government ought to bury cash so that people could have the remunerative work of digging it up. When everyone was out spending again, as they ought properly to be, the economy would recover. And basically, Keynes was right.

After World War II (during which Americans saved roughly a quarter of their income), the U.S. economy went into overdrive. In his 1954 study *People of Plenty: Economic Abundance and the American Character*, David M. Potter said of the American that "society expects him to consume his quota of goods—of automobiles, of whiskey, of television sets—by maintaining a certain standard of living, and it regards him as a 'good guy' for absorbing his share, while it snickers at the prudent, self-denying, abstemious thrift that an earlier generation would have respected." Or as William Whyte put it two years later in *The Organization Man*, "thrift is becoming a little un-American."

Self-control met its Waterloo in the 1960s, whose worthy liberations have happily outlived most of the decade's intellectual (and sartorial) excesses. The emphasis in those noisome days was on escaping not just the tyranny of capitalist-inflected social control, but also aspects of self-control that seemed of equally dubious provenance. The youth culture's embrace of consciousness-altering drugs can be seen as a turn to pharmacology for help in overthrowing a superego so insidiously effective we might not even be aware of its string-pulling and repressiveness, so familiar and even comfortable were its constraints. The interest in Eastern mysticism, meditation, free love, and other means of getting over and around ourselves—in letting it all hang out—was part of the same revolutionary upheaval. Brink Lindsey sums up the consequences with something like mimetic exuberance: "Freed from physical want and material insecurity, Americans in their millions began climbing Maslow's pyramid. They threw over the traditional Protestant ethos of self-denial and hurled themselves instead into an utterly unprecedented mass pursuit of personal fulfillment, reinventing and reinvigorating the perennial quests for belonging and status along the way. The realm of freedom, once imagined as a tranquil, happily-ever-after Utopia, turned out to be a free-for-all of feverish and unquenchable desire."

The sixties were followed by the seventies—and relentlessly rising prices, a powerful force for discouraging delay of gratification. Inflation, after all, creates the expectation that everything will be more expensive tomorrow, so the sensible thing to do is buy today. Saving is foolish, since your money will be worth less later on. But borrowing is smart, because a dollar borrowed today can be paid back with cheaper dollars down the road. Remember, money is only worth what it will buy, and when inflation is entrenched, everyone believes the value of money is eroding.

Inflation leapt up in America as a new generation—the baby boomers—were coming of age, the product of a new, more relaxed approach to child rearing. Parents who had grown up making the sacrifices required by the Great Depression and the Second World War would create a child-centered suburban paradise for their offspring in the sunshine of the great postwar economic boom. For complex reasons, that boom yielded to the stagflation of the seventies—which in turn led to the election of Ronald Reagan as president.

Recall that his opponent in 1980 was the incumbent Jimmy Carter, a Baptist regarded by many voters and comedians as a scold. Carter was self-control personified, lusting only in his heart and showing great restraint in the Iran hostage crisis. He chastised the electorate for indulgence and malaise, and even allowed himself to be seen in a beige wool cardigan, urging us to turn down our thermostats. Carter seemed to embody Aristotle's distinction between the continent man, who resists harmful indulgences he would dearly love to embrace, and the temperate man, who is simply refraining from excesses he probably wouldn't enjoy anyway. Expecting such a temperate president to get elected twice was probably asking a lot of the voters.

The gilded presidency of Ronald Reagan was something else again. It was not about limits or asceticism or self-restraint, except to the extent that people were supposed to be responsible for themselves. To Reagan, material desires were not shameful but perfectly legitimate and worthy of pursuit. Reagan cut taxes, said no to unions, and expanded on the deregulatory impulses of the previous administration. The heroic Paul Volcker, who was Federal Reserve chairman under both presidents, ruthlessly expunged inflation and demolished giant swaths of industrial obsolescence by jacking up interest rates.

Baby-boomer energy, unfettered capital, technological innovation, and a huge and growing pile of pension-fund assets fueled an economic boom that persisted, with a few hiccups, right into the first few years of the twenty-first century. It was helped along by cheap imports from Asia, an influx of hardworking immigrants, and what would later come to seem an insanely accommodating monetary policy espoused by

Volcker's libertarian-leaning successor, a former clarinet player named Alan Greenspan. The effect of all this was huge, perhaps even revolutionary, as the historian John Patrick Diggins explains: "With the 1980s came America's 'Emersonian Moment,' when people were told to trust not the state but the self and to pursue wealth and power without sin or shame. Far from being a conservative, Reagan was the great liberating spirit of modern American history, a political romantic impatient with the status quo."

Unfortunately, his administration's emphasis on individual financial empowerment and deregulation left us vulnerable to ourselves.

The Recent Crash

"Lead us not into temptation," Jesus says in the New Testament, "but deliver us from evil." There may have been evils from which Reagan delivered us, but there is little doubt that, as Diggins concludes, "Reagan led America into temptation," and we've hardly stopped spending ever since.

A few numbers tell the story. Home equity debt rose from $1 billion in the early 1980s to more than $1 trillion by the time of the 2008 crash. Since the early Reagan years, overall household debt more than doubled as a percentage of gross domestic product. The national savings rate hit zero in 2005 and 2006, although it's risen since. From the time of Reagan's first inauguration, personal bankruptcies per capita have risen sixfold. There were more than a million in 2008 alone.

How did all this happen? It wasn't just that Reagan legitimized consumption, although he did. More concretely, the Reagan era vastly expanded the freedom of choice we enjoy—and must cope with—as consumers and investors. Now, to a greater extent than ever before, we are masters of our own finances. Traditional employer-paid and -managed pensions have increasingly given way to self-directed retirement vehicles that individuals must fund and manage themselves, putting the onus on workers not just to set aside the money but to figure out how to invest it. Borrowing has become much easier. Once-exotic mortgage products have been made widely available to citizens who are often only dimly able to understand them.

Most people are ill-prepared for this brave new world. When I taught graduate students for a semester at a top university, I was amazed that they mostly didn't know a stock from a bond, or even a deposit from an investment. They weren't clear on where the government gets money, either. (They assumed taxes were levied mainly on wealth rather than income.) If these well-educated and worldly young adults were so completely in the dark about money, what does that say about everyone else?

But knowledge is no guarantee of prudence. "If there was anybody who should have avoided the mortgage catastrophe," writes Edmund Andrews, "it was I. As an economics reporter for the *New York Times*, I have been the paper's chief eyes and ears on the Federal Reserve for the past six years. I watched Alan Greenspan and his successor, Ben S. Bernanke, at close range. I wrote several early-warning articles in 2004 about the spike in go-go mortgages . . . But in 2004, I joined millions of otherwise-sane Americans in what we now know was a catastrophic binge on overpriced real estate and reckless mortgages."

By now it's a familiar story. Alan Greenspan and the Chinese made borrowing too easy, unfettered bankers chose greed over sobriety, and consumers snapped up McMansions financed by loans they could never repay. In 1980, the year Reagan was elected, American household debt stood at what must have seemed the enormous sum of $1.4 trillion. In 2008 the figure was ten times larger. Is it any wonder there were more than a million consumer bankruptcy filings that year? Or that the nation's banking system came close to collapse? The result of all this excess is a population hungover from its recent intoxication with spending and flabbergasted by the bill from the wine merchant.

There was a time when debt carried a stigma and bankrupts were practically pariahs. Americans lived in what some have called a culture of thrift, their spending constrained not just by modest incomes and frugal social mores but by a variety of thrift-oriented institutions and practices, from local building and loan societies (remember *It's a Wonderful Life?*) to hefty down-payment requirements and usury laws that capped the interest rate a lender could charge. A dense web of regulations kept banking simple, sleepy, and modestly profitable.

But the inflation of the seventies and the deregulation of the eighties, along with a rapidly changing society, gradually replaced this culture of thrift with a culture of profligacy, which is especially dangerous for working-class Americans. Barbara Dafoe Whitehead, a scholar whose interests seem to include self-control, writes, "The potential 'small saver' has been left behind as prey to new, highly profitable financial institutions: subprime credit card issuers and mortgage brokers, rent-to-own merchants, payday lenders, auto title lenders, tax refund lenders, private student-loan companies, franchise tax preparers, check cashing outlets and the state lottery. Once existing on society's margins, these institutions now constitute a large and aggressively expanding anti-thrift sector that is dragging hundreds of thousands of American consumers into profligacy and over-indebtedness. America now has a two-tier financial institutional system—one catering to the 'investor class,' the other to the 'lottery class.' "

Consider the rise of credit cards, financial instruments rivaled only by home equity loans as a way to get ourselves into trouble. Before the crisis, the average American family had thirteen of them, and 40 percent of U.S. households carried a credit card balance, up from just 6 percent in 1970. Credit cards are (usually) extremely profitable for banks, and until the recent near-death experience of the nation's financial system, credit card come-ons were ubiquitous. When I got a notice from the New York State Department of Motor Vehicles to renew the registration on my car, for example, it came with an ad from Discover, which offered an enticingly low initial interest rate (of zero) and various other blandishments if only I would sign up for a card.

What an egalitarian achievement: reckless overspending became a course open to practically every American, just like reckless investing. Changing attitudes toward debt, the end of usury laws, increasing paper wealth from rising stock and home prices, and stagnant incomes for many Americans all played a role. By the time of the crash, only 24 percent of Americans were debt free, compared with 42 percent half a century earlier.

While there are many culprits in the resulting financial crisis, it clearly represents a colossal failure of self-control, and by saying so I do not mean to exonerate the rich and powerful, who certainly behaved recklessly. John Mack, chairman of Morgan Stanley, even admitted publicly, "We cannot control ourselves." But neither do I mean to excuse the working- and middle-class families who, encouraged by profit seekers of every stripe, piled loan upon mortgage upon credit card and apparently never gave a thought to the morrow. And when it was all over—when it all came crashing horribly down, as it inevitably had to—people blamed the banks for lending them all that money, and the government for allowing the banks to do so. Where, we wailed, were the grown-ups? More to the point, where is Pogo when we need him to remind us that, "We have met the enemy and he is us."

Self-control and Social Change

*Any contract lenient enough to allow termination of hopeless marriages
cannot at the same time be strict enough to prevent opportunistic switching.*

—ROBERT FRANK

Franklin and Eleanor Roosevelt's marriage lasted for forty years,
ending only with the president's death in 1945. Would the Roos-
evelts have been happier divorced? It's hard to say. All we know
is that they stuck together through thick and thin, and that a lot of good
came of their sometimes painful partnership.

It was a different story for Franklin and Eleanor's five children, who
had twenty-nine kids—and racked up nineteen marriages and fifteen
divorces along the way. The evolution of matrimony from something
like an ironclad contract into an arrangement as likely to be broken as
not says a lot about the modern dilemma and the way social changes
have altered the self-control landscape.

As Dorothy recognized in *The Wizard of Oz*, we're not in Kansas
anymore. We don't live the small-town life that was once so madden-
ingly effective at constraining behavior. The role of women is radically
different from what it was even fifty years ago. Americans today are
also richer, more mobile, and more likely to live alone. On average they
spend many more years on this earth—as Franklin Roosevelt probably

would have done with modern medical care. Premarital sex is taken for granted, as is birth control and a little youthful experimentation with drugs. (Think of all the politicians who "didn't inhale.") Homosexuality has come out of the closet. Second careers, second homes, second spouses, and even second childhoods are commonplace.

These changes are part of a tectonic social adjustment: a shift, in the developed world, away from tradition and received social structures in favor of personal choice and self-invention. In the non-Islamic world, at least, church and ideology no longer provide much in the way of traditional limits on individual behavior. Communism, with its tyrannies large and small, is dead, and as a character in a Donald Barthelme story once remarked, opium is now the opiate of the people.

Amen, let us hasten to add; who wants someone else to tell us what to do? It's the same with money; although lots of people are ready to criticize affluence, nobody I know truly craves the opposite. But the result of these changes is that each of us must rely more on ourselves for the kind of restraint that was once imposed externally, back in the bad old days. In those days, "we still inhabited our parents' moral universe," the historian Tony Judt recalled recently in describing how circumscribed life was before the social revolution of the 1960s. "Dating was difficult—no one had cars; our homes were too small for privacy; contraception was available but only if you were willing to confront a disapproving pharmacist. There was a well-founded presumption of innocence and ignorance, for boys and girls alike. Most boys I knew attended single-sex schools and we rarely encountered women."

What accounts for this great change? Simply put, our social arrangements are freer now because we can afford them to be. As the political scientist Ronald Inglehart writes, "In a major part of the world, the disciplined, self-denying, and achievement-oriented norms of industrial society are giving way to an increasingly broad latitude for individual choice of lifestyles and individual self-expression."

That's a great achievement, but it comes at a price. Emile Durkheim, the father of modern sociology, warned in 1897 of the dangers that come with freedom, affluence, and technology—in particular, of a dangerous condition he called anomie (from the Greek *anomia*, lawlessness). Anomie means lacking clear norms, standards, or ideals. Aristotle stressed the importance of *telos*—one's purpose or goal—but anomie is a kind of Aristotelian vacuum, a demoralizing condition of purposelessness often brought on by rapid change. Durkheim felt that people should live in a web of interlocking networks and institutions that would provide a structure of values; without these values, we might fall into purely selfish and carnal behaviors. "The more weakened the groups to which [a man] belongs," Durkheim observed, "the less he depends on them, the more he consequently depends only on himself and recognizes no other rules of conduct than what are founded on his private interests."

It was a vision far different from the world so many of us live in today. "A Durkheimian society," psychologist Jonathan Haidt tells us, "would value self-control over self-expression, duty over rights, and loyalty to one's groups over concerns for outgroups." The hierarchical family was the model for that society, but it's on the wane in most of the developed world outside of Asia. The rise of divorce had undermined parental authority by giving children leverage to pry loose disciplinary constraints, if only by playing one parent against the other. And the willingness of adult offspring to move far away from parents—and vice versa, when retirement comes—has further weakened ties that once circumscribed behavior more tightly. In much of the world, the family's role has evolved from one of economic production to emotional satisfaction, transforming its inherent bias from discipline to indulgence. Families are less likely to be intact, and when a father is present he is less likely to be the authority figure he might have been in the days of patriarchy. My sense is that this role hasn't been taken up by mothers, although it is sometimes outsourced: witness the popularity of kids' martial arts classes, in which an instructor chosen for his ability to beat the crap out of everyone demands deference, punctuality, politeness, and respect—just as patriarchs were wont to do at home.

This change in the purpose of the family has encouraged the development of youth culture, which inevitably devalues patience, prudence, and other stodgy-sounding values associated with maturity. "Abandon" is a virtue in such an environment; it's not just what the young do, but what the non-young may embrace, if only to prove to themselves and others that they aren't old. We may color our behavior, in other words, for the same reason that we color our hair. Once boys in shorts yearned to dress like men, but now grown men dress themselves like boys. In the twentieth century, the historian Eli Zaretsky writes, people "separated from traditional familial morality, gave up their obsession with self-control and thrift, and entered into the sexualized 'dreamworlds' of mass consumption on behalf of a new orientation to personal life."

The Matrimonial Knot

Franklin and Eleanor Roosevelt were married in 1905, when young men and women typically lived at home—or boarded in someone else's home—until they wed, often turning over much of their earnings to their parents. In those days, for better or worse, only one in ten marriages ended in divorce.

The evolution of marriage since then illustrates the complex effects of technology, affluence, and social change on the problem of self-control. In the century since Franklin and Eleanor tied the knot, readily available birth control—the pill may yet be seen as the most momentous technology of the twentieth century—enabled us to have sex more easily outside of matrimony. Women got the vote and, eventually, legal abortion and other rights. Their growing earning power undermined the traditional patriarchal structure of marriage. Changing divorce laws (enacted by popularly elected legislators) made it easier to dissolve an unhappy union like Franklin and Eleanor's. And divorce long ago ceased to be a one-way ticket to social disrepute.

In Franklin and Eleanor's day, marriage was a fairly effective pre-commitment device. It was binding, and it constrained behavior by (ostensibly) putting other potential partners off-limits and raising the price of any breakup. Old-fashioned marriages were kind of like old-fashioned corsets: attractive, perhaps, but uncomfortably rigid once you got yourself into them, and most confining for women. Easily dissolved modern marriages are very different, for absent a lot of impulse suppression by both participants, the partnership will collapse. Marriages today probably consume self-control just as much as they bolster it—if not more so.

Despite all these changes, Americans still love marriage—as they always have. "There is certainly no country in the world," Alexis de Tocqueville wrote in the 1830s, "where the tie of marriage is more respected." Yet never before has marriage had less importance as an American social institution. There are fewer marriages per capita, they happen later, and, unless trends change, half of all marriages today will end in divorce.

Still, we refuse to give up on it. We are more marriage oriented than most comparable countries; Americans overwhelmingly want and believe in matrimony. But we're probably also more obsessed with personal fulfillment than people in most other places, which might make us likelier to seek out something new rather than live with discontent. These conflicting values of ours make for a turbulent conjugal landscape. Americans have high rates of both marriage and divorce, less-enduring cohabitation arrangements (and more of them), and a higher rate of childbearing by women who are not living with the baby's father. The churn rate of our domestic relations has rendered family life in the United States uniquely unstable. "No other comparable nation," the marriage scholar Andrew J. Cherlin observes, "has such a high level of multiple marital and cohabiting unions."

Would you be surprised to learn that America's high breakup rate might have something to do with self-control? For there are really two states of matrimony in America—one for those with education, and a much less stable one for those without. (Imagine them as the Denmark and Iraq of nuptials.) The divorce rate among college-educated women—probably the Americans who would score highest in any test of self-control—is much lower than it is among women without undergraduate degrees. And education is associated with better impulse control.

Americans sometimes lament the prevalence of divorce. Yet there is little tolerance for the idea of reversing no-fault divorce laws—even though Americans have a shorter wait for a no-fault divorce than couples in almost any other Western nation, and as we've already seen, speed kills self-control. But there is little evidence that reversing no-fault divorce would make much difference except to perpetuate the very worst marriages—to the detriment of women. Besides, where no-fault divorce is barred, couples often concoct whatever faults the legal system requires. Easing the financial burdens of the poorest married couples might help; then again, Americans have been poorer in the past and divorced less.

The really big change isn't in the law but in us. I think we're more willing to put our own happiness first. People who find their marriages unfulfilling want to split up, and there is no longer much social pressure to keep them together. Should there be? Probably. A little social pressure can do a world of good, as it has against smoking, and as with smoking cessation, third parties would benefit. For implicit in the way marriage has changed in the past half century is a shift in priorities that favors adults at the expense of kids.

While there is debate over how bad divorce is for children (some researchers argue that the problem for kids is domestic strife or poverty or family instability rather than marital dissolution), I am not aware of anyone arguing that our high rate of coupling and uncoupling is good for children. What we do know is that, for kids, divorce goes along with more suicide, delinquency, drug and alcohol addiction, poor school performance, domestic abuse, and other problems. Children of divorce are themselves more likely to divorce when they grow up.

The picture is even bleaker when you look at cohabitation. America's high rate of family reshuffling is unique in the industrialized world. In splitting up so often, we may be transferring significant costs to children, kicking the can of misery down the road to the next generation in our restless search for fulfillment today. If so, we are beggaring the future on behalf of the present, just as we have done with our over-spending and our over-warming of the planet.

There is no simple answer. What we've lost in our modern domestic arrangements is a strong if inflexible structure for channeling our actions to the benefit of others, even if we later change our minds about things. What we've saved are the lives of a good many women. The economists Betsey Stevenson and Justin Wolfers, partners who study marriage but so far have declined to engage in it, have found that "total female suicide declined by around 20 percent in the long run in states that adopted unilateral divorce." Domestic violence rates in those states also fell by about a third from 1976 to 1985. Unilateral divorce may also have helped reduce the murder of women. Violence was reduced so much, the economists concluded, that it must have gone down not just because some bad relationships ended, but because it fell in ongoing ones as well. Easier divorce, it seemed, was forcing men to treat their wives better. This would not have surprised Montaigne, who claimed that in Rome, "what made marriages honoured and secure for so long a period was freedom to break them at will. Men loved their wives more because they could lose them."

It's not even clear, in the age of divorce on demand, whether the legal part of marriage matters much anymore. An acquaintance of mine tells of having attended a large, lavish wedding as one of the very few guests in on the bride and groom's secret—which was that their wedding was a sham, since it had everything except the marriage license. The couple had decided that being legally married would result in too much of a tax penalty, and that they could have all the advantages without giving any role to the state. But keeping the secret was crucial, for if someone had let the cat out of the bag, it would have undermined the social pressure they wanted to bring to bear on themselves in favor of staying together.

For better or worse, some people are trying to rehabilitate marriage as a powerful commitment device. Three states—Louisiana, Arizona, and Arkansas—permit "covenant marriages," a type of marriage that is harder to get into and quite a bit harder to get out of. Covenant marriage seems to be largely a creature of Christian evangelism, and relatively few people choose it in the states where it's available. Those who do might be the least likely to get divorced in any case. But perhaps the concept, or something like it, deserves wider availability, and not just for the sake of the kids. There is some evidence that people are happier with the choices they make when those choices are irrevocable. (Covenant marriages can be ended, by the way, but usually only on very limited grounds, like imprisonment or adultery.) Covenant marriage tries to reassert the commitment function of marriage, which as an institution used to be something different from mere legally sanctioned cohabitation. And in general I like the idea of government offering people voluntary ways to constrain their own behavior, something I'll talk about a lot more later.

Meanwhile, people can do this sort of thing for themselves. A prenuptial agreement, for example, might contain a legally binding pledge to give a big chunk of the marital assets to some third party (who would know of the arrangement and strive to collect) in the event the marriage collapses. A *Wall Street Journal* blog reported on a similar real-life example that might also help stave off divorce—a prenup that imposes hefty fines for infidelity: "the spouse that cheats has to pay the other a percentage of his or her assets."

The family's decline probably contributes to another phenomenon that stealthily undermines our self-regulatory capacities: loneliness. "To be free is often to be lonely," W. H. Auden rightly observed, and we find ourselves today very free indeed. Social isolation seems to be increasing, and researchers have implicated it in overeating, poor diet, drug and alcohol abuse, bulimia, and suicide—all of which reflect a fundamental mispricing of the future compared with the present. Lonely people have a harder time concentrating (attention management is a key element of self-control), are more likely to divorce, and they get into more conflicts with neighbors and coworkers. The lonely also exercise less and sleep less efficiently.

Loneliness not only subverts behavioral self-control but also weakens the human organism's unconscious ability to control its own systems for optimal health. Loneliness "disrupts the regulation of key cellular processes deep within the body," reports the psychologist John Cacioppo, who has studied social isolation for years. It harms our immune systems, degrades cardiovascular performance, and may be "hastening millions of people to an early grave," even if only because the lonely are so much less able to resist harmful foods and intoxicants. In a study purporting to be a taste test, for example, lonelier people ate more cookies and rated their flavor more highly. Thomas Buddenbrook, the aging patriarch of the eponymous family in the novel by Thomas Mann, had a similar problem with loneliness and smoking. In explaining to his doctor—in 1874!—why he can't give up his beloved cigarettes, this most public of men complains of isolation: "One is so frightfully alone . . ."

Ultimate Ends

If the purpose of the family has changed, so too has the purpose of life, even if we don't often think about it. The historian Darrin McMahon has noted "the steady erosion of other ways of conceiving of life's purpose and end," such as virtue or honor, instead of just pleasure. "In a world that places a premium on good feeling and positive emotion, these other ends have nowhere near the power to channel and constrain our choices that they once did. The same may be said of religion—long considered the ultimate end—but which today, even in places like the United States, where religious observance remains strong, is more often than not treated as a means to a better and happier life."

Some religious constraints seem absurdly arbitrary, of course; my favorite is the ban on blended cloth in Leviticus. Yet most traditional religions, in one form or another, also usefully emphasize sobriety, sexual restraint, moderation, and mindfulness generally. Buddhism, for example, recommends a variety of sensible measures for avoiding temptations, including looking out for them in advance. It was no less than Mark Sanford, freshly back from a visit to his paramour on the pampas, who observed that, "God's law is indeed there to protect you from yourself."

South Carolina's straying governor notwithstanding, people who have religious faith may well have more self-control. Maybe it's because religions tend to deemphasize the here and now in favor of one's eternal soul or, at the very least, participation in some mystical unity, the grandeur of which makes overspending and marital infidelity seem petty and foolish. The very notion of an afterlife encourages future-mindedness and, once upon a time, made people defer gratification right up until they were dead, which I am prepared to admit is probably a little too long.

It's obvious even to an infidel like me that religion is a useful way for people to find meaning, or belonging, or even just solace in a harsh and chancy world—and in the absence of religion people are more likely to seek those things by pandering to their own less-welcome desires. Take away religion and you seem to create a vacuum that shopping and the like rush to fill. Spiritualism, which is flourishing, isn't the same thing; it doesn't forbid much of anything except perhaps self-awareness. And religious practice without genuine faith doesn't seem to work either; apparently rituals have to be faith based, like any other placebo, to have any benefit.

Where religion does persist in the Western world, it's less bent than it used to be on telling us what to do and what not to do. In a movement that started perhaps a century ago, modern pastors more than ever are rolling out a feel-good version of the old-time religion which says, essentially, that what you're doing is pretty much okay and by golly you ought to feel good about it. In this they are only responding to the marketplace, which wants the same good feelings from God as it does from movies. (Think of *I Am a Fugitive from a Chain Gang* or *All Quiet on the Western Front* or even *Von Ryan's Express.* Commercial pictures today aren't produced with such unhappy endings. Tragedy is out.)

Traditional religious practices persist in places, but here, too—as the Amish discovered—the challenges of modernity have ratcheted up the pressure on the *self* in *self-control.* Take the custom of *shomer negiah* among the Orthodox Jews, who consider interactions between unmarried men and women so combustible that they are forbidden even to

touch one another. The practice evolved for a different world, one
in which the faithful lived in closer-knit communities, nuptials were
arranged by family, and young adults didn't remain single for long. But
the world has changed, with the result that Orthodox Jews of both sexes
find themselves struggling to remain chaste—well into their twenties
and thirties.

"Historically, people got married much younger," says Rabbi Yosef
Blau, who counsels students at Yeshiva University, "so the whole notion
of being physically mature and holding back expressing it was not really
applicable. The level of control expected is greater than ever because
society functions so differently."

The Greek Way

In working on this book I discovered a mountain of scientific research on self-control—research that continues even as you read these words. Neuroscientists are working to unravel the biology of temptation and restraint, while psychologists have studied the ability of small children to postpone gratification—and then followed these kids into middle age, discovering that youthful self-control predicted success in later life. Other researchers have looked at the effect on self-control of loneliness, glucose, urban living, mobs, exhaustion, and countless other factors. Still other scientists have implicated self-control deficits in divorce, crime, obesity, and addiction. Their findings are fascinating and can help us understand who we are and how we should live. Soon enough we'll get to them. But after marinating in these issues for a while, I discovered that the very best guides to weakness of the will held no tenure, had no graduate degrees, and dealt with the problem without magnetic resonance imaging devices for peering into the skulls of undergraduates.

The ancient Greeks nailed it anyway. They grasped its importance, built it into their social system, and thought about it in sophisticated ways. They saw clearly that self-command is about time but also freedom, and that pleasure, like so many things, is only bad when taken to extremes. Most of all, they recognized human weakness without letting themselves off the hook.

The Greeks' profound concern with all this was manifest early on, long before the classical period of Plato and Aristotle, when Homer took appetite and self-mastery as his themes in his two great epic poems. Both *The Iliad* and *The Odyssey* are shot through with the recognition that people are weak, no matter how strong they may be on the battlefield. Even gods, after all, are subject to desire. Think of Ares and Aphrodite, snared in their lovemaking by Aphrodite's husband, Hephaestus, who chains them in their shame for all the gods to see. Temptation bedevils all of us. But if *The Iliad* is about the consequences of yielding to it (Helen, after all, is temptation personified), *The Odyssey* is about the heroism a man can show in mastering temptation, and it is this second epic which no serious student of self-control can afford to ignore.

The Hero

Who else but Odysseus could be the star of this story? As a hero, Odysseus had it all—strength, courage, and enough sex appeal to turn the head of more than one goddess. His best-known qualities—the ones that have defined him for the ages—are shrewdness (it was "wily" Odysseus, as Homer often called him, who cooked up the Trojan horse caper that ultimately ended the war) and tenacity, for his relentless drive to reach home. But his greatest strength is the combination of these two things, which form the basis for his extraordinary self-mastery.

What Odysseus had was *enkrateia,* which means roughly "self-command." *Enkrateia* seems to be about conflict: between the parts of oneself, but also between freedom and slavery, for defeat meant subjugation. This is what happened to women after a lost war, and weakness of the will shamefully implied emasculation. (For the Greeks and others, temptation was routinely seen as female.) The connection between *enkrateia* and virility is long standing, and since temptation was always a threat, masculinity was ever shadowed in peril. Self-mastery was how you kept your balls, and it took vigilance. "Miserable wretch," Socrates says at one point in alarm, "are you reckoning what will happen to you if you kiss a beautiful youth: instantly to be a slave instead of a free person."

Odysseus is shrewd, but his genius is the way he puts his wiles at the service of his determination, in the case of the Sirens even turning those wiles against himself. Our hero, you'll recall, is on his way home from the sacking of Troy. Knowing he won't be able to resist the song he's about to hear, he finds a way to enforce his own wish not to succumb to it—a wish he knows perfectly well he will soon repudiate under the spell of the music. *The Odyssey*, in fact, is all about temptation, and Odysseus survives the decade-long journey—he alone of all his men—back to Ithaca because when it counts, he can resist. Again and again they are waylaid by their appetites, getting high by eating lotus, getting themselves turned into pigs—living symbols of excess!—at a feast, and most tragically devouring the cattle of Helios, which they slaughter despite their leader's warnings.

In *The Odyssey*, impulsiveness always leads to problems, and even Odysseus himself succumbs occasionally—as when he taunts Cyclops during his getaway from the giant's cave, revealing his identity and thus allowing Poseidon to take revenge—but that only makes him human. Part of the guy's charm is that he isn't some willpower superhero; he can be rash as well as prudent, and when he's challenged, his cleverness sometimes deserts him, especially as the result of his desire for renown. Nor does he shy away from pleasure—he indulges happily with Circe, for example. He's no ascetic; his talent is for knowing when to indulge and when not to, which is why he is something of an ideal. "Whenever a present or future hurt may be avoided, or an advantage gained, his self-restraint is never wanting," one nineteenth-century critic observed, with only a little exaggeration, "but, failing this, he nowhere shows himself unwilling to gratify either his appetites or his passions."

The Polis

Self-control remained an obsession in the later "classical" period, around the fourth century BCE, the time of Plato and Aristotle, which is what we mostly think of when we think of ancient Greece. Greek ethics in this period boils down to a single phrase: *meden agan*, or nothing to excess. Someone who adhered to this principle was said to possess *sophrosyne*, which means something like temperance or self-mastery. A person who wasn't *sophron* must have had some moral deficit and lacked a kind of integrity. The classicist Helen North in her wonderful study of the subject, which appeared in the immoderate year of 1966, nicely described the key components of *sophrosyne* as "the control of appetite by reason and the harmonious agreement within the soul that this control should be exercised."

So having *sophrosyne* means that you have a grip on your desires *and you are glad that you do*. It's not about self-denial; rather, the emphasis here is on finding a place between too little control (always a danger) and too much, which is not so great either. Implicit in subordinating appetite to reason is the idea of deferring gratification. "*Sophrosyne* is related to the Greek tendency to interpret all kinds of experience—whether moral, political, aesthetic, physical, or metaphysical—in terms of harmony and proportion," North explains. "It is an expression of the self-knowledge and self-control that the Greek polis demanded of its citizens, to curb and counterbalance their individualism and self-assertion."

The idea here is not to suppress individuality or freedom but only to keep them within bounds to avoid personal and social chaos. Plato understood this when he argued in *The Republic* that citizens and the state should have the same four cardinal virtues: wisdom, courage, justice, and *sophrosyne* (sometimes rendered as "self-discipline"). "Self-discipline stretches across the whole scale," he wrote. His ideal republic was not a democracy. Thus, his ideal of *sophrosyne* lay not just in men's control of their desires "for the pleasures of eating, drinking, and sex" but also in men's "obedience to their rulers," which in the absence of freedom can seem cowardly or subservient.

But *sophrosyne* in a democracy is something else again, something honorable and freely chosen yet also essential, as it was in fourth-century Athens, where it could be a badge of freedom and virility (at least for the minority of Athenians who were free men). Called "the fairest gift of the gods" by Euripides, *sophrosyne* came to be seen as an Athenian virtue, one identified not just with democracy but also with upward mobility and maturity.

Perhaps the most direct and formidable argument for it comes in Plato's *Gorgias*. Socrates's foil in this great dialogue is Callicles, a proto-Nietzsche of sorts who argues shamelessly that happiness comes from self-indulgence. People praise self-restraint out of cowardice, in his view, and an inability to satisfy their passions. He held that convention is a mere expedient of the weak, and laws are merely the ropes that society's pathetic majority use to bind the strong. In his view, the temperate "are really fools, for how can a man be happy who is the servant of anything? On the contrary, I plainly assert, that he who would truly live ought to allow his desires to wax to the uttermost."

Hedonism is a virtue for Callicles, but one available only to the strong—to the few, in other words. His is a vision of goodness restricted to the elite, who are practically defined by the ability to give rein to their pleasures. But Socrates's emphasis on self-mastery makes virtue available to all. Self-control obviates the need for tyrannical power to feed one's passions; advocating *sophrosyne* only requires making each person his own ruler, an act that would prove enormously empowering— and appealing to those who were neither slaves nor aristocrats. As North tells us, "The same spirit as animates the reforms of Solon (the insistence on measure, the balancing of one party against the others, the instinct for moderation . . .) leads to the adoption by the emerging middle class of the virtue that symbolizes their innermost aspirations." The Athenian conception of self-control was thus a bourgeois phenomenon, and some flavor of *sophrosyne* would remain identified with the middle-class forever after—which probably accounts for some of moderation's more recent disrepute.

The political importance of self-control was particularly evident in the compact city-state known to the Greeks as the polis. The polis was a small place, lacking in privacy. People went about on foot; servants and family members were everywhere. Athens at its ancient peak was a prime example, a polis of just a few thousand native citizens (and thousands more women, children, and slaves). Day-to-day life in classical Athens went on with minimal state supervision—there were no police officers, censors, or curfews—but your fellow polis-dwellers were all around you, and they were watching. "Each and every inhabitant was a potential agent of the polis," the classicist James Davidson tells us, adding that the courts depended on witnesses, including domestic servants, to attest to almost anything that might be contested—and most everything was.

Outside the legal arena, there was the matter of public opinion. People of similar social station would tend to know—and talk to—one another. Reputation would matter enormously. "It is in the growth of the polis that we see conditions especially favorable to the development of *sophrosyne*," North tells us. "The polis by its very nature required a much greater exercise of restraint."

Contrast the intimacy of the polis, however suffocating, with the disinhibiting anonymity and vastness of the modern city—or perhaps worse, the modern sprawling suburb, with its blur of traffic and ubiquitous big-box stores dispensing goods as if they were Pez. If the polis enforced *sophrosyne* by its intensely personal nature, the modern city is much more likely to be a breeding ground for the affliction known as *akrasia*, and ever since the ancients put a name to it, it has given philosophers fits.

The Problem

To the Greeks, *akrasia* simply meant a lack of self-command, so that your desires run away with you contrary to the dictates of reason. The akratic acts against his own better judgment. And this is where the problems occur, because how could anyone do such a thing? Surely your judgment simply changed. As Socrates says in the *Protagoras*, "No one goes willingly toward the bad."

Yet who among us hasn't? It's a thorny problem. Philosophers disagree over what it takes to be akratic, or whether akrasia even exists. Socrates was perhaps the most famous dissenter; although his views seemed to evolve (and we mainly know what Plato tells us), he mostly insisted that you couldn't choose a course of action you didn't think was good. If you seemed to make such a choice, you were probably just acting on faulty or insufficient knowledge. Akrasia thus was a kind of ignorance.

Perhaps Socrates took this somewhat idealistic view because he excelled at self-restraint, especially where the urges of the body were concerned—and he must have had plenty of temptation, given that he was surrounded by admiring young men whose charms were not lost on him in a culture that countenanced homosexuality under certain circumstances. In Plato's *Symposium*, one of several Socratic dialogues that belong on any self-control reading list, we learn that Socrates has spent the night under the same cloak as a willing—nay, eager!—Alcibiades, the fairest of youths, yet made no overtures. And this wasn't for want of desire on the part of the philosopher, who discloses in another *Symposium* (this one by Xenophon) "that he does not remember a moment of his life during which he was not in love."

Socrates may have been strictly correct about akrasia, but human experience suggests that if he was, it was only on narrow technical grounds, and even then the case is hardly closed. "Of Socrates," wrote the philosopher E. J. Lemmon, who was obviously a believer, "we can say that as a plain matter of fact he was just wrong—acrasia [sic] does occur, or in Aristotle's phrase, knowledge just is, however sad this may be, frequently dragged about by desire."

Traditionally, akrasia was rendered in English as "incontinence," but perhaps owing to the snickering inspired by the word's urinary tang, it's more often translated on this side of the Atlantic as "weakness of the will," although this leaves out cases of what might be called negligent absence of the will. The term *incontinence* can capture these and has other advantages too, not least the vivid way it conveys a humiliating loss of control, a failure of the muscles charged with holding things in until the appropriate time and place can be found to let them out.

Psychologists have lately likened willpower to a muscle, complete with speculation about how to build it up and under what circumstances even the strongest wills become exhausted, but there are some important differences. You can resist murdering your exasperating next-door neighbor forever, but sooner or later, if you can't find a bathroom, no power at your disposal will keep you from wetting your pants. Moral fiber and muscle fiber have only so much in common. As John Dewey says, "We need to discriminate between the physical and the moral question."

Akrasia is a mysterious affliction, neutralizing principles, anesthetizing inhibition, and blurring farsighted vision so that you can do the kind of thing for which you might hate yourself in the morning. It often involves ignorance, but largely as the result of self-deception: *just this once; it's not that fattening; I'll stop smoking tomorrow; my wife will never know.* Akratic self-deception can be dangerous, as we learned all too recently from the bankers who, in the period leading up to the crash of 2008, had every reason to have faith in their complex (and little understood) financial technologies instead of focusing on the risks. "Faith," Friedrich Nietzsche tells us, "is the will not to know." Yet the bankers' ignorance is hard to distinguish from incontinence, for they surely acquiesced in their own deception just as I might acquiesce in violating my own diet.

Anyway, akrasia simply isn't supposed to resemble a banker. I prefer to think of it as a young woman in dark glasses, strategically torn jeans, and flip-flops, bearing a Starbucks cup as she emerges painfully into the blinding light of day. But here I am only indulging in some age-old masculine stereotyping, for literary history is littered with powerful females portrayed as tempting men away from self-mastery—and in the process, threatening their manhood. There's a seductress of knights in *The Faerie Queene* by the name of Acrasia, for example, a "false enchauntresse" reminiscent of Circe, who waylaid Odysseus and his men. Given what we know about male impulsivity, it might be fairer to portray akrasia here as a raw-boned slacker dude fueled by Walmart cola and focused intensely on a video game, thumbs twitching madly in the basement of his mother's house in the middle of the night.

Yet Edmund Spenser's conception of akrasia as seducer remains essentially sound even from the relatively gender-neutral perspective of our own times. Or perhaps the seducer is really temptation itself, and akrasia describes the process of being seduced—of acquiescing to our own subversion by doing the thing we should not, possibly against at least some of our own wishes. We go along in spite of ourselves, perhaps in both trepidation and relief, giving in as if to a wayward lover whom on principle we ought to resist. Like such a lover, akrasia is habit-forming; one episode tends to lead to another and therefore threatens to make us into something we might not want to be. "We are what we repeatedly do," Will Durant wrote in summarizing Aristotle on this score. "Excellence, then, is not an act but a habit."

The Guru

Aristotle (384–322 BCE) grew up in Macedonia and at seventeen became a pupil of Plato, who in turn had been a pupil of Socrates. After two decades at Plato's Academy, Aristotle was hired by King Philip of Macedonia to tutor his teenage son, who would become Alexander the Great. But what matters here is that, for all who lie awake at night wondering about the problem of self-control, Aristotle was the sage of sages, for self-mastery was central to his ethical system as well as his conception of the good life: "I count him braver who overcomes his desires than him who conquers his enemies, for the hardest victory is the victory over self." Aristotle's work on this subject, in his *Nicomachean Ethics*, shines a beacon so strong that it illuminates our lives to this day.

To Aristotle, the object of life was *eudaimonia*, a form of happiness that he was careful to distinguish from mere pleasure or amusement. He had in mind something larger, something we might call a good or virtuous life, which philosophers lately have sometimes described as human flourishing. And he recognized that pleasures taken to excess could threaten this life, leading to misery. The solution was to live according to the mean, avoiding both excess and deficiency.

Notice that too much and too little are *both* considered vices (although "one of the extremes is always more erroneous than the other"); this implies that the good life isn't made of continuous self-denial—or for that matter, the mindless suppression of zeal. On the contrary, what Aristotle is talking about here is something like suitability about doing the right thing at the right time in the right way for the right reasons. The implication is that there are times when immoderate actions are precisely what the situation calls for; the devil is in knowing when this is. Ideologues see such circumstances everywhere: "I would remind you that extremism in the defense of liberty is no vice," Barry Goldwater famously said in accepting the Republican presidential nomination in 1964. "And let me remind you also that moderation in the pursuit of justice is no virtue."

So the mean isn't just about ordering a medium coffee or leading a life of mildness. To modern ears moderation sounds dull, but, in fact, it can be heroic; to Aristotle, the moderate person—the person who moderates his behavior to the occasion—is "magnificent," the immoderate merely vulgar. Finding and adhering to this mean will not be easy, and even with the best of intentions we find ourselves veering toward one pole or the other. Getting it right takes knowledge and effort, just like achieving happiness, and cultivating good habits can help us with this challenge. In keeping with his emphasis on deeds, Aristotle intuited what psychologists would later demonstrate, which is that one right choice piled on another would raise the likelihood of future right choices, resulting eventually in the edifice of a good life. "Refrain tonight," Hamlet urges his mother. "And that shall lend a kind of easiness/To the next abstinence; the next more easy;/For use almost can change the stamp of nature/And either master the devil, or throw him out."

Aristotle also understood that living the sort of virtuous life he had in mind—perennially holding the reins of one's appetites and emotions, indulging them when appropriate and suppressing them when not—imposes an enormous burden for any of us by ourselves. So he emphasized the role of friends—not acquaintances, or contacts, or drinking buddies, but real friends. These serious friendships take time to develop, he recognized, and we are unlikely to have many of them, but they're invaluable because they foster virtue. Besides, happiness is not something that happens overnight, or as the result of some quick fix. "The good for man," Aristotle argued, "is an activity of the soul in accordance with virtue . . . in a complete lifetime. One swallow does not make a summer; neither does one day."

It's striking how much Aristotle anticipates the questions that bedevil us today, not just in everyday life but in the lab as well. He tries to address, for example, to what extent we are responsible for our happiness. "Is happiness something that can be learnt, or acquired by habituation or cultivated in some other way, or does it come to us by a sort of divine dispensation or even by chance?" Might it be hereditary, in other words? Or are we just victims of happenstance, subject to the whims of fate (the arrival of a fortune, the loss of a loved one, the curse of ill health)? Aristotle allows for these things, noting that misfortunes, if they are numerous and severe enough, can have an impact; it always helps to have the gods smile on us. But he defines happiness as "a kind of virtuous activity of soul," and this activity is clearly within our powers to undertake. On that basis, we're heavily responsible for our own happiness—and even at least partly for our dispositions. "Wickedness," Aristotle says flatly, "is voluntary."

It's fair to say that the disease model of addiction never gained any traction with Aristotle. In *The Nicomachean Ethics* he carefully analyzes voluntary (as opposed to compulsory) behavior and moral responsibility. "An act is compulsory," he writes, "when it has an external origin of such a kind that the agent or patient contributes nothing to it."

Examples might be a person on a sailboat carried off by the wind, or someone on the street thrown into a van by kidnappers.

While recognizing some gray areas—sailors might have to toss cargo overboard to save themselves in a storm, a voluntary act mandated by circumstances—Aristotle takes a pretty hard line on most behavior. He has no patience for the notion that pleasure can have a compulsive effect on us because "it would make all acts compulsory." Even going to the dentist results in the pleasure of keeping one's teeth. Nor is ignorance any excuse, unless it's a very particular kind of ignorance; for example, shooting your enemy because you hadn't yet learned that a cease-fire was signed. Beyond this, ignorance of right and wrong, including the ignorance induced by drunkenness or rage, is simply inadmissible.

Yet ignorance, for Aristotle, was not something to gloss over lightly (as we must unfortunately do here); on the contrary, his analysis of it made it possible for him to answer Socrates's question of how someone could fail to restrain himself even if he knows that what he wants to do is such a terrible idea.

The answer is that while we may possess knowledge, we are not always using it. I may know, for instance, where we hide a spare key at our house, or how to say "grapefruit" in French. But as I sit here typing, imagining an impatient reader, I am not using this knowledge, and, in fact, researchers have found that people who were made to think of self-discipline (by having to unscramble sentences about it) immediately made more future-oriented snack choices than those given sentences about self-indulgence. Put in mind of what they already knew—in effect, pushed to *use* their knowledge—they acted more in keeping with it.

But why don't we have this knowledge when we need it—at a bar, for instance, or a casino? Aristotle seems to have understood perfectly what scientists like George Loewenstein would later prove about hot and cold states, observing that "outbursts of anger and sexual appetites and some other such passions, it is evident, actually alter our bodily condition, and in some men even produce fits of madness."

That's no excuse, of course. In general, Aristotle was impatient with excuses and finger-pointing. He noticed our inconsistent tendency to

take credit for worthy actions while blaming things outside ourselves—
drugs, circumstances, fate—for the unworthy things we do. Aristotle
thought we ought to own up to both and implies that we're responsible
for a lot more than we typically admit. We're responsible for our moral
states, for example; a pattern of dishonesty and dissipation will lead
to actions in keeping with these traits, yet we're responsible nonetheless, because we create the patterns that we are victims of. We might
have formed different habits. We might even have formed different
dispositions, since as Aristotle asserts (and some modern psychologists
also contend), "we ourselves are in a sense partly responsible for our
dispositions."

Aristotle won't even exonerate us for how we look, a stance that
should carry particular sting for modern-day Americans. He notes
that blindness from birth or illness is beyond reproach, but not the loss
of eyesight from too much drinking. Similarly, we bear responsibility
for our appearance when it is shaped by our own acts or omissions.
"Nobody blames those who are naturally ugly," he observes, "but we
do blame those who become so through lack of exercise and care for
their appearance."

As you might imagine, Aristotle had a good deal to say about incontinence. Akrasia, he contended, is of two kinds. The first type is the one
that beset John Cheever when he reached for the bottle despite his earlier resolve not to. It's happened to all of us. We resolve to work, but sit
down to watch an inning of the ball game, and get up nine innings later,
having known the whole time that we were supposed to be doing something else. Or perhaps we've resolved to eat a healthier diet, but then
find an excuse to make gluttons of ourselves. This all-too-familiar form
of akrasia Aristotle called *astheneia,* which means, roughly, weakness.
The weak person does what is bad in full knowledge of what is good,
and therefore lives in conflict with himself. He knows appetite ought to
submit to reason; his problem is what most of us would call willpower.

The second type of akratic, Aristotle said, suffers from *propeteia,* or
impetuosity, the psychology of which is very different from *astheneia.*
This impetuous akratic acts without even thinking of whether he does

good or ill. His appetites are simply allowed free rein, inevitably to the detriment of himself and others—if only because he belongs to them, rather than vice versa. He is led by them blindly, like a bull by a nose ring.

Responsible people tend toward *astheneia*, but the irresponsible, almost by definition, are given to *propeteia*, and much of the time, when we decry a lack of self-control in others, this is the kind of akrasia we are criticizing. "He's so thoughtless," we might say in anger or disgust. We all know people like this; the akratic of this type makes noise in theaters, has a terrible temper, gets into fights, can't keep a job, lies all the time, is a stranger to sexual fidelity, and so forth. Extreme cases qualify for a medical diagnosis: antisocial personality disorder. Such impulsive akratics do not get much sympathy; we tend to forgive lapses in willpower more readily than indifference, perhaps because weakness at least reflects good intentions.

But Aristotle implied that failing to enact your will was no less a shortcoming than not bothering to have one. In doing so he was pointing out the terrible ethical pitfalls of reckless action—much as Harry Frankfurt would later, in calling such a person a wanton. Hannah Arendt would make a similar connection while covering the 1963 trial of Adolf Eichmann in Jerusalem. Eichmann, it seems, had not reflected much on the morality of his actions, prompting Arendt to make the sobering observation that "such thoughtlessness can wreak more havoc than all the evil instincts taken together."

Drinking It All In

For all their philosophizing, the ancient Greeks understood the importance of social structures in enabling individuals to keep themselves in line. In ancient Athens, as James Davidson reminds us, "appetites were managed constantly and minutely through a series of ubiquitous practices. Each cup should contain more water than wine, each mouthful more bread than meat."

The utility of these practices, so many of which have been swept away in the haste and atomization of modern life, is apparent in the tradition of the symposium itself, which was basically a highly ritualized drinking party. The protocol for these events was well established and shows how helpful ritual can be in promoting pleasure by keeping it within bounds. Except for a ceremonial taste of undiluted wine at the beginning, the wine was always mixed with water to produce a drink perhaps as potent as modern beer, and the number of kraters (urns, basically, for mixing wine) was limited in advance, often to three. The size of the cups and the pace of the drinking was controlled as well, and the aim was socializing rather than inebriation, although everyone must have gotten a buzz. Plato's *Symposium*, in fact, opens with a discussion of how the guests, still hungover from the previous night's antics, are going to drink. The Greeks apparently knew instinctively that these decisions were best made in advance, in front of one another, and in the sober light of reason.

8

The Marshmallow Test

Walter Mischel came to study self-control by a circuitous route. Like Sigmund Freud and Billy Wilder, both of whom plumbed the murky depths of temptation and desire before him, Mischel was from Vienna and left under similar circumstances, although at a much younger age. Mischel was just a boy, and his is a classic story of its type: the prosperous and assimilated Jewish family impoverished and humiliated by the Nazis, the lucky escape to America, the sight of Manhattan breathtaking from the boat, the small store in Brooklyn, the unrelenting toil and sense of displacement, the brilliant son, the odd jobs in the garment business and in a department store, the awakening to literature. His overprotective mother, in Europe seen mainly on a divan with an ice pack on her head, was here transformed into a formidable businesswoman, shucking off her Old World vapors while instilling in the boy (just as Freud's mother did) the belief that he could do anything. He could paint, for example, and never mind that there was no money: "Oil colors were too expensive, but I found that Jell-O, my mother's favorite fare, mixed the right way, especially the reds, could work reasonably, and a mostly Jell-O self-portrait at age 17 still hangs unfaded and uneaten in my Manhattan apartment."

Mischel wrote those words as an old man at Columbia University, where he is still conducting research into self-control. But in the 1950s he was a young psychologist at Ohio State University when his then wife obtained a grant to study spirit possession in the Orisha religion of Trinidad. Trinidad seemed a lot more exciting than Ohio, so Mischel went along, spending summers there from 1955 to 1958. Orisha was then known as Shango, and Mischel reports that while the psychological tests he tried to administer were a waste of time, Shango and its practitioners were fascinating. In their religious ceremonies, he observed an intentional loss of control: "Laborers and domestic servants of the British by day became 'possessed' at night by the mix of saints and African gods whose spirits 'rode' them as they danced in hypnotized states, enacting their godlike roles, with the irresistible drums pounding and the rum bottles passing."

Mischel spent his time in a section of Trinidad where the people were either of African or East Indian descent, both groups having found their way to the Caribbean as the result of British colonialism. Members of each group lived with their own kind, and each appeared to have its own values and stereotypes: "It did not take much listening to note a recurrent theme in their characterizations of each other. In the eyes of the East Indians, the Africans were just pleasure-bent, impulsive, eager to have a good time and live in the moment while never planning or thinking ahead about the future. Reciprocally, the Africans saw their East Indian neighbors as just working for the future and stuffing their money under the mattress without ever enjoying today."

His curiosity piqued, Mischel went into the local schools and began to study children of both ethnic groups. He started interviewing kids to discern such things as their family situation, their motivation to achieve, and their intelligence. Then he did something hugely consequential.

When students completed Mischel's questionnaire, he showed them two potential candy rewards, one costing just a penny and the other ten cents. He'd already learned from the students that, as expected, they much preferred the ten-cent candy, except the rewards now came with a catch: Mischel explained that he didn't have enough of the better candies just then, so students would be given a choice of taking a penny candy now or the vastly more desirable ten-cent candy in a week. He then recorded their choices and correlated them with other factors he was studying.

In the first paper to emerge from this research, in 1958, the results were consistent with the cultural pattern he'd previously observed. Mischel studied children ages seven to nine. Of the black students, twenty-two out of thirty-five chose the smaller, immediate reward. Of the Indian students, these proportions were almost exactly reversed: twelve of eighteen held out for the larger candy. Mischel and later commentators speculated that these results might be a function of the students' doubt that the later reward would ever materialize. Bolstering this notion was the remarkable finding that all eleven students without a father at home (ten of whom were black) chose the immediate reward, suggesting that the lack of a reliable male parent impaired confidence in the promises of grown-ups—and was a better predictor than ethnicity of what choice a child would make. (It's also possible that men who live apart from their families are more prone to immediate gratification and that their children have inherited this impulsive bent.)

Subsequent research on race and delay of gratification has produced mixed results; a 1983 survey in the *Journal of Black Psychology* found no clear pattern. But an interesting study in Atlanta underscored the importance of trust. Bonnie R. Strickland reported in 1972 that black sixth-graders were much less likely to choose a larger, later reward than white students were—when the promise of a later reward came from a white experimenter. When the experimenter was black, however, black students were dramatically more willing to delay gratification, although still at a level well below that of white students, whose willingness was unaffected by the experimenter's race.

Today Walter Mischel is a towering figure in the quietly sizzling realm of what might be called self-control studies. The technique that he used in Trinidad would come to be known as the "delay of gratification paradigm," which basically means offering someone the choice of a small, immediate reward or a larger, later one—often much larger but not much later, so that the later reward is unequivocally a better deal—and has become the standard method of probing people's ability to postpone rewards and exercise self-control. As a result of his summers in the Caribbean, Mischel wrote a series of papers looking at the relationship between delay of gratification and attention, intelligence, age, family structure, and income—papers, in other words, that addressed some of the most important questions in the field. More important still, his visits to Trinidad were the start of a lifelong effort to understand the problem of self-control experimentally. This effort would result in a body of astonishing research, most of it built on the foundations he established in the Caribbean. A lot of what we know (or suspect) about self-control today can be traced back to Mischel's earliest efforts, which is one reason they're worth exploring today.

Another is that one distilled nugget of his research, colloquially known as "the marshmallow test," would eventually become a staple of preachers and pundits. The test presents kids with a choice of one treat now or two if they can just wait a while. Mischel's findings with this test have prompted a series of motivational books, and DON'T EAT THE MARSHMALLOW was emblazoned on T-shirts in a Philadelphia charter school. The test would come to have political implications, too, like a modern version of Aesop's fable of the ant and the scarab beetle (better known to us today as the story of a thrifty ant and an improvident grasshopper), but anointed by science. We'll get to the marshmallow test in a minute. The point, for now, is that Mischel's research shows with stunning clarity just how important self-control is in people's lives.

What commentators rarely pay much attention to is the troubling question raised by Mischel's research. Self-control matters, sure. But does his work show that we should exercise more of it? Or that we can't, because our capacity for it is inborn? And if it is inborn, doesn't that turn all the homilies citing Mischel's work into parables about the hopelessness of predestination? "It's highly likely to be like most things in life are turning out to be," says Mischel, "which is, yes, the wiring makes a difference. And yes, the experience makes a difference. And the wiring and the experience are interacting and changing each other."

But we're getting ahead of ourselves. Let's go back instead to Mischel's time at wintry Harvard, that Puritan-inspired institution a world away from balmy Trinidad. It was at Harvard that he and his associates managed to complete some fascinating studies among Boston-area children. In this work, Mischel built on what he'd learned in Trinidad and used some of the same general techniques. In a study focusing on temptation, for instance, elementary school boys were invited to play an arcade-style game in which they were to shoot a toy ray gun at a disabled rocket. Each child was assigned to keep score for himself while the experimenter was out of the room, supposedly busy with paperwork. But the game was set up so that no matter how skillfully the weapon was fired, it was impossible to score enough points to win a badge at any of the three levels of highest expertise. The game, in other words, almost cried out for the kids to cheat. And cheat they did.

Mischel and Carol Gilligan, his coauthor (who would someday become famous for raising alarms about the supposedly inferior treatment of girls in school), also offered the children a series of choices between smaller, immediate rewards or larger, later rewards. The children's responses enabled the researchers to grade their ability to delay gratification. Mischel and Gilligan found that the kids best able to do so were also least likely to cheat. And of those who did cheat, the ones best able to delay gratification waited longest before chiseling.

In other studies of Boston-area children, Mischel and his colleagues found that kids who were better able to delay gratification—typically, those who chose to wait a bit for an unequivocally superior reward instead of grabbing for the smaller one immediately—tended to be more intelligent, more socially responsible, and more ambitious for achievement. As Mischel put it in the deflating language of science, "The obtained concurrent associations are extensive."

But in the early 1960s, Mischel began to find Harvard's psychology department less and less hospitable. "The place kept getting crazier," Mischel wrote later, and "it was impossible to work." The reason, basically, was Timothy Leary, with whom Mischel got along well at first, since the two shared an interest in personality assessment. But Leary soon moved on to matters psychedelic, while the newly minted PhD Richard Alpert was on his way to becoming Baba Ram Dass. "Mattresses suddenly replaced several of the graduate student desks," Mischel writes of those days, "and large packages from Ciba chemicals in Switzerland began to arrive in the department mail."

In 1962, Mischel moved to Stanford, where he would undertake the experiments for which he is now famous. He spent nearly twenty years there with his second wife, with whom he had three daughters in rapid succession. Watching the girls grow up made him wonder all the more about how rewards enable people to delay gratification—and about the development of willpower, "a term that as a psychologist I still put into quotes."

Stanford University's new Bing Nursery School proved the ideal place to explore these issues. Not only did it put a group of young kids close at hand; it even came equipped with big one-way observation windows. Mischel already had a broad sense of how his Bing experiments would be carried out; he would use the techniques he'd employed in Trinidad. But this time he drew on his own daughters for some of his hypotheses. Perhaps more important, at Stanford he had time on his side, for over the succeeding decades Mischel and an ever changing cast of colleagues and graduate students would follow up on the Bing alumni, with remarkable results.

The experiments ran from 1968 to 1974, a time of turmoil outside the nursery walls—a period spanning Vietnam and Watergate, the assassinations of Robert Kennedy and Martin Luther King Jr. A total of 653 children participated during those years, of whom 316 were boys and 337 girls, and on average they were a few months past their fourth birthday. In a typical experiment, Mischel or one of his associates might play with a four-year-old for a few minutes and then sit the child at a table. On this table there might be three distinct things: a single marshmallow, a pair of marshmallows, and a bell. The experimenter would explain that he had to leave for a bit and that the child would have a choice. If he waited for the adult's return, he could have the pair of marshmallows. But if he didn't want to wait, he could summon the grown-up by ringing the bell—in which case he could only have one marshmallow.

The experimenter would then leave the room for up to (usually) fifteen minutes. In some tests, the rewards were left exposed on the table, but in others they were removed from sight. In some, the children were even given advice (sometimes good, sometimes bad) on how to hold out. In all cases, the crucial measurement was: How many seconds would it take for the child to ring the bell?

The mostly middle-class Bing children in these experiments were around four and a half years old, an age at which it's hard to delay gratification—in part because there's still a lot of brain development ahead, but also perhaps because little kids haven't yet learned any strategies for keeping temptation at bay. The experimenters tried various suggestions during the different experimental configurations and discovered that telling the children to contemplate the treat's arousing properties—the luscious sweet flavor, for instance—not only cut delay times, at least when the rewards were exposed, but narrowed differences between children. And in the absence of any advice from the experimenters, the children tried their own strategies, some sensible and some not.

Self-distraction generally was effective. Some of the kids with the longest delay times covered their eyes or rested their heads on their arms. Others talked to themselves, turned their backs and sang songs, made up games with their hands and feet, tried to go to sleep to make the time pass, or climbed under the table to escape temptation. One boy took to kicking the table; "it's a very male response," says Mischel. Another boy, confronted with Oreos, seized one, pried it open, licked out the cream and then reassembled the cookie on the tray.

Mischel, an elfin figure who nowadays resembles a distant cousin of Yoda in *Star Wars*, spent hours watching the kids squirming and extemporizing from behind the nursery school's one-way glass. He learned that what determined how long they could hold out before ringing the bell (if they rang at all) was how the children handled the challenge mentally. "We saw that what mattered was what was in their heads, and that trumped what was actually in front of them: The duration of delay depended on specific types of 'hot' or 'cool' mental representations and the ways in which attention was deployed during the delay interval."

The idea that the brain is divided into "hot" and "cool" areas has gained some currency among researchers. The notion is that the cool areas, probably associated with the hippocampus and frontal lobes, correspond to what philosophers might call reason. They are rational and generate planned, advantageous behavior. The hot areas are more primitive, and develop earlier in young children. These areas, associated with immediate survival and operating more reflexively, take care of appetitive processing, fight-or-flight reactions, and other instant responses to stimuli. What Mischel and some other researchers think nowadays is that children held out more effectively when they were able to shift processing from the hot to the cold brain systems. In a recent interview, Mischel put it this way: "The same child who can't wait a minute if they're thinking about how yummy and chewy the marshmallow is can wait for 20 minutes if they're thinking of the marshmallow as being puffy like a cotton ball or like a cloud floating in the sky."

Clearly there's a lot to be learned about self-control from these Bing Nursery experiments: attention management helps, focusing on the attractive qualities of the thing to be resisted does not, and keeping the desired object out of sight helps, too. So does thinking of the thing in an abstract way—the crunchy, salty pretzels might be construed as tasteless miniature logs. State of mind matters, sure, but the important point is that we have some control over our states of mind, even at the age of four.

Even more interesting is what Mischel and his colleagues discovered some years later, in follow-up studies of the same Bing four-year-olds: the best performers on the marshmallow test had developed into the best-adjusted adolescents.

"Those who had waited longer in this situation at four years of age were described more than ten years later by their parents as adolescents who were more academically and socially competent than their peers and more able to cope with frustration and resist temptation . . . Parents saw their children as more verbally fluent and able to express ideas; they used and responded to reason, were attentive and able to concentrate, to plan, and to think ahead, and were competent and skillful. Likewise they were perceived as able to cope and deal with stress more maturely and seemed more self-assured. In some variations of this laboratory situation, seconds of delay time in preschool also were related to their Scholastic Aptitude Test (SAT) scores when they applied to college."

Mischel hasn't published the size of the SAT difference between those who could wait and those who couldn't, but he's told some people that it was 210 points—which would be huge. And there was more. The kids with the shortest delay scores, according to Mischel, had lower grade point averages, more school suspensions, and "were most likely to end up as the bullies." The ability to delay gratification also predicted body weight: kids with the higher delay scores were thinner. (This last finding was bolstered recently in two separate studies involving more than 1,800 children. Like Mischel, the researchers offered four- and five-year-olds a bigger treat if they could wait, discovering that kids less able to delay gratification were more likely to be fat by the age of eleven.)

By now Mischel knew he was really onto something, and he continued to follow his Bing Nursery subjects into adulthood. In another study, this time when the kids had reached an average age of twenty-seven, Mischel and his colleagues looked at sensitivity to rejection, which can be seen as a measure of social anxiety, and how it related to their performance years earlier as four-year-olds. The study, which covered 152 Bing alumni, found that rejection sensitivity caused problems for those found to have it—unless they had also had high delay-of-gratification scores at Bing, in which case rejection sensitivity didn't seem to matter much. Highly rejection-sensitive individuals with *low* delay-of-gratification scores as tykes—these were the kids who just couldn't wait—were found later in life to have lower educational attainment and more use of cocaine or crack.

About those four-year-olds: You're probably wondering how long they managed to hold out in the face of all those marshmallows, pretzels, and so forth. In one paper that followed up on 185 of the kids, Mischel and colleagues reported that this group on average managed to delay gobbling their treat for 512.8 seconds, or less than nine minutes. On the whole, Mischel has said, depending on the goodies at hand and other circumstances, his four-year-olds held out for seven or eight minutes. But some could hold out for much longer—perhaps as long as twenty minutes.

Walter Mischel is a pioneer, but he isn't the only one who's noticed the many ramifications associated with self-control in the young. Take school performance, for example. A number of researchers have found self-regulatory abilities to be associated with grades.

Angela Duckworth and Martin Seligman are psychologists at the University of Pennsylvania's dubious-sounding Positive Psychology Center, which actually isn't dubious at all; Seligman is director and pretty much inventor of the positive psychology field, which studies the emotions, actions, and institutions that contribute to happiness. People do in fact have some control over their mental states. We know, for example, not only that emotions cause facial expressions, but that the arrow of causality runs in reverse as well, so that putting on a happy face really can make you happier. It doesn't take a PhD to know that cultivating good thoughts helps, too. Long before we had a Positive Psychology Center, the Roman emperor Marcus Aurelius observed: "Such as are thy habitual thoughts, such also will be the character of thy mind; for the soul is dyed by the thoughts."

In a 2005 study of 140 eighth-graders at an ethnically diverse magnet school, Duckworth (a former schoolteacher) and Seligman first graded the kids on self-discipline by using ratings from their parents and teachers and from the students' own responses to a questionnaire that asked such things as, How hard is it for you to break bad habits? This all happened in the fall, near the beginning of the school year. In spring the researchers came back and found that self-discipline was correlated with school attendance, grades, standardized achievement test scores, and eventual admission to a competitive high school.

Duckworth and Seligman repeated the study with another 164 eighth-graders, this time adding a delay-of-gratification task and an IQ test. Self-discipline turned out to be a vastly better predictor of grades than was IQ—not surprisingly, since doing well in school requires sustained effort, putting off fun when it's time to do homework, and steady work toward the long-range goal of a high grade at term's end. Self-discipline also more accurately predicted attendance, how much time was spent on homework, and even at what time each evening homework was commenced. Self-discipline was also a much better predictor of how much TV the kids watched; the higher the self-discipline score, the less time in front of the tube. Afterward, the psychologists did not mince words.

"Underachievement among American youth is often blamed on inadequate teachers, boring textbooks, and large class sizes," they wrote. "We suggest another reason for students falling short of their intellectual potential: their failure to exercise self-discipline . . . We believe that many of America's children have trouble making choices that require them to sacrifice short-term pleasure for long-term gain, and that programs that build self-discipline may be the royal road to building academic achievement."

Duckworth and Seligman found something else pretty interesting. They knew that girls consistently get better grades than boys in K–12 schooling, yet fail to outperform boys on achievement or IQ tests. So they wondered if self-control might play a role. After analyzing their data, they concluded that in their study, at least, it did. The girls were more self-disciplined, "and this advantage is more relevant to report card grades than to achievement or aptitude tests."

These results are no flash in the pan, and some have speculated that, just as boys do worse in school for want of self-control, American students lag their foreign peers for similar reasons. Again, when it comes to school, self-mastery matters. Raymond Wolfe and Scott Johnson, for example, looked at thirty-two personality variables in a group of students and found that self-control was the only one with any real ability to predict grades in college. Self-control was a better predictor than SAT scores; only high school grades did a better job foretelling how students would fare at college, and the researchers recommended "that the global trait of self-control or conscientiousness be systematically assessed and used in college admissions decisions."

Kids with good self-control also grow into adults who get along better with others. In one study, published in 1999, teacher ratings of kids' self-control at ages four to six predicted which kids would be more popular. And work by Mischel and Yuichi Shoda showed that a four-year-old's ability to defer gratification was associated with better relationships as a young adult. Other studies show that preschoolers with more self-control have more social competence and less negative emotional arousal; that high-schoolers with high self-control have fewer eating and drinking problems; that college students with high self-control get better grades; and that preteen and teenaged boys with low self-control are at greater risk of aggressive behavior and delinquency.

Shortfalls in self-control are also implicated in heroin addiction, alcohol abuse, and overspending among the young. The criminologist Travis Hirschi writes that among high school students, self-control "consistently predicts behavior analogous to crime: truancy, cheating on exams, being sent out of a classroom, driving while drinking, auto accidents, bike-skateboard-rollerblade accidents, broken bones, shooting dice for money, drinking alcohol, smoking tobacco, and smoking marijuana."

Walter Mischel, meanwhile, the man who started it all, is still in hot pursuit of the mystery of self-control. With funding from the National Science Foundation, he and coinvestigators around the country have launched an ambitious effort to expand our knowledge about something, which, based on the marshmallow experiments, has already been established as a surpassingly important human characteristic. Using surveys and magnetic resonance brain scans of the now-grown

Bing children, researchers are investigating the brain structures that enable people to exercise self-control. The scientists are also conducting genetic tests to try to figure out to what extent the ability to defer gratification is hereditary.

For there is unquestionably a genetic component, and modern technology makes it cheap and easy to tell which gene variants people have. The study will draw subjects from Mischel's preschoolers dating back to the early 1970s, all of them in their late thirties and early forties now, and will focus especially on two groups: one that's shown a high level of self-control over the years, and another that's shown the opposite.

Mischel's plan raises a crucial question. If self-control is so important for kids, can it be taught? There is every reason to believe that it can. Nobody seems to think it's 100 percent hereditary, after all. Mischel contends that good parenting plays a large role—even in everyday matters like not snacking before meals. And researchers have already found some value in programs aimed at teaching children "executive functions," which is psychological jargon for self-control. Adele Diamond evaluated a fascinating program called Tools of the Mind, developed by psychologists Deborah Leong and Elena Bodrova. The program asked students to plot their play intentions in writing, and their days were filled with various other games and activities designed to promote planning, focus, and delay of gratification. In a study of 147 kids roughly divided between those in Tools of the Mind and those not, Diamond found that after two years the program participants did quite a bit better on tests of executive function—suggesting they really did learn some self-control.

Other schools have embraced the gospel of self-control as well. The renowned KIPP (Knowledge Is Power Program) chain of charter schools, which has succeeded in inner-city neighborhoods where other schools have failed, has made self-control one of its core "character strengths." The KIPP school in Philadelphia gave its students T-shirts with the words DON'T EAT THE MARSHMALLOW lettered across the front.

Diamond says kids today may need such training because old-fashioned styles of self-organized free play taught self-control skills in ways that modern, parent-organized sports and in-home electronic play may not. On the other hand, martial arts, music lessons, or other activities requiring sustained attention probably help. Says Diamond: "I think a lot of kids get diagnosed with ADHD now, not all but many just because they never learned how to exercise self-control."

The Seesaw Struggle

My great religion is a belief in the blood, the flesh, as being wiser than the intellect. We can go wrong in our minds. But what our blood tells and believes and says, is always true.

—D. H. LAWRENCE

If you don't control your emotions, your emotions will control your acts, and that's not good.

—MARIANO RIVERA

The exaltation of human passion has a long history in the Western Hemisphere. Around the time the United States was born, the rise of Romanticism launched a celebration of the self—and all that is wild, primitive, and instinctual—that hasn't abated. To this equivocal tradition, the story of Daedalus and Icarus offers an ancient and pessimistic rebuke.

It's a familiar tale. Father and son, as you'll recall, were imprisoned on the isle of Crete. Daedalus, who crafted the waxy wings the duo would use to escape by air, warned his son not to fly too close to the sun, which could melt the wax, nor too close to the sea, which could dampen the feathers. Like so many parents since, the experienced Daedalus was urging moderation, lobbying quite literally for the middle way, which is inevitably anathema to youth. Sure enough, once airborne, Icarus giddily soared higher and higher, climbing for the heavens, until the wax melted and he plunged tragically into the sea.

Can you think of a better self-control story? You have the conflict between reason and emotion, planning and spontaneity, and of course maturity and youth. The tragedy was abetted by a technology that bestowed freedom but in exchange demanded self-restraint. The whole thing shows how difficult it can be to find and keep to the middle way— how in the heat of the moment crucial knowledge that we possess can be lost to us. It's also a story about foresight; it wasn't just passion that led to disaster, for it was Daedalus's skill and planning that had brought the two of them to that pass. As is so often the case, the prudent and the imprudent are implicated in one another's suffering. When Icarus kills himself, he kills a little of his father as well—the father who might have looked ahead just a little further, to foresee what a young man, intoxicated with the father's great invention, might end up doing to both of them.

The story of Daedalus and Icarus is the story of self-control in a nutshell, for each represents one of the two eternally warring camps whose seesaw struggle comprises the history of our topic. On one side are the forces of premeditation—of reason, of calculation, of foresight, of sobriety, of tomorrow. Arrayed against them are the armies of instinct—impulse, passion, intoxication, and most of all, the forces of today. Each works in some ways on behalf of the other, but for the most part they have been at loggerheads. The waxing and waning of their fortunes is of interest here not just for historical reasons but because beliefs matter; people's attitudes about self-control influence how much of it they are likely to exercise—and to expect from one another. While there is no clear winner in the enduring conflict between moderation and release, a pattern is discernible: over time, a growing emphasis on the self as the locus of control, rather than outside authorities such as tradition, family, or king.

In This Corner, Moderation

We've already seen that the party of self-control was founded by the Greeks; even Epicurus, who is better known nowadays as the pre-Christian patron saint of hedonism, emphasized that while it was important to be happy and fed, pleasures must be taken in moderation if we are to avoid becoming enslaved to our appetites. The Romans, for all their excesses, were concerned with self-control as well. "Who then is free?" Horace asked rhetorically. "The wise man who is master of himself, who remains undaunted in the face of poverty, chains and death, who stubbornly defies his passions and despises positions of power, a man complete in himself, smooth and round, who prevents extraneous elements clinging to his polished surface."

The Romans pursued this conception of freedom by expanding the Stoicism they inherited from the Greeks into a pattern for living based on stringent emotional self-regulation. To the Stoics, what mattered was not what happens to you but how you handle it. Self-command is required to overcome the dangerous misinformation of our emotions, and because for the most part the self is the only thing that we *can* command. We have no control, ultimately, over what other people do or think, or whether there will be an earthquake tomorrow. What we can influence is our understanding of these circumstances and how we respond to them. "If you are distressed by anything external," said the Roman emperor and Stoic Marcus Aurelius, "the pain is not due to the thing itself, but to your estimate of it; and this you have the power to revoke at any moment."

Well-disguised tendrils of Stoicism reach right up into modern life—in the serenity prayer, for example, as well as in the rise of cognitive behavioral therapy ("deal with it!") and the increased popularity in the West of Buddhism, which urges us to cast off desire and free ourselves of anger. A version of Stoicism has long been a component of the masculine ideal. Yet Stoicism itself, in our therapeutic age, remains in bad odor, done in by its reputation for cultivated apathy and tight-lipped suffering. And in truth, Stoicism represents an unhealthy form of extremism, for in rejecting the passions rather than moderating them, or at least cherry-picking to distinguish the desirable from the undesirable, it departs tragically—and inhumanly—from Aristotle's principle of the mean. The idea is not to stamp out the passions but to regulate them.

The early Christians, so ready to turn the other cheek, were big on self-control but, unlike their pagan predecessors, believed the idea was to live in obedience to God, as the Jews had insisted before them—except without succumbing to worldly temptation. Failures of the will were thus not so much lapses of judgment or forgetfulness but a kind of rebellious vanity—bad nonetheless, and likely to be punished, but bad for different (and ultimately more tenuous) reasons. Instead of akrasia, what we had was sin. Suddenly, self-control depended on faith.

When the Reformation came along—as yet another rebellion against temptation—it jacked up the stakes considerably, placing the onus for control firmly on the self. Like old-fashioned marriages, transgression was not something a Protestant could easily undo. "A tremendous historical influence was actually exerted by the absence in Judaism and ascetic Protestantism of anything like the confessional," Max Weber wrote, explaining that absent any means of obtaining release from sins, these religions "favored the evolution of an ethically rationalized pattern of life."

So did the Enlightenment, which emphasized reason over the passions and self-mastery for all. Philosophers such as John Locke and Jean-Jacques Rousseau saw society as a social contract in which it was necessary for the self to be its own master—for otherwise the state might have to do the job. The Enlightenment placed even more of the burden of control on the self than the Reformation did. And in doing so, it paved the way for the burgeoning world of capitalist enterprise, which gave people powerful incentives to regulate their own behavior. As Adam Smith observed, it made everyone into an entrepreneur, even ditch diggers, who had to sell their services just as merchants had to sell their wares, and in the world of business, it is important to be reliable, predictable, sober, even bland. In Smith's vision, people would moderate their appetites because doing so would be profitable.

The factory revolution rationalized life more than just ethically, getting everyone to live by the clock, show up at the right time and place, and get the job done. Early capitalism may have driven people to drink—or to laudanum, the opium tincture so popular in Victorian England—but what was needed most of all was sober workers, and eventually they emerged. Capitalism encouraged rationality, forward-looking calculation, and deferred gratification, sowing patiently today in order to reap tomorrow. In capitalism one eschewed romping in the meadows—heck, one eschewed meadows altogether—to hunch over a dirty, noisy machine or a numbing set of ledgers. It was all about self-control. Under capitalism, habits (and displays) of sobriety, thrift, and foresight enabled people, firms, and nations to thrive.

Surely a match made in heaven, capitalism and the Reformation were united in the Puritans, those doughty pioneers who are known mainly for establishing a tyranny of virtue in what we now regard as the prelapsarian paradise of the New World. The Puritans exist in the popular mind as a kind of Protestant Taliban, invoking God and Scripture to instill their pathological fear of pleasure in an entire nation. Thus they often take the rap for the way Americans seem to lurch between reckless hedonism and frantic self-censure; if only we'd been allowed to enjoy ourselves way back in the seventeenth-century colonies of Massachusetts, we might have acquired the crucial sense of moderation we so often seem to be missing now. "The Puritan is never popular," John Dewey observed, "not even in a society of Puritans."

In fact, the Puritans play an important role in this story—just not that particular role. It was not their supposed loathing for good times that accounts for the difficulties of their successors in this fat land. On the contrary, the Puritans knew how to have fun, and the desperate fulminations of censorious Puritan divines, passed down to us in their sermons, are evidence of that. No, the Puritans matter to us here because it was their worldly asceticism, to borrow a phrase from Max Weber, that laid the foundation for the astonishing affluence to come.

What matters most about the Puritans is not any dire role they supposedly played in the etiology of American excess. It was the way they
embodied the thing that made all this excess possible—the thing that
would later be called the Protestant ethic, but that was really just the
culture of discipline that produced the wealth that made the sybaritic
world of modern America practically inevitable. Seeking virtue rather
than wealth, they couldn't help accumulating riches.

The power of that culture is vividly apparent if you compare the
Puritan colonies in Massachusetts to the wretched English settlement
in Jamestown, Virginia, which was rife with the selfishness and sloth
the Puritans so despised. Where the Puritans were conscientious, the
Virginians cut corners. The Puritans insisted that everyone work, and
even Governor John Winthrop made a point of being seen doing manual labor. But many of the Virginians were "gentlemen," which meant
physical labor was the thing they defined themselves by *not* doing. The
Puritans maintained social cohesion and emphasized not just creating
wealth but building institutions. The Virginians mainly wanted to find
gold and get rich quick.

The Puritans were enterprising, but they strove for a moral capitalism constrained by community institutions. They accumulated wealth,
but they also invested in human capital, mandating that any town of
fifty families or more should have a school. They founded universities,
established printing presses, and in their heyday devoured books: as
historian Bruce Daniels writes, "New England was surprisingly liter-
ate, probably more so than any other region in the Western world." Life
expectancy in New England was significantly longer than in the South,
and there was a lot of what we like to call today "social capital," or
community involvement and trust, the virtue of which was hammered
home regularly from the pulpit. "The chastising efforts of ministers
such as Cotton Mather," the historian Stephen Innes tells us, "helped
increase the likelihood that the Bay Colony would remain a capitalist
commonwealth—a society that demanded deferred gratification and a
link between individual and collective well-being."

While the Puritans invested in education, the Virginians insisted on ignorance. Their governor, the Puritan-hating William Berkeley, "rejoiced in 1671 that in his colony, unlike Massachusetts, 'there are no free schools nor printing, and I hope we shall not have these [in a] hundred years; for learning has brought disobedience, and heresy, and sects into the world, and printing has divulged them, and [produced] libels against the best government.'"

The Puritans' notion that their labor exalted God meant they didn't need much time off, so they purged some eighty holy days from their calendar, increasing the number of workdays to more than three hundred and trashing the traditional two-to-one ratio of work to leisure (which had prevailed from China to Rome and right up into modern America) in favor of something approaching four to one. Not only did they work twice as much as other people, but they placed huge importance on doing a good job—on exercising care and producing quality. The result isn't difficult to predict: in practically no time, these patiently manic lords of discipline had transformed their unpromising strip of the New World into an agricultural, trading, and manufacturing powerhouse so dynamic that before long it was an economic competitor with the mother country.

In their seriousness, inner steel, and faith-driven earning power, the Victorians—on both sides of the Atlantic—were the Puritans' natural heirs. Although lacking the egalitarianism of their American cousins, British Victorians were very much like the Puritans in that they were communitarians as well as colonizers and people of action given nonetheless to introspection. And like the Puritans, they exalted self-control practically above all else.

The Victorian ethos evolved from the evangelical movement that sought to constrain sex, drinking, and idleness in the early nineteenth century, creating an environment in which clean living was next to godliness. Evangelism, especially on the part of women, was quite successful in cleaning up bad behavior, most of it by men.

Above all, the Victorians were sophisticates when it came to self-control. They understood, perhaps better than we do, that the flesh is weak, and that even the best of us need structures—social, religious, professional—to help us stay out of trouble. The Victorian enterprise, says James Q. Wilson, was really "a massive private effort to inculcate self-control in people who were confronting the vast temptations of big-city life. The Victorians thought that people had a fallible human nature that would often lead them to choose self-indulgence over self-restraint. The task of society was to emphasize the latter in order to minimize the former."

The moralistic values of the era (and the social system in which they were embodied) grew up in response to the increasingly commercial and impersonal world of modernity ushered in by the Industrial Revolution. This isn't all we have in common with our Victorian ancestors; they too lived through technological upheaval, and we share their tendency to moralize. There was a lot of signaling in Victorian behavior, as there is today, and a certain tribalism, but even individuals on the bottom rungs of society had the prospect of advancement if they, too, embraced sobriety, thrift, sexual restraint, and other Victorian values— values designed, as Peter Stearns tells us, "to enable an increasingly self-conscious middle class, eager to distinguish itself from the urban lower classes and new immigrant populations, to identify respectable strangers. In addition, they served a population aware that earlier, face-to-face community supervision had become less effective in an urban society."

Yet for all their awareness of human weakness, the Victorians were optimistic about self-mastery (they had conquered much of the world, so why not the self?) and regularly exhorted one another to exercise it. No one did so more tirelessly than Samuel Smiles, the great nineteenth-century Scottish self-improvement guru whose books on the subject included *Self-Help* (which appeared in the landmark year of 1859, when readers first encountered John Stuart Mill's *On Liberty* and Charles Darwin's *On the Origin of Species*), as well as *Duty* and *Character*. "No man can be free who is in debt," he tells us in yet another work, *Thrift*. "The inevitable effect of debt is not only to injure personal independence, but, in the long run, to inflict moral degradation."

All this said, there was quite a large gap between Victorian ideals and the Victorian reality of saloons, narcotic patent medicines, and prostitution—a reality that can be glimpsed in the story of Jekyll and Hyde, to say nothing of the Sherlock Holmes stories. Compared to London or New York of that era, the modern metropolis is buttoned-up indeed. But that reality may in itself have bolstered the values we think of as characteristically Victorian, since it was important for people to try to stay out of trouble—and demonstrate to others that they were succeeding.

And in This Corner, Release

The triumph of capitalism was a triumph for self-control, for in the long run the system made people free as long as they regulated themselves. But it called for quite a lot of regulation indeed—which is where the allure of release comes in. The trend toward that release was once known as Romanticism, a movement in European cultural life that emphasized feeling over thought, passion over reason, and extremes of all kinds over moderation. Romanticism was about youth, ecstasy, nature, and instinct, and it is with us still. Like most revolutions, it would someday eat a goodly number of its children.

Romanticism was also a reaction to the rationalist juggernaut of capitalism. On all sides, it seemed, people were supposed to uphold elaborate social rituals, conform to the schedule of business, and get along as part of a mass society built on science and materialism. The Romantic revolution was a rebellion against all this, an early hippie movement that valued nature and imagination and individual consciousness. It was interested in the unique, the quirky, the ethnic, the ugly, and the extreme. Self-control was something one wanted less of, not more. The challenge, in fact, was to throw off the fetters of upbringing and rationality in order to experience beauty anew, in all its morning freshness.

In terms of sex appeal, it's hard to compete with the Romantics and their Byronic locks, tortured souls, and youthful good looks. Everyone chafes at society's restrictions sooner or later, and Romanticism held up the bright banner of freedom, waving it defiantly at opponents who looked by comparison like a bunch of old farts. Messages that appeal to the emotions are always the most powerful, and the Romantics managed to combine passion with skill in music, poetry, and art in ways that seduced an entire civilization. Events would play into their hands as well; a series of increasingly violent wars, revolutions, and other cataclysms made the measured response of Classicism look artificial and inadequate.

Romanticism, in short, has provided the cultural capital for the party of release for more than two hundred years. Romanticism changed the way people think about self-control, in many ways for the good. Passion, after all, should not be prejudged as bad, and received structures are not always worth upholding. Self-control isn't supposed to be about blind obedience. On the other hand, an ideology of excess will inevitably have its excesses. Consider, in 1923, D. H. Lawrence's assault on the "snuff-coloured" moderation of Ben Franklin. In Lawrence's defense, Franklin drove many literary types crazy, provoking attacks by Edgar Allan Poe, Henry David Thoreau, Herman Melville, and Mark Twain. But none went as far as Lawrence in his *Studies in Classic American Literature*.

"Resolve to abide by your own deepest promptings," Lawrence urges, in his own version of Franklin's list of virtues, "and to sacrifice the smaller thing to the greater. Kill when you must, and be killed the same: the *must* coming from the gods inside you, or from the men in whom you recognize the Holy Ghost."

Parts of Lawrence's attack reflect the absence of God from Franklin's motivations, the seemingly bloodless calculation he substituted for Puritan zeal. But the attack is against what is Puritan in Franklin as well as what is not, and perfectly captures the change in thinking that eventually would take us from "a penny saved is a penny earned" to "let it all hang out." Here is what Lawrence gives as his "creed":

That I am I.
That my soul is a dark forest.
That my known self will never be more than
a little clearing in the forest.

That gods, strange gods, come forth from the forest into
the clearing of my known self, and then go back.
That I must have the courage to let them come and go.

We didn't get from Franklin to Lawrence overnight. The triumph of
the passions took a long time; in the second half of the nineteenth century
the forces of control seemed firmly, well, in control, although even then
a Romantic strain ran through the arts and was woven subtly into popular attitudes. But things were changing. Affluence was a rising tide that
would lift expectations, including expectations for personal freedom.
And forces in favor of control would suffer a series of devastating blows
in the middle nineteenth and early twentieth centuries—under the very
noses of the Victorians—from three of the period's most important
thinkers. Charles Darwin's earthshaking work made it harder for people to continue thinking of themselves as so very different from other
animals and, for better or worse, placed us at the mercy of evolution and
instinct. Karl Marx, Darwin's contemporary, placed us at the mercy of
implacable economic and historical forces—but believed we were destined to throw off the chains of capitalism.

And then Sigmund Freud came along.

10

Let My People Go

We're bringing them the plague, and they don't even know it.

—Attributed to Sigmund Freud, on landing in America

I n the battle between inhibition and release, both sides might with
some justice lay claim to Freud, who insisted that "living freely"
was never the goal of psychoanalysis, and that conflicting desires
are "not resolved by helping one side to win a victory over the other." In
fact, Freud was a near-perfect specimen of nineteenth-century Austrian
Homo bourgeois, with its strange blend of Puritanism and aestheticism,
and he admired both the cool, self-possessed, gratification-deferring
English gentleman and his rational-seeming, lawmaking, and law-
abiding society.

Self-control was Freud's great topic. Liberation was a goal, but the
point of it was not license but choice. Nonetheless, over time Freud's
ideas proved empowering mainly to the liberationist view, which
gained serious traction in the twentieth century. Ever since Freud, and
in some ways even in spite of him, social critics and popular culture
have leapfrogged one another in full flight from constraint, denigrating
self-control even as the widening scope of human freedom made it ever
more important that we exercise it.

It must be said that Freud's timing was impeccable; in the twentieth century there would be much to give credence to any who doubted human rationality. After the shocking madness of the Great War, which blew up Victorian ideals in the trenches along with millions of disillusioned men, psychoanalysis quickly suffused the consciousness of the age. The doctor in Rebecca West's first novel, *The Return of the Soldier* (1918), explains it all for us—with some exasperation—when he arrives to treat an amnesiac home from the front. Speaking to the soldier's wife and cousin, he says:

> "The mental life that can be controlled by effort isn't the mental life that matters. You've been stuffed up when you were young with talk about a thing called self-control, a sort of barmaid for the soul that says, 'Time's up, gentlemen,' and 'Here, you've had enough.' There is no such thing. There's a deep self in one, the essential self, that has its wishes. And if those wishes are suppressed by the superficial self—the self that makes, as you say, efforts, and usually makes them with the sole idea of putting up a good show before the neighbors—it takes its revenge. Into the house of conduct erected by the superficial self it sends an obsession."

Freud was especially a sensation in America, where his renown spread from the moment he delivered his famous Clark University lectures of 1909. His talks sold well in book form and psychoanalysis erupted as a hot topic in popular magazines, quickly becoming a prominent aspect of the culture. By 1924, when the murder trial of Leopold and Loeb was in the headlines, the *Chicago Tribune*'s flamboyant publisher Colonel Robert McCormick cabled Freud with an offer of $25,000 (a princely sum in those days) "or anything he name come Chicago psychoanalyze" the killers. McCormick even offered to charter a steamship for the trip.

Freud declined, but later that year was beseeched by the Hollywood producer Samuel Goldwyn with the staggering offer of $100,000 to write for the screen or come to America as a kind of consultant. The idea apparently was that Freud was an expert in Hollywood's two main concerns, romance and laughter; Goldwyn characterized him as "the greatest love specialist in the world." The *New York Times* memorialized the great man's response in early 1925: FREUD REBUFFS GOLDWYN. VIENNESE PSYCHOANALYST IS NOT INTERESTED IN MOTION PICTURE OFFER. But playing hard to get probably only amplified his renown. "By the mid-1920s," his biographer Peter Gay reports, "Freud had become a household name."

In the decades to come, Freud's ideas would grow into orthodoxy here, becoming the core of medical training in psychiatry and subtly permeating the larger culture. By the 1950s, Freudian therapy was firmly established in this country, and its basic doctrines were familiar even to those who had never reclined on an analyst's couch. For literary critics, the encounter with Freud was practically "transference" at first sight; classics such as *Moby-Dick* were subjected to psychoanalytic review, and psychobiography became a trendy approach to writing lives. Popular culture was perhaps more ambivalent, offering laymen's explanations in paperback but mocking Freud and his ilk in *New Yorker* cartoons and Hollywood movies. The Chad Mitchell Trio even made musical fun in their "Ballad of Sigmund Freud."

It's probably true that Freud's momentous (and only) visit to America opened the door to the self-indulgent culture of therapy and victimization so often decried in this country today, but it would be foolish to lay all the blame on Freud, who in some ways merely helped us get where we were determined to go. Americans were already obsessed with the unconscious, faith healing, mesmerism, "mind cure," and other such inner mysteries when he got here. These had been percolating through society since before the Civil War, when Americans who might once have worried over the condition of their souls became increasingly interested in their psyches. By the time Freud arrived, Eric Caplan writes, "mental therapeutics was already integrally woven into the fabric of American medicine and culture."

Yet there's no doubt that Freud had a big impact. It was Freud, after all, who gave us the psychopathology of everyday life, and a hundred years later we've come to see everyday life as pretty darned psycho-pathological. In particular we now regard extreme forms of appetite as diseases, a notion once largely reserved for drug and alcohol abuse but since expanded to so many other forms of excess. Without Freud, too, it's hard to believe that shyness could have become "social anxiety disorder," sadness could be medicalized as depression, and society's most fortunate members—rich, well-educated white people—would feel the need to take so much Prozac, Paxil, and other drugs to help them get through their privileged days. The American Psychiatric Association already considers 48 million of us to be mentally ill, and while it may often seem that the correct number is closer to 300 million, the sheer magnitude of the official diagnosis gives one pause. Isn't it possible we are confusing human diversity with disease? More subtly, what is the price we pay in lost agency when we are so ready to abdicate an important chunk of ourselves to illness, experts, and pharmaceuticals?

Doctor, Heal Thyself

What makes Freud especially interesting for our purposes is the way in which his life and thought bring together so many of the issues involved in grappling with the problem of self-control in the modern world—a world his ideas have done so much to shape. Freud himself, at least superficially, was a paragon of unwavering self-mastery. Yet his iron grip on himself often looks like a form of overcompensation. His fixation on sex—indeed, his life's work—suggests the wish fulfillment dream of a sexually repressed Victorian paterfamilias.

The two appetites that consistently defeated his self-control were his hunger for renown and his lust for tobacco. For Freud's patients, of course, the bigger problem was his inability to rein in his boundless longing for fame and fortune. We now know, for instance, that he couldn't resist massaging the facts of his cases until they took the form that most suited him—until they looked like a "cure," even if in fact none had been effected. And he seems to have had little control over his anger and impatience at criticism; on the contrary, he was quite ready to pathologize dissent and if necessary shun the incorrigible. "It appears over and over," writes Peter Gay, that Freud's life "was a struggle for self-discipline, for control over his speculative impulses and his rage— rage at his enemies and, even harder to manage, at those among his adherents he found wanting or disloyal."

In many respects he was quite successful at subduing himself. As a boy he was a superb student, and as an adult he pursued success by single-minded devotion to work. Although Freud's ideas were unconventional, he always desperately craved recognition and social status; he even managed to feel disappointment at not having been awarded the Nobel Prize. In his personal life, the good doctor was a classic nineteenth-century bourgeois, presiding patriarchally over a Viennese household full of women and children whom he dominated. But Freud was also a man aboil with his own powers, and more conscious than most people of his own lusts and dark impulses. There was plenty for him to keep under control, including a ferocious temper and his own sexual desires. (His self-restraint was surely tested, in those early and less ethically rigorous days of analysis, by attractive female patients who sometimes tried to seduce him.) But he managed. In fact, in the full flower of adulthood, he ran his life with the kind of efficiency and attention to schedule worthy of a Teutonic railroad.

He had "an air of power disciplined," Gay tells us. "Even Freud's mustache and pointed beard were subdued to order by a barber's daily attention. Freud had learned to harness his appetites—his volcanic emotions, his lust for speculation, and his restless energies—to the single-minded pursuit of his mission . . . His heroic effort at self-mastery in the service of concentrated work had chained him to a most precise timetable. Like the good bourgeois he was, and was not ashamed of being, 'he lived' in his nephew Ernst Waldinger's words, 'by the clock.'"

In a typical day, Freud would rise by seven a.m. and see patients until noon. At the stroke of one p.m., as Gay tells it, "the family assembled around the dining-room table; Freud appeared from his study, his wife sat down facing him at the other end, and the maid materialized, bearing the soup tureen." After lunch there was a walk, then more work and patients, often until nine p.m. Supper would be followed by a brief card game or a walk, perhaps a stop in a café, and then writing, reading, and editorial work. He went to sleep at one a.m. Even recreations were scrupulously planned and scheduled, and on weekends there was a program as well, which included university lectures, letter writing, and a visit to his mother. Is it any surprise the very idea of America was repugnant to him? It must have been painful for such a deeply cultured and rigorously self-programmed person, one so very rooted in the cozy cosmopolitanism of Vienna, just to think about such a vast, unruly, improvisatory sort of place.

Although Freud used cocaine right up into the 1890s to treat his own psychic demons, which must have been fearsome, he doesn't seem to have been hooked. But his obsessive smoking was something else again—an addiction of choice if ever there was one—and would blight his old age, eventually taking his life.

Freud started smoking when he was twenty-four, influenced by his heavy-smoking father, and by the time his love affair with tobacco was in full bloom, he was consuming an astonishing twenty cigars daily. Smoking was central to his life and work; he claimed not to trust men who abstained. It was the topic of the very first session of Freud's Wednesday Psychological Society, the Viennese cabal that built psychoanalysis into a movement. Meetings of this circle were conducted in a room "so thick with smoke," Freud's son Martin recalled, "it seemed a wonder that human beings had been able to live in it for hours, let alone speak in it without choking."

Freud was urged to stop for health reasons as early as 1894, when, at the age of thirty-eight, he developed heart troubles. He quit, but only for seven weeks. Cigars were just too important for sustaining the energy and concentration he depended upon. Without them, he felt, he could not write or think. "I ascribe to the cigar," he wrote, "the greatest share of my self-control and tenacity in work."

At one point Freud quit for fourteen months, far beyond the reach of the most serious cravings, thereby proving he could abstain if he wanted to. But he didn't want to, which is why he went back after all that time—and kept smoking even as surgeons removed more and more of his lower face. Even at the end of his life, racked with pain from the oral cancer that was killing him, he insisted that cigars had "served me for precisely fifty years as protection and a weapon in the combat of life . . . I owe to the cigar a great intensification of my capacity to work and a facilitation of my self-control."

For a long time the good doctor's attitude toward smoking embodied his own ideas about resistance. Or perhaps it was an example of what he called "knowing and not knowing," in an echo of the Greeks who talked about having knowledge (*smoking is killing me*) that is deactivated by pleasure. Or maybe it was just a death wish. It's noteworthy that in Freud's day, suicide was a popular option for accomplished Viennese, particularly Jewish ones. "Between 1860 and 1938," William Johnston tells us, "an astonishing number of Austrian intellectuals committed suicide," including Otto Weininger and three of Wittgenstein's seven siblings (the Wittgensteins were Catholic but of Jewish descent). It was the ultimate rebellion against the future-mindedness otherwise so characteristic of Vienna's accomplished Jews, since suicide obliterates the future altogether. And a timely suicide played an important role in Freud's life. When, in 1883, a promising young Jewish neurologist (and friend of Freud's) named Nathan Weiss hanged himself in a public bath, it created an opening in neurology on the medical faculty at the University of Vienna, which Freud applied for and got.

Freud was shocked by Weiss's suicide but was on the same course himself, albeit in slow motion, thanks to his cigars. In 1923, at the age of sixty-six, Freud detected a growth in his mouth. In all likelihood he knew what it was; he had first noticed a painful swelling on his palate in 1917, but it went away—supposedly after lighting up a cigar from a coveted box presented by a patient. This time, when he consulted a physician friend about the problem, Freud warned him: "Be prepared to see something you won't like." This doctor recognized the growth as malignant but told Freud it was a nasty leukoplakia—a benign growth, although often a precursor of cancer.

Despite Vienna's wealth of medical talent—and Freud's connections—
he chose to have a superficial outpatient procedure performed by an
inept rhinologist named Marcus Hajek, who botched even this limited
operation. In the hospital, owing to lack of space, the dazed and blood-
ied analyst was compelled to lie on a cot in a tiny room shared with
a mentally retarded man—a man who happened to be a dwarf. There
Freud commenced hemorrhaging. He tried ringing the bell to summon
help, but it was out of order. Fortunately, his roommate raced out of
the room to summon a nurse, and Freud's life was saved. He would live
through thirty-two more operations relating to his cancer before finally,
in agony, asking his doctor to help him terminate his life. The suicide
of his friend Weiss launched Freud's life's work, and his own suicide
would end it.

Freud's Self-control Legacy

Although much of his life's work hasn't stood the tests of time or science, one of Freud's ideas in particular has proved quite durable: the
idea that we don't—and can't—know what goes on in our very own
minds. Freud didn't invent the idea of the unconscious; on the contrary,
it was well established, by Schopenhauer and others, long before Freud
came along. But with his thrilling emphasis on sexuality and dreams, he
was surely its greatest popularizer, however uncomfortably. (He later
wrote that psychoanalysis in America "suffered a great deal from being
watered down," and "many abuses which have no relation to it find a
cover under its name.") And to the extent we came to believe our subconscious was in the driver's seat, we lost some faith in our own agency.

Another effect of the Freudian enterprise was to help overthrow
the power of received morality—what might be called the morality
of taboo—and to free us, for better or worse, from the automatic identity and authority of family. At the same time it sought to awaken us
to the drives we didn't know we had—particularly sexual drives. By

lifting the burden of shame under which these were buried while questioning received morality about them, Freud's work made us both more and less free, and in this way it jacked up the pressure on the *self* in *self-control*. To the extent we find ourselves free from arbitrary-seeming social constraints, we need only to constrain ourselves. But to the extent we can't control—or even know—what's in our own minds, the unanalyzed masses are left less capable of the job after Freud. Freud's legacy is liberating, but with its focus on dreams, childhood trauma, and murky impulses, it undermined the power of the only thing left to take the place of Victorian social constraint and received taboo, and that is the power of the rational self.

Although Freud's emphasis on primal guilt might have resonated with the Puritans, he nonetheless gave religion a good hard shove out the door, and despite all its failings, it can be a useful inhibiting force. Freud was a classic patriarch, yet he did as much as anybody to overthrow patriarchy, including the patriarchy of God; in Freudian mythology, the father was for boys a terrifying figure, always threatening castration, and frustrating their desire for their mothers. We no longer take the Oedipus complex very seriously, but we do seem to have thrown over patriarchal strictures right along with the patriarch (who may not any longer be living with his children anyway).

We also got from Freud (and psychology in general) a much more nuanced view of transgression, one that takes account of various personal and social forces and is more likely to see "wrongdoing" as illness. The result is a more refined sense of justice—along with a new willingness to see ourselves as victims. As Willard Gaylin has observed, "the extension of sociological and psychological exculpation will essentially prove self-defeating if it becomes all-inclusive. The law demands some acknowledgement of self-control."

Freud probably accelerated the easing of sexual mores—which was one of his main goals—and his ideas may have played a role in reforming treatment of the mentally ill. Nor is it altogether his fault that where he proposed autonomy, we derived license. But even if he didn't mean to, he propelled us toward the individualism that we insist upon in modern life, at the expense of the social fabric that individuals must depend upon. Freud's focus on disinhibition is only to be expected; his patients came from the Viennese bourgeoisie, were often women, and had to cope with stifling layers of social constraint. "The great majority of his patients," wrote the psychologist Robert R. Holt, "were probably overcontrolled people (as he was himself) whose problem with respect to moral constraints was not to get control over unethical behavior but to learn to relax their too-severe self-discipline."

Psychology today is still disinhibiting, and one reason is the nature of the confidant. Once upon a time, confiding meant spilling the beans to a friend or clergyman, but the rise of therapy as a market-oriented specialty has given the affluent a class of willing professional confidants who can be hired with all the advantages of a commercial transaction. Therapists are paid not to tell and not to judge. At the very least they affect a certain moral neutrality—the moral neutrality of the marketplace, which is oddly enough the therapeutic milieu. Aside from the expense, which is often covered by health insurance, we seem to like the new system—so much that in a 2008 Harris poll nearly three in ten American adults reported having received treatment or therapy from a mental health professional.

For all the ways Freud's legacy might have undermined self-control, there was one hugely important way in which he had the opposite effect. If the goal of psychoanalysis was autonomy—in Freud's words, "to uncover repressions and replace them by acts of judgment"—then the mission of Freud's enterprise was to get us to recognize our desires and decide what we think of them. Doing this means forming desires about our desires, or the second-order preferences we spoke of earlier in this book. Forming and upholding these is what self-control is all about. In Harry Frankfurt's terms, Freud wanted each of us to become a person rather than a mere wanton—a noble goal indeed, even if it means accepting a large additional burden on the *self* in *self-control*. Seen in this light, the intent of Freud's bizarre enterprise (aside from making him famous) was to give each of us the power to say yea or nay to our own impulses as well as to the received constraints that might have bound them.

In a sense, Freud sought to banish Aristotle's thoughtless form of akrasia. In Freud's holy trinity of id, ego, and superego, the ego represents a middle way, the part of ourselves beholden neither to instinct nor taboo, the part whose job is to balance drives, ethics, and the needs of others. And it was this part that Freud tried to exalt. For all his failings, Freud gave us a shorthand that enabled him to say in a single sentence—his explanation of psychoanalysis—what's taking me an entire book: "Where id was, there ego shall be."

11

The Intimate Contest

"I must try to conquer myself," said his wife, with the sigh natural to this purpose.

"As you only have your own power to do it with, it sounds as if it would be an equal struggle."

—IVY COMPTON-BURNETT, *PARENTS AND CHILDREN*

The struggle for self-control is exciting because it's all about conflict. What sets it apart is that the conflict is mainly with yourself.

So, imagine that your friends want you to join them in robbing a bank—not by inflating your income on a mortgage application, but the old-fashioned way, at gunpoint. You sense this is a bad idea; you have moral qualms, you're worried someone will get hurt, and you're unsure how you will avoid getting caught. Still, you agree to go along—they're your friends, after all—but you're of two minds, and your acquiescence comes with deep misgivings.

As you approach the bank with your compatriots, all of you in grotesque Simpsons masks, adrenaline surges through your system. Your palms are sweating; you're nearly overcome by a powerful desire to cast down your canvas satchel and run. Instead, with a superhuman effort, you force yourself to go inside and shout, "Stick 'em up!"

Now if we go back in our fantasy to the moments before you entered the bank, and if (it's a fantasy, remember) we peel back the lid of your skull in order to peer inside, we might find that you were quite literally of two minds about the whole thing. Perhaps your frontal lobes, where the future is accounted for and your powers of planning and reasoning are believed to reside, took a dim view of the whole bank thing, foreseeing all kinds of potential trouble. But your limbic system—the parts of the brain mainly responsible for your emotions, including your amygdala, where fear springs up—took an entirely different view. It was terrified mainly by the prospect of being cast from your circle of friends and revved up by the excitement of making a withdrawal—all that money! all that danger!—at the point of a gun.

Or perhaps it was the opposite—it's hard to tell, looking at the simmering pile of gray matter stewing there in your skull. Perhaps your frontal lobes, after some initial reluctance, were enlisted in the planning of the heist, while your limbic system was clucking away in feathery terror at the prospect of being shot or incarcerated. If only we had a functional magnetic resonance imaging device to produce brain images showing which parts of your gray matter lit up when, we might at least get a clearer picture of what's going on in there.

Enough of the bank robbery. The really shocking thing is that *you are almost always* of two minds—at least two, as a matter of fact. One is a wild and crazy guy, pleasure lovin' but prone to violent squalls of temper that come and go with unsettling suddenness—think of the young Harvey Keitel. The other is your insurance-buying self, the one that plans ahead, shuns credit, and slathers on the sunscreen (*and* brings an umbrella anyway, just in case)—maybe the young Michael Moriarty. The two of you are the Odd Couple. Or really you're like Felix and Oscar's New York apartment, sheltering the Odd Couple in your very own body. Quick, which one do you want to be in charge? (You should know that, just like in the movie, Oscar's name is on the lease.)

Like most ideas, this notion of ourselves as divided isn't new, and traditionally it swans around cloaked in Manichean garb, which is of course black and white. The Persian prophet Zoroaster, in perhaps

600 BCE, held that good and evil are born into all of us, and versions of this idea are so widely found in the world's religions that they are practically a theological commonplace. Dualism comes naturally to creatures who are divided into males and females and live every day through cycles of light and dark. But there's something more at work, something people have perhaps always sensed inside themselves.

There is the sound of our internal voices, for instance, which we have to listen to all day and which we sometimes struggle to refute, suppress, or divert. For most of us this self-talk is almost synonymous with consciousness, yet we recognize a *listener* as well who is not the *speaker* inside of us, even though both inhabit the same corporeal space. (This unending self-talk is important; Socrates said his inner voice, or *daemon*, kept him on the straight and narrow.)

Then there's the feeling that the mind and body must be separate things, a notion that has come to be called Cartesian dualism, for the great French philosopher René Descartes, its most renowned exponent (and a powerful advocate of self-control as central to moral virtue). B. F. Skinner's radicalism ironically led him down this familiar path, except he postulated a divide between *managing* self and *managed* self, because, he said, "we must specify who is controlling whom." Body and soul, reason and passion, yin and yang, Abbott and Costello—the dualist vision beckons in every generation.

The State of the Union

Dualism has its uses. The distinction between *psyche* and *soma* helps us separate ourselves from the natural world enough to embrace some kind of ethics apart from the law of the jungle. The same distinction also comforts us with the sense that the world is more than it seems. Dualism entitles us to believe we aren't just flesh and blood, and thereby underwrites our faith in the sanctity of human life—while also permitting us (metaphorically, at least) to stave off death, for while the body clearly dies, the part that isn't body might live on. Dualism, in short, opens the door to immortality.

Thinking of ourselves as dual also enables us to separate ourselves from the part we (or others) disapprove of, as Dr. Jekyll sought to do by periodically spinning off Mr. Hyde. This notion of ourselves as divided lets us indulge the sanctioned part of ourselves while maintaining plausible deniability—like the country squire John Worthing in *The Importance of Being Earnest,* who maintains a racy urban alter ego named Ernest for fun and games in London. Saint Paul laments in his letter to the Romans, "I do not do what I would like to do, but instead I do what I hate . . . so I am not really the one who does this thing; rather it is the sin that lives in me."

Perhaps this is what the Hollywood publicist was alluding to when, in announcing that his client was going into treatment, he said: "After 20 years of sobriety, Robin Williams found himself drinking again." How shocked Williams must have been by this discovery!

Similarly, when Bernard Madoff was sentenced to one hundred and fifty years behind bars for what may have been the single largest financial fraud ever perpetrated, his wife issued a statement in which she confessed to a kind of bigamy: "My husband was the one we (and I include myself) respected and trusted with our lives and our livelihoods . . . Then there is the other man who stunned us all with his confession and is responsible for this terrible situation . . . The man who committed this horrible fraud is not the man whom I have known for all these years."

When her husband(s) broke the news, she might well have asked, "Bernie, what possessed you?" For once upon a time we might have laid such sinful actions at the door of Satan—*the devil made me do it!* We're too sophisticated for that now, so we call this inciteful creature the id or our inner child or the reptilian brain or some other equally mystical term.

Economists, who are always concerned with motivation and choice, embraced the two-self model long ago, starting with Adam Smith, who placed a heavy emphasis on self-control in his *Theory of Moral Sentiments,* in which he describes dividing himself into a spectator and an actor, the one judging the other. A similar split is evident in the research of George Loewenstein, a professor of economics and psychology at Carnegie Mellon University (and the great-grandson of Sigmund Freud), who sees our selves as divided between an affective system and a deliberative system.

In a series of remarkable papers, often with such other leading self-control researchers as Dan Ariely and Kathleen Vohs, Loewenstein has explored what he calls the "cold-to-hot empathy gap." A "cold" state is basically the absence of physiological need or arousal, so that being cold means not being hungry, not being aroused sexually, or being so cold that it's painful. On the contrary, it means being okay, calm, not desperate. Think of it as your sated self. Being in a "hot" state means being subject to any of these "visceral" conditions— subject either to drives such as hunger or lust, emotions such as anger or fear, or bodily sensations such as pain.

It turns out that when we're in a cold state, we seriously underestimate the power of a hot state to shape our behavior. In fact, when we're cold, we underestimate the power of a hot state on someone *else's* behavior. In a cold state, we can't even make sense of the "heat-induced" actions we've taken in the past ourselves. The same is pretty much true of our hot states, which seem to numb us to our cold selves. Experiments have borne this out again and again with respect to food, sex, and drugs.

Odysseus might have predicted as much. He thought Calypso was great at night, in the light of his passion's fire, yet during the day he sat by the shore and wept for home, where Penelope was holding the suitors at bay. In his hot state, inspired by the gorgeous goddess at hand, he was practically a different person than in the cold light of day.

Evidently, that's true of most men when it comes to sex. Loewenstein and Ariely paid thirty-five male undergraduates to answer questions in aroused and unaroused states—and found huge differences. Men who were aroused (by masturbating without orgasm) were much likelier to agree to sex with men, fat women, and people they hated. They were more eager for bondage, spanking, and anal sex and were a lot likelier to find cigarette smoke attractive. They were also more willing to do bad things in order to get laid. They were vastly more likely, for instance, to lie about being in love and to encourage a woman to drink. They were more than twice as likely to keep trying after a clear "no" from a woman, and more than five times as likely to slip her a drug.

The whole disturbing business is reminiscent of Shakespeare's *The Rape of Lucrece*, when Tarquin, considering whether to commit the dirty deed, "holds he disputation / 'Tween frozen conscience and hot burning will." His desire is "past reason's weak removing," clearly suggesting a hideous failure of self-control, yet while he knows there will be trouble later, he can't seem to imagine beforehand just how bad he'll feel afterward, when "hot desire converts to cold disdain."

What's interesting about Loewenstein's findings here is the suggestion that the self is so deeply divided between hot or cold that in one state we are a stranger to ourselves in the other. "These kinds of states," he says, "have the ability to change us so profoundly that we're more different from ourselves in different states than we are from another person."

Richard Thaler (perhaps the father of behavioral economics) and H. M. Shefrin, in a classic paper called "An Economic Theory of Self-Control," envision the individual at any point in time as a farsighted planner and a myopic doer: "The resulting conflict is seen to be fundamentally similar to the agency conflict between the owners and managers of a firm." In a corporation, the hired managers might act more in their own short-run interests (as "myopic doers") than in the interests of the shareholders who pay their salaries. We saw this very problem in the recent financial crisis. The chief executive of a bank, for instance, might encourage risky loans that generate high short-term profits—and a rich year-end bonus—even though the borrowers might later default, to the detriment of the shareholders and everyone else.

Plato, in *The Republic*, gives another view of this conflict between the side of us that plans and the side that acts. He suggests human nature must contain two elements, one better and one worse, otherwise the idea of self-mastery is absurd: "For if you're master *of* yourself you're presumably also subject *to* yourself, and so *both* master *and* subject." Elsewhere Plato says, "Each is an enemy of himself," and victory in this struggle is crucial, for "being defeated by oneself is the most shameful and at the same time the worst of all defeats."

Implied in all this doubleness is the sense that our wholeness is made of two parts—which in turn suggests that neither can live without the other. Consider the Judaic concepts *yetzer ha-ra* and *yetzer ha-tov*. *Yetzer* means impulse, and *yetzer ha-ra* is our appetitive side; it's not simply or inherently evil, as is sometimes thought, but it can be a source of evil, as you can imagine. It's our drives, our needs, our instinctual hungers. Next to passionate *yetzer ha-ra*, dutiful *yetzer ha-tov* is kind of dull. It's the ethical force; our conscience, in common parlance, which reminds us of God's law as we are about to fall short of it.

A rabbi I know, Jonathan Kligler, tells of a revealing legend from the Talmud about these uneasily coexisting impulses. The story is that once upon a time in a Jewish community the pious men were fed up with the wild behavior induced by *yetzer ha-ra*, so they decided to take action—by hunting it down once and for all. Once it was captured and caged, they thought at last they had secured the triumph of *yetzer ha-tov*, but their satisfaction was short-lived, for it soon became clear that something spooky was going on. Eggs went unhatched, houses unbuilt—life came to a standstill. The reason was obvious—as hard as it was to live with *yetzer ha-ra*, living without it was impossible. What to do? After some debate, it was decided: they put out its eyes and then turned it loose. George Ainslie, the psychiatrist and self-control pioneer, loved this story when I told it to him. A Gentile psychiatrist—there are a few, evidently—Ainslie immediately saw the wisdom of the rabbis' action: "They let it go, but they blinded it first, so *yetzer ha-ra* can only see what reason shows it."

Were the creators of *Star Trek* steeped in such Talmudic lore? They might well have been, judging from the classic first-season episode "The Enemy Within," in which a transporter malfunction divides Captain Kirk in two, one good and one evil. Fortunately for both the universe and the series, Bad Kirk doesn't triumph, but the surprising thing is that Good Kirk can't live without him, and until the two are reunited, the captain's life is endangered. Evidently, the starship's captain needs his *yetzer ha-ra*.

So do the rest of us. The neuroscientist Antonio Damasio has studied patients who have suffered damage to their orbitofrontal cortex, the part of the brain just above the eyes and a region heavily implicated in both emotions and decision making. Damasio found that such damage often left a patient's intellect intact but cut off his emotional life, suggesting a creature something like *Star Trek*'s Mr. Spock.

Sadly, the result isn't a dispassionate reasoning machine but a lost soul without the ability to make the most basic decisions. These patients found themselves shorn of preference or motivation; without any intuitive, *feeling* basis for choosing one option over another, they suffered a kind of existential paralysis—much like that of Jacob Horner, the protagonist in John Barth's early novel *The End of the Road*, who often seems to lack the blessed autopilot that keeps the rest of us going on an everyday basis. Horner's motivation is so completely undermined by existential doubt that he finds himself subject to random paralysis—in a train station, for example—simply because in a universe without sense or meaning, there's no good reason for choosing one action over another. As William James observed, "There is no more miserable human being than one in whom nothing is habitual but indecision, and for whom the lighting of every cigar, the drinking of every cup, the time of rising and going to bed every day, and the beginning of every bit of work, are subject of express volitional deliberation."

But there's something else about that Talmudic legend, something not so obvious at first but important nonetheless. In the contest of *yetzer ha-ra* and *yetzer ha-tov*, there is a missing actor, one we might as well call the referee. The yetzer twins are a metaphor for our dual natures, but they imply a third player who must adjudicate their competing demands. And although a threesome is probably never as satisfying as people imagine (and of course I'd have no way to know), three is the number we've been stuck with for a long, long time.

Three's a Crowd

Plato lays it all out in the *Phaedrus*, the dialogue in which Socrates poetically describes a tripartite soul by using the famous metaphor of the charioteer struggling to control a pair of winged horses, one good and the other bad:

> The right-hand horse is upright and cleanly made; he has a lofty neck and an aquiline nose; his colour is white, and his eyes dark; he is a lover of honour and modesty and temperance, and the follower of true glory; he needs no touch of the whip, but is guided by word and admonition only. The other is a crooked lumbering animal, put together anyhow; he has a short thick neck; he is flat-faced and of a dark colour, with grey eyes and blood-red complexion; the mate of insolence and pride, shag-eared and deaf, hardly yielding to whip and spur.

The *Phaedrus* has its fans, but is there really any more profound or beautiful exposition of the soul's tripartite nature than "Donald's Better Self"? In this 1938 cartoon classic, which is to Plato what *It's a Wonderful Life* is to Sartre, Donald Duck is portrayed as a youngster caught in a battle between two sides of himself. The action (which you can see for yourself on YouTube) opens with him asleep in bed. When his alarm goes off he goes on sleeping, but an angelic Donald look-alike rises cheerfully from his body, turns off the alarm, and wakes Donald up with some prim little hand claps and talk about school. This character is a bit of an odd duck; although referred to throughout as a *he*, Good Donald has a markedly feminine air, including what seems to be a woman's voice (it might as well be Eleanor Roosevelt's, from the patrician sound of it) and a schoolmarmishly large derriere. Good Donald is the sort who's always given self-control a bad name; on the way to school, he's the very picture of sanctimony, strutting with his beak in the air, hands pressed together, and eyes lidded heavily in rapturous self-approval.

On the other hand, there is no gender confusion about blue-collar Bad Donald, who appears soon enough. If Good Donald is clearly feminine, in keeping with traditional ideas about women as a civilizing force, Bad Donald, the gravel-voiced devilish side, is all man, with horns and an arrow-shaped tail, which stands phallically erect. When he diverts Donald from his pious progress toward the schoolhouse, it is not just to go fishing but (apparently) to whisper dirty jokes in his ear, which Donald pretends to get and like.

Bad Donald is determined to rescue Donald—who is eager to be rescued—from the emasculating uprightness that Good Donald seems determined to inflict. Bad Donald not only encourages bad behavior but laughs as his naïve charge exerts himself to demonstrate his manliness with a pipe. "Take another puff! Be a man!" Bad Donald urges, promising that the tobacco will put hair on Donald's feathery chest. Donald promptly gets sick and succumbs to paroxysms of regret: "Why did I do it?" he moans more than once, his remorse placing him in a great tradition of self-pitying sinners that includes such sainted predecessors as Paul and Augustine. Donald is soon back on the path to virtue, which is synonymous here with education (literally, the path to the schoolhouse). As is so often the case in morality tales, good is stronger than evil, and Donald now cheers on Good Donald, who soon overcomes his unwillingness to vanquish Bad Donald with fisticuffs, at which point the remaining Donalds merge into one and go off to school.

That same year, Donald, very much a grown-up this time, stars in a short titled "Self-Control," which is about how hard it can be to control one's temper. Seen together, the two films are handy allegories for the two main causes that Aristotle laid out for weakness of the will: pleasure and anger. In "Donald's Better Self," the pleasures are sleeping late, skipping school, fishing, sharing a raunchy laugh, and smoking tobacco, although in the cartoon, of course, pleasure sometimes goes too far and leads to regret. In "Self-Control," a smarmy radio guru gives listeners—including Donald—some sensible advice on controlling anger, advice to which Donald is susceptible because he already has regrets about his previous tantrums. But in this case our hero finds happiness only when he gives up counting to ten and lets himself blow. Here, too, there is pleasure at work—the pleasure of indulging one's temper.

The amazing thing is that, in both films, Donald Duck and Sigmund

Freud are on the same page. It was Freud, after all, who held that repression could lead to illness, and it is Freud who is our best-known proponent of the tripartite self. Freud borrowed his big ideas, for the most part, and it's a wonder he came up with this one before Walt Disney. But he was steeped in the classics and had the example of Plato's *Phaedrus*, not to mention the great nineteenth-century neurologist John Hughlings Jackson. Jackson quite explicitly saw the self as double, consisting of subject consciousness and object consciousness. But he saw the central nervous system as having a three-part hierarchy reflecting evolutionary history—much as scientists do today. He called the parts lowest, middle, and highest, based on their stage of evolutionary development, and postulated that the highest part, which allows the most self-control, relies on the prefrontal cortex.

"I am large. . . . I contain multitudes."

But is the self merely a trio? Walt Whitman claimed to contain multitudes, and George Ainslie sees the self as a kind of gang—"a huge, disorganized and shapeless society of lusts and impulses," as Lawrence Durrell put it in *Justine*—or better yet, a market made of competing interests, one that functions like "a bazaar of partially incompatible factions, where, in order to prevail, an option has not only to promise more than its competitors, but to act strategically to keep the competitors from later undermining it." In other words, it's a bargaining process.

On this basis, it's not difficult to conceive of the self as a practically infinite number of entities stretching forward and back in time. The philosopher Derek Parfit has suggested that our future selves are tantamount to different individuals, and as such aren't entitled to any more deference than anyone else, although he does acknowledge that it matters how far off in time any of your particular selves happens to be: "My concern for my future may correspond to the degree of 'connectedness' between me now and myself in the future . . . since connectedness is nearly always weaker over longer periods, I can rationally care less about my further future."

Those future selves may never even come to be; accident or disease might intervene, and your awareness of this possibility can only undermine your present concern for your future incarnations. Even if they do come to be, they may look and act and think and feel altogether different from the way you do today, with different memories and experiences and preferences. They will have the advantages of prior experience, saving, and investing, offset perhaps by the disadvantages of greater age, in a mix you can't begin to fathom or predict.

Now imagine that the lot of you are staying at a hotel, one right after another. Clearly, you'll only need one room. And so every morning the old version of you checks out and every afternoon the newest one checks in, to be succeeded daily by an even newer self, in a cycle that continues year after year until death. The problem is, there's no cleaning staff, and frankly the place is getting a little rank. *If only the guy before me had cleaned up!*

But now *you're* in the room, and you don't want to clean up, either. *Do I really have to?* You begin to wonder: *Just what do I owe to my later selves?* The only one who can straighten up, after all, is the current occupant, but why make such a sacrifice? What you want now is a drink and a bath; any later guests can fend for themselves. Ah, but every day you go on this way, the room deteriorates further. One of you has got to sacrifice for the good of the others; yet if you think only of the current occupant, there's no reason you can't indulge yourself endlessly in the here and now, the others be damned.

The problem with this thinking is that it will shortly immiserate all of you. Yet it's foolish to pretend that our "selves" are really of so little consequence to one another, or as distant from us as some long-ago ancestors. We know that we'll become them, and they have a claim on us—and so we're motivated to clean, giving them not just a tidy room but the memory of having done the right thing, which they're more likely to do again. The close connection among these selves, to

Ainslie, explains willpower, for if we didn't care about our future (or past) selves, why on earth would we bother?

The funny thing is that what you might think of as a cost to your current self—some pleasure forgone in favor of strangers-to-come—may actually be a benefit to that self. There is satisfaction to be had from doing for others and in thinking of yourself as a disciplined person. There is also pleasure in anticipating some future reward. Indeed, the pleasure of anticipation often outweighs the pleasure of the reward itself.

The dashing Shane Frederick, who studies these issues at Yale, notes that our attitude toward the future is complex, and that we do not automatically accelerate pleasures and postpone pains. That's the pattern with, say, alcohol consumption (pleasure now, pain later), but with jogging, it's the opposite: we embrace pain now for pleasure (in the form of fitness, etc.) later. With education, similarly, there is suffering today and financial reward tomorrow. With tanning, we get pain (sunburn) today, followed by pleasure (tan) followed by pain (long-term skin damage).

While anticipating a reward is rewarding in itself, it's unclear how much we value this pleasure. Frederick notes that when we order something online, faster shipping costs more, not less; while we may enjoy anticipation, we don't seem willing to pay extra to prolong it. And of course not all anticipation is pleasurable; anticipation of pain can be awful, and sometimes the dread is worse than the thing dreaded. This is why people often prefer to get bad experiences over with rather than, in effect, prolonging them with miserable expectation.

Weighing now versus later can get complicated, as I learned from my twin boys when they were around ten years old. Confronted with a plate of pasta and meatballs, a favorite dinner at our house, both boys tended to eat the meatballs last. Saving up the best part sounds simple enough, but the issues embedded in their decision illustrate the uncertainties that beset all of us when deciding whether to forgo gratification.

Delay, for instance, might make the hoarded meatballs less tasty. They could get cold, or they might not seem quite as delicious after one's appetite has been dulled by a plateful of spaghetti. Meat and starch might be more rewarding in tandem—and, in fact, the boys never asked for a dinner of meatballs alone. There could be an earthquake after you eat the spaghetti but before you get to the meatballs, wiping out the cherished hoard. Or your evil twin could decide to gobble his, thus removing the most obvious means of retribution, and then steal one of yours.

In weighing these issues, we rely on memory and imagination to cope with an uncertain future. We recall past experiences, we try to project how we would feel if this or that occurred, and we call upon the knowledge we have gained by living. All of this requires a sense of ourselves as contiguous across time and suggests it would be a mistake to dismiss out of hand the needs and desires we are likely to have tomorrow. For as Hillel must surely have said somewhere, if I am not for my future selves, then who will be? But if I am only for my future selves, then what am I?

The Mind-Body Problem

our flesh
Surrounds us with its own decisions

—PHILIP LARKIN

There is no better illustration of Philip Larkin's observation than the case of a forty-year-old schoolteacher who came to the attention of neurologists at the University of Virginia. The man had lived quietly with his wife and stepdaughter until something changed—and his thoughts were captured more and more by forbidden forms of sex.

Troublesome thoughts are hard to control, as we shall see, but these were not the usual harmless longings and spicy fantasies that roost pleasantly in the minds of so many men. These were edgier, more insistent, and soon the man began to act on them, in some sense against his own will. He started by collecting pornography, then advanced to soliciting prostitutes and visiting massage parlors, until, at last, his obsession came to focus on children. The man was a schoolteacher, remember. When he turned his attentions toward his own prepubescent stepdaughter, her mother called the police—and he was soon removed from the home and convicted of child molestation. As a last-ditch effort to avoid prison, the bizarrely changed schoolteacher signed up for group therapy, but soon got himself ejected for propositioning women at the program. There was now no option but incarceration. He spent his last night of freedom in a suicidal terror that he would rape his landlady no matter how hard he tried not to—and he was tortured by headaches so bad that, finally, he drove himself to the hospital.

As it turned out, the stress of his predicament wasn't to blame, although it might have given anyone a migraine. What the man had was an egg-sized tumor in the right lobe of the orbitofrontal cortex, which is a part of the human brain closely associated with judgment, impulse control, and social behavior. When surgeons excised the lesion, his pedophilia vanished along with his interest in pornography, prostitutes, and rape. (When it grew back, his troubles returned until the doctors operated yet again.)

What the surgery did was restore the man's ability to control himself, something the rest of us, with our vastly more mundane failings and transgressions, have to manage without medical intervention. And while few of us fall as fast or as far as the unfortunate Virginia schoolteacher did, his story raises many of the oldest and deepest questions about the ability of each of us to regulate our behavior. "We're dealing with the neurology of morality here," said Russell Swerdlow, one of his physicians.

If a tumor could induce such a lapse, after all, to what extent could the man be held responsible for his strange behavior? And if a section of the brain is the seat of our willpower, what if that section is naturally more developed in some people than in others? Even in the absence of a tumor, self-control is surely at some level a physical process, unless you happen to believe in something like a soul that exists apart from flesh and blood. But if weakness of will is a mere physical shortcoming, how can it also be a moral failing? Given the rapidly unraveling mysteries of genetics, neuroscience, and human behavior, how much self-control can any of us accurately claim to have? The issue is far from academic; Dr. Swerdlow has since been approached by defense attorneys hoping he could find something exculpatory in the brain scans of their clients. The first lawyer to bring him such a problem represented a defendant who had prostate cancer.

. . .

In order to answer these questions, we have to understand a little something about the nature of the brain and how it got the way it is. For the essential problem is that, Descartes notwithstanding, there is no mind-body distinction. It's all body, and it evolved to live in a world very different from the one in which we dwell today. As the great Rexford Tugwell observed in 1922, a decade before he went to work for Franklin Roosevelt, "Man is equipped with the psychical and physical make-up of his first human ancestors; he is the sort of being who functions best in the exhilarations and the fatigues of the hunt, of primitive warfare, and in the precarious life of nomadism . . . Strangely and suddenly he now finds himself transported into a different milieu, keeping, however, as he must, the equipment for the old life."

Or as the psychologists Leda Cosmides and John Tooby put it: "Our modern skulls house a stone-age mind."

Evolution Made Me Do It

Try to imagine how different your problems would be if you lived eons ago on some African savannah. Think of a camping trip lasting around seven million years. In this environment—the one for which we evolved—people lived as hunters and gatherers in small nomadic bands or clans. Life was shorter and also simpler. There was no refrigeration and relatively little, aside from finding food, to tax our powers of concentration. Amphetamine abuse, bulimia, compulsive shopping, and all the other pathological flora of modern life were inconceivable. Distractibility ("Hey, wasn't that a tiger?!") might have been a favored adaptation, right along with impulsiveness. A slower metabolism and a preference for fats and sweets were an evolutionary advantage, not a threat to your health or social standing.

"The self," the psychologist Mark R. Leary tells us, "did not evolve to exert the amount of control that we require of it in modern life. To begin with, our lives are filled with far more choices and decisions than the lives of the individuals in whom the modern self first appeared. Spending their entire lives in the same clan, wandering the same territory, planning only a day or two ahead, and practicing the same cultural traditions, our prehistoric ancestors would not have confronted the innumerable choices that modern people must make every day."

Self-control is largely a matter of timing; we can do (or not do) most things at any point between *right now* and *never*, and by exerting our will we can make sure the timing is in accord with our overall best interests. But choices between now and later are challenging for people because of how the human brain developed.

The earliest vertebrate brains were pretty simple, consisting of some clumps of nerves that handled such literally vital aspects of life as breath and heartbeat. Over time, additional brain structures evolved—the thalamus, hypothalamus, amygdala, and hippocampus. This new layer of structures, which wrapped around the old, is known as the limbic system. *Limbus* is Latin for border, which is ironic because this particular part of the brain isn't too interested in the boundaries we or others set for ourselves. This limbic overlay is sometimes called the emotional brain, for it is the seat of our basic drives and deals with memory, emotion, thirst, hunger, fear, and some motor functions as well as our circadian rhythms. The whole package carried us along for millennia on something like autopilot.

Eventually, in response to the increasing complexity of mammalian life, the more social mammals developed yet another layer, the neocortex, which grew to surround the limbic system. This is the wrinkled gray matter most of us think of when we visualize a brain. The relatively enormous frontal section of this newish overlay has to do with emotions as well, but it also has remarkable powers of reasoning, planning, and problem solving. It's the seat of what have been called our executive functions, which include our ability to regulate our emotions, control impulses, focus on what we need to, and delay gratification.

The foremost area of the frontal lobes, the prefrontal cortex, is especially important for most of this stuff. Bigger in humans than in other primates, it has been implicated in working memory, organization skills, planning and strategizing, decision making, and reactions to punishment or reward. It also plays an important role in empathy and insight. If the intellect has an address, it is the prefrontal cortex. By any reasonable standard, this is the seat of the self, the thing you really mean when you think about you.

You would not design the system in this layered way from scratch, but that's evolution for you, piling one thing on another, the way Microsoft stacked Windows precariously on top of DOS years ago. (Remember the C prompt?) The new system works well enough, but it's no match for the massively parallel capabilities of the much older parts of our brain, which coordinate a symphony of organic processes without conscious intervention. Danger? Your heart rate suddenly accelerates and your eyes widen, all by themselves. Grabbed a hot pot handle? The signal to jerk your hand away bypasses the conscious parts of your brain to get where it's going faster.

The parts of the brain are all tightly connected, of course, and occupy the same snug and heavily fortified cabin between the ears and behind the eyes. But despite their close quarters, their seemingly long association, and the amazing feats we associate with them (the ability to understand relativity, for example, or troubleshoot Microsoft Windows), the various brain structures do not always work in perfect coordination. In fact, often they butt heads, or perhaps we should say lobes.

Consider a study of fourteen Princeton undergraduates conducted a few years back by the brain scientist Samuel McClure and colleagues. The researchers stuffed the students—one at a time—into a large device called a functional magnetic resonance imaging scanner, which provides color images graphically depicting brain activity. Then the students were presented with a series of choices between smaller sums of money given sooner and larger amounts given later—classic intertemporal choice questions of the kind asked by Walter Mischel. These questions are usually of the type, "Would you rather have $10 now or $15 in seven days?" The sensible answer is to wait a week for the much larger sum; it's not every day that you're offered a guaranteed 50 percent return on your investment in just a week.

I wonder sometimes about what these questions really measure. For example, what if there are external factors that skew the students' answers—say, an invitation to a movie showing only that night that a student might not otherwise have the cash for? But most professional students of self-control regard these questions as a reasonable tool for assessing someone's ability to defer gratification—and a measure of how extensively we discount the future. So, what McClure and his associates found, right there in living color, was that decisions involving a possible immediate reward ignited increased activity in brain areas associated with emotion—specifically, the classic limbic structures that are heavily supplied by the body's dopamine system (which are also associated with impulsivity and addiction). Like serotonin, dopamine plays a central role in self-regulation; it's the way the brain gives us pleasure to reinforce the things likely to both propagate our genes and, if taken to excess, do us in.

Dopamine is fascinating stuff; this neurotransmitter appears to be at the heart of our problems with impulse control. The brains of people with Parkinson's disease are almost entirely dopamine-free, and sufferers can find it difficult or impossible to make their bodies do something like reach for a glass. On the other hand, certain drugs (like cocaine or amphetamines) work to make more dopamine available, and heavy users find it difficult to *stop* themselves from doing something—in particular, taking more drugs. High levels of dopamine have been implicated not just in drug abuse but in compulsive behaviors as well. A small number of Parkinson's patients have developed such behaviors from their medication (which is intended to restore some of the brain's dopamine). Max Wells, a retired physician from Austin, Texas, claimed in a lawsuit that his medication triggered a gambling addiction that cost him $14 million. Others have found themselves getting carried away with eating or sex.

Predictably, all the decisions made by participants in McClure's study activated parts of the brain associated with abstract reasoning;

these were smart young adults, and they were trying to figure things out. But when the students picked the *delayed* option in a given choice set, the calculating parts of their brain—regions of the lateral prefrontal cortex and posterior parietal cortex—lit up more powerfully. When students chose the *immediate* reward, the emotional and calculating parts of the brain both were activated, with a slight edge to the emotional part. "There are two different brain systems," McClure said at the time, "and one of them"—the more emotional—"kicks in as you get really proximate to the reward."

Freud would have taken quite a bit of comfort from this, I imagine; he always nursed hopes that science would somehow find anatomical correlatives to the metaphorical structure he dreamed up for the human psyche, and what McClure is suggesting, if you squint, looks a little like Freud's ego and id. We really are of two minds (if not more!), and these two brains see the world very differently; they have very different priorities, and they often try to subvert one another. The limbic brain gives us reasons to rationalize actions we know may be unwise. The calculating brain might take actions to prevent the seething limbic brain from becoming roused.

"Our emotional brain has a hard time imagining the future, even though our logical brain clearly sees the future consequences of our current actions," explains David Laibson, a Harvard economist who worked on the study. "Our emotional brain wants to max out the credit card, order dessert and smoke a cigarette. Our logical brain knows we should save for retirement, go for a jog and quit smoking. To understand why we feel internally conflicted, it will help to know how myopic and forward-looking brain systems value rewards and how these systems talk to one another."

Modern life, with its cacophony of temptations and demands, is a far more complex (and hospitable) place for us than the environment we evolved in, which is a good thing, for in the evolutionary environment you'd probably be dead by now. The downside is that modern life places far more pressure on the *self* in *self-control* because of what the Nobel Prize–winning ethologist Nikolaas Tinbergen called "super-normal stimuli." Tinbergen studied animals to determine, for example, what it was about potential mates that was most attractive, and then produced dummies with this characteristic exaggerated. What he found was that the imitation was more appealing than the real McCoy. Geese with an instinct to retrieve eggs removed from the nest will try to retrieve a volleyball if it has the right markings. A bird will feed a fake chick before it feeds its own if the dummy's beak is opened wider and has more dramatic coloring.

We live in a world of such supernormal stimuli today. In affluent countries, supernormally appealing rewards—heavily sweetened lattes, unnaturally large breast implants, mesmerizing computer games—appeal to our evolutionary instincts with captivating force far beyond that which we evolved to withstand. The relatively low cost of such refined products as sugar, cocaine, and even gasoline means that the only thing between us and our instincts is a thin membrane of will-power, or an even thinner membrane of mindfulness.

The problem, as Mark Leary attests, "is not that our modern lives are worse than those of prehistoric humans but, rather, that our lives require a far greater amount of self-control. As a result, we sometimes push our efforts to control ourselves past the self's ability to respond . . . The result is not only occasional failures of self-regulation, some of which are disastrous, but also a chronically low level of self-control strength."

Humans evolved with the capacity to look ahead and guide them-selves accordingly, deferring gratification when it seemed useful to do so, but we didn't evolve to cope with a world in which we could obtain luscious foods at a moment's notice, encounter thousands of strangers in a single afternoon, or spend next year's earnings with a few swipes of plastic. Modern life simply requires an unnatural degree of self-control, and one of its side effects is self-control fatigue.

To fully appreciate how well we manage in spite of our evolution-ary handicaps, you have to look past the run-of-the-mill lapses that all of us are subject to sooner or later. Look instead at just how badly our

self-control can fail us as the result of illness or injury, as was the case
with the Virginia schoolteacher described at the beginning of this chapter. In fact, brain injuries going back to the nineteenth century have
taught us a lot about our executive functions generally and about self-
control in particular. The most famous example in the annals of medicine is the remarkable Phineas Gage.

Ouch!

On September 13, 1848, Phineas Gage was the handsome twenty-five-
year-old foreman of a work crew building a section of the bed for the
Rutland and Burlington Railroad just south of Cavendish, Vermont,
where the crew was methodically blasting its way through a large section of rock that stood in the way. They did this by drilling holes in the
stone and filling them with powder and fuse. This material was gently
tamped down, then sand was added as a kind of buffer, after which a
tamping iron would be brought to bear for more serious packing. This
was an iron cylinder 42 inches long and weighing 13½ pounds. For most
of its length, it was 1¼ inches wide, but it narrowed to a point of about
a quarter inch at one end.

At 4:30 p.m., Gage for some reason—fatigue? distraction?—began
using this bar to tamp a charge into a hole without the crucial sand. A
spark was triggered by the collision of the metal against the rock, and
the resulting explosion propelled the tamping iron like a rocket, straight
out of the hole and clear through young Gage's head.

All things considered, he was extraordinarily lucky. The bar entered,
point first, just below his left cheekbone and penetrated the brain
behind the socket of his left eye. The force of the missile was such that
it exited through the top of his head and landed 20 to 25 yards behind
him. Along the way, it knocked out a chunk of his frontal lobes.

The precise nature of Gage's brain damage will never be known, but
an enormous amount of scientific ingenuity has been devoted to trying
to figure it out. Unfortunately, no autopsy was performed—but we are

getting ahead of ourselves, because, if you can believe it, the tamping-bar accident didn't kill him.

Gage, apparently an exceedingly robust specimen, may have been unconscious for a while, but sooner or later he was driven by his men in an oxcart to the nearby inn where he lived. He dismounted without any help and from the inn's porch told his story to those who gathered around. When Dr. Edward Higginson Williams turned up, Gage greeted him by saying, "Doctor, here is business enough for you."

Gage's luck held; about an hour later, Dr. John Martyn Harlow arrived, and over the months ahead, this man's deft handling of Gage's serious infection—long before the invention of antibiotics—saved the patient's life. It's also thanks to Harlow, mainly, that we know of the psychological consequences following Gage's unfortunate encounter with the tamping rod.

Preceding the accident, according to Harlow, Gage was quite a guy: efficient, energetic, capable, temperate in his habits, of "a well-balanced mind," and a favorite of his men and his employer alike. Afterward, however, he was almost literally a different person; Harlow tells us he became obstinate, profane, capricious, "impatient of restraint or advice" that happened to go against his own desires, and "a child intellectually" with "the animal passions of a strong man." The change was so complete that, according to those who knew him, he was "no longer Gage."

It seems likely that, by some standards, he *was* no longer Gage, because the iron rod had damaged the section of the brain that, to a great extent, made him who he was. It was the section that enabled him to look ahead, to make plans and carry them out, to exercise patience and reason—the section, in other words, where self-mastery lived. In a sense, Gage lost a hunk of his personhood on that fateful day in 1848. He lived another twelve years, until May 1860, but was never able to perform his earlier work. He spent some time in Chile, was for a while an attraction at P. T. Barnum's American Museum (a freak show with pretentions) in New York, exhibited himself and his iron bar (which he always kept close by) across New England, and worked on farms near San Francisco. Epileptic seizures ultimately did him in, concluding an erratic life riven in two by the railroad accident more than a decade earlier.

Subsequent brain injury cases have only fortified the belief that the prefrontal cortex is the seat of our supervisory functions as well as our ability to conceive of the future. In general, people with frontal lobe damage tend to be more impulsive, less disciplined, lacking in short-term memory, and easily distracted, especially from tasks requiring sustained attention. They often have a disturbed experience of time and have problems forming goals and making plans. Depending on what specific part of the frontal lobes have been damaged, these individuals may also be unable to foresee the consequences of their own actions (which underlines the importance of imagination and working memory in self-control for the rest of us), and perhaps as a result, they are more prone to making decisions based on the prospect of instantaneous reward. Sometimes they appear "stimulus bound," or unable to act without the prod of some environmental demand.

Three brain circuits in particular seem to be involved in all this: the ventromedial orbitofrontal cortex, the dorsolateral prefrontal cortex, and the anterior cingulate cortex. Damage to the ventromedial orbitofrontal cortex, which is strongly connected with the limbic system, often results in a myopic view of the future, poor impulse control, distractibility, bad judgment, and uninhibited emotionality. Often these patients—and Phineas Gage appears to have been one—know right from wrong but can't guide their behavior accordingly. Rules and manners are flouted and people see these unlucky individuals as selfish or immature. In patients with dorsolateral prefrontal cortex damage, the ability to compare outcome and intention can be destroyed or seriously compromised, as if an important aspect of the patient's imagination has been shattered; victims may suffer dorsolateral syndrome, which is characterized by flatness of affect and indifference to pain. Damage to the anterior cingulate cortex, finally, has been associated with obsessive-compulsive disorder and schizophrenia, which are characterized by poor impulse control.

The Lobes Impaired

Accidents like the one that befell poor Phineas Gage aren't the only way your frontal lobes might not be up to snuff. Another cause might be medical treatment. In the middle of the twentieth century, for example, lacking good therapeutic options for mental illness, physicians performed thousands of lobotomies. One common technique (skip ahead if you're reading this while eating) was to pound an ice pick up into the brain through an eye socket and move it around blindly. Previously troubled patients seemed to emerge pacified, but the result, perhaps not surprisingly, was the dull demeanor typical of dorsolateral syndrome.

Recent research (which will come as no surprise to exasperated parents) has demonstrated that teenagers have frontal lobes that aren't ready for prime time, either, as is perhaps evident from their driving record: in the United States, mile for mile, teens are four times more likely to have an accident than adult drivers, and auto accidents are the leading cause of teenage deaths.

Teenagers are different from you and me, and the differences are more than skin-deep. Aside from acne, one big difference is that teens don't have a fully formed prefrontal cortex. From birth, the human brain is growing and changing to meet the demands of a complex environment. We are born with a plethora of synapses, which are the things that connect nerve cells in the brain. In fact, we're born with more than we need. Some synapses transmit excitatory information, which increases the likelihood that the receiving neuron will send an impulse to another neuron. But other synapses are inhibitory, and these reduce the likelihood that the receiving neuron will fire. Our extra synapses get pruned as we grow up, and in this process it's mostly excitatory synapses that are eliminated—with the result that the balance shifts over time toward inhibitory circuits, leading us away from the action bias associated with impetuous youth. There is probably some poignant trade-off here; as

William Wordsworth (along with Natalie Wood) reminds us, "nothing can bring back the hour of splendour in the grass."

But those changes are only the beginning, for during adolescence the branching of neurons becomes much more complex in the prefrontal cortex. The myelin sheathing on nerve fibers, which protects them but also makes them much faster conductors, increases throughout the brain, but increases last in the prefrontal cortex, where it doesn't happen until well into a person's twenties. Adolescence is also a time of hugely increased dopamine connections to the prefrontal cortex, which is important because this particular messenger chemical is implicated in many behaviors involving risk, reward, novelty, and self-control. Behavioral tests and magnetic resonance imaging studies confirm that teenage brains aren't very good at certain inhibitory tasks.

There are other brain differences between teens and adults, differences that make self-control all the more difficult for young people, but you get the general idea. All this science is merely piling up physiological evidence for something parents and teachers have long known, which is that teens often are impulsive, risk loving, and uninhibited. But at least we now know the reason: it's their brains. This realization may be helpful to parents and teens alike, although it says little for the youth culture we all seem to inhabit—a culture that arises from the part of society least capable of subjugating impulses.

In addition to youth, poor executive function has been associated in some studies with lower socioeconomic status. Such a correlation, if it exists, might occur because poverty is associated with factors that undermine people's self-regulatory capacities: stress, poor nutrition, lead poisoning, or some other means as yet unsuspected. It could be the result of prenatal smoking, alcohol, or drug abuse. Or it could even occur because executive function is partly hereditary and people are poor because nature dealt them a bad hand in this department.

Genes

The connection between poverty and heredity is controversial, but there is little doubt that self-control is significantly inherited. Genes affect almost every aspect of behavior, so why not this one? There is evidence, for example, that the dopamine receptor gene DRD2 is associated with impulsivity; kids with one form of this gene have more behavior problems and are less likely to go to college. Research has also shown that certain versions of DRD2 and several other genes are more common in conscientious people, a group that shows such signs of self-control as persistence, responsibility, and dependability.

Hormones, neurotransmitters, and many other potentially relevant biological factors are at least partly genetic as well, as are some other self-control-related characteristics, such as novelty-seeking and, especially, intelligence. The ability to defer gratification is strongly associated with intelligence, and Yale psychologist Jeremy Gray, who has studied this connection, says intelligence is 50 to 80 percent hereditary (although some psychologists say the proportion is lower). "Some portion of delay discounting is heritable," Gray told me in an interview, referring to how strongly people prefer larger-later to sooner-smaller rewards. "I'd be amazed if it turned out to be different."

The scientific case on this is not closed, but the evidence seems to support his view. In a twin study, for example, UCLA neuroscientist Paul Thompson and his colleagues found that the structure of certain regions of the brain—including the frontal region, which is critical for self-control—is highly heritable, so much so that environment was considered to have only a negligible effect.

As we face fewer external restrictions in our lives, the role of genetics in human behavior probably grows larger, for each of us is freer than we would have been in the past to follow our inherited talents and predispositions. Women endowed with intelligence and ambition are no longer limited to becoming homemakers or schoolteachers. Black people, in the past more cruelly constrained by the color of their skin, can become president. Given this reality, the genetic dimension of self-control may well be growing in influence compared with other factors.

Consider the implications. Willpower appears to be the result of genes, environment, or some interaction of the two—just like the tumor that shattered the Virginia schoolteacher's sexual self-restraint. Whatever the formula, it's hard to see how I can be held responsible if I can't resist temptation. Justin Gosling, in a slender philosophical volume called *Weakness of the Will,* puts the point succinctly: "If I am physically too weak to lift a weight, it is not my fault if I fail; so why does the same not hold if I am too weak of will, suffering, as it were, from debility of spiritual muscle?"

This is precisely the trouble with delving into the neuroscience of self-control. Delve deeply enough, and you may decide pretty quickly that we don't have any self-control at all.

Self-control, Free Will, and Other Oxymorons

So convenient a thing it is to be a reasonable Creature, *since it enables one to find or make a Reason for every thing one has a mind to do.*

—BENJAMIN FRANKLIN

Think back, if you can bear it, to college philosophy class. Back then, somebody was always ready to claim that there's no such thing as free will. These people—and of course they can't help themselves, or so they presumably believe—argue that everything is caused by the things that have come before, and thus the future is entirely determined, which is why their stance is known as *determinism*. Like the poor, it seems, determinism is always with us. "Men are deceived in that they think themselves free . . ." Benedict de Spinoza wrote way back in 1677, "an opinion which consists only in this, that they are conscious of their own actions and ignorant of the causes by which they are determined."

The implication is that the term *self-control* is meaningless. Unfortunately, the case for humans as automatons has been growing lately, bolstered by an unsettling mountain of research suggesting that the conscious mind is as much biological yes-man as ship's captain. As Jonathan Miller concluded, "Human beings owe a surprisingly large proportion of their cognitive and behavioral capacities to the existence of an 'automatic self' of which they have no conscious knowledge and over which they have little voluntary control."

Freud was right about this much at least: an awful lot of the time this automatic self really is the one in the driver's seat. The Yale psychologist John Bargh, for example, has conducted a series of hair-raising experiments in which he's managed to induce behaviors in people so easily (and so thoroughly without their knowledge) that it seems to scare even him. Bargh is a nice, thoughtful guy with a courtly demeanor and a large frame topped by a boyish thatch of dark hair, and as we sat in his office in New Haven I had the sense that he leads a perfectly normal life as a middle-aged dad. Yet this innocuous-seeming individual has spent years of his life undermining the bedrock notion of human autonomy.

Primed Numbers

One classic Bargh experiment involved having a research assistant greet participants while holding a beverage. The assistant casually asks each subject to hold the drink, ostensibly so that the assistant can have a free hand for writing. Some participants were handed a hot cup of coffee and others were given an iced version of the same drink. Then the subjects were given a packet of information on an individual and were asked to assess the individual's personality traits. Guess what? Those who had held the hot coffee rated the person as significantly warmer. Bargh has done a lot of this stuff and has reached a simple conclusion: "We have much less volition and autonomy than we think."

What's at work here is a phenomenon called priming, whereby behavior is activated through the power of unconscious suggestion. In recent years the psychology literature has been flooded with priming studies, all of which suggest that we literally have no idea what we're doing, or at least no idea why we're doing it.

Priming is amazingly easy. For example, when Bargh and colleagues exposed people to words related to rudeness, those individuals were vastly more likely to interrupt a subsequent conversation than people exposed to words associated with politeness. Even more vividly, in the course of an ostensible language test, people were exposed to stereotypes of the elderly. Sure enough, the folks who were primed this way walked more slowly down the hall when leaving and couldn't remember as much about the room where it had been held (compared to individuals in a control group who were not similarly primed).

Want another? In 2004, the psychologist Alan Kay and colleagues recruited students to take part in an investment game. Half the students played at a table with a briefcase and leather portfolio on it—and they were far more tightfisted than the other half, who played at a table with a backpack on it. Apparently the briefcase generated businesslike competitive behavior while a backpack telegraphed the opposite.

A year later, Dutch researchers had students fill out a questionnaire in a room that contained—out of sight—a bucket giving off the faint odor of a citrusy cleaning product. Afterward, the students were given a snack. Lo and behold, students who'd been smelling the cleaning fragrance were three times likelier to clean up afterward than members of a control group who completed the questionnaire in a room *without* the cleaning scent. The remarkable thing is that in all these studies, the subjects, who were as easy to manipulate as puppets on a string, had no idea they were influenced at all. Bargh draws an analogy to what they used to say about Bob Feller's fastball: you can't hit what you can't see.

The Dutch cleaning study brings to mind my personal favorite, which has to do with what business school professors Chen-Bo Zhong and Katie Liljenquist call the Macbeth effect. The professors divided a group of sixty students in two and asked half to recall in detail an incident from their own past in which they behaved unethically. The other half was asked to recall an incident of ethical behavior. Both groups were also asked to describe their emotions. Then they were given six fragments of words to complete. Three of these fragments could make cleaning-related words such as *wash, shower,* and *soap,* or they could form more neutral words such as *wish, shaker,* and *step.* So here's the Macbeth effect: the students who'd wallowed in their own unethical behavior proved much more likely to complete the word puzzles with cleaning words.

In another study described in the same paper, participants were told they were taking part in research on handwriting and were asked to copy a first-person short story. Half were given a story about helping a coworker; the other half were given a story about sabotaging a coworker. Participants then rated the desirability of various products, which included batteries, candy bars, Post-it Notes, and a variety of cleaning products including Windex and toothpaste. Participants who were given the sabotage story rated the cleaning products higher, but there was no difference between groups for the non-cleaning products.

In a third study, also reported in Zhong and Liljenquist's paper, participants went through the same ethical/unethical handwriting rigmarole but this time were offered a choice of taking one of two "gifts" afterward: an antiseptic cleaning wipe or a pencil. Can you see where this is going? Yup. In fact, two-thirds of those who'd been given the "unethical" passage chose the wipe, compared to one-third of the comparison group. "These three studies provided evidence for the Macbeth effect," the authors write. "Exposure to one's own and even to others' moral indiscretions poses a moral threat and stimulates a need for physical cleansing."

If the moral climate matters, so does the work climate. A variety of studies have shown that priming for achievement makes us work longer and harder and increases our persistence in overcoming obstacles. Bargh and his colleagues, for instance, found that giving people a bogus word-search task involving terms like *strive* and *succeed* made them work more at a Scrabble task. In another experiment involving a faked power failure, those primed for achievement were more likely to get back to work than those without such priming.

As I said, people intentionally primed in this way have no idea they've been influenced—and when asked, they stoutly deny it, inventing alternative rationales for their actions. Brian Wansink, Cornell University's guru of food cues (he's actually a professor of marketing), has found more or less the same thing with respect to what he calls "mindless eating." In a series of revealing experiments, he's shown that people are influenced in how much they eat by a variety of external cues—usually without their knowledge. "The big danger," he's said, "is that we all think we are too smart to be influenced by environmental cues."

But we're not, as Wansink has proven. He can influence how much you eat by manipulating the number of people sitting with you, their intake, your portion size, the lighting in the room, the music, or the variety and arrangement of foods on the plate. Low light, always disinhibiting, tends to make people eat more, as does eating at a table full of linebackers who consume mountains of food. Montaigne was probably right when he wrote, "Most of my actions are done by example, not by choice."

More surprisingly, Wansink has shown that he can get people to eat dramatically more M&M's simply by putting ten different colors into a bowl instead of seven (consumption increased 43 percent). Heck, he can just vary the arrangement; in a study using six flavors of jelly beans, he was able to boost consumption (69 percent!) just by mixing them up rather than presenting the same six flavors in some organized array. The truth is that people eat for all kinds of reasons that have nothing to do with whether they're hungry. It doesn't even seem to matter whether the food tastes good, as Wansink also has shown. Moviegoers ate a third more popcorn if they were given a large bucket than if they were given a medium one—even though the popcorn was two weeks old. "Nobody has any self-control," says Marion Nestle, a professor of nutrition and food studies at New York University. "Everyone, everyone, when presented with larger size portions will automatically eat more calories."

We can't control our thoughts any more reliably than we can control what we eat. When Leo Tolstoy was a boy, his adored older brother Nikólenka challenged him to stand in a corner until he could stop thinking of a white bear, a challenge the young Tolstoy accepted even though, he later wrote, he "could not possibly manage" to keep the ursine creature out of mind. In 1987, the psychologist Daniel Wegner discovered that American college students have the same trouble. At Trinity University in San Antonio, where he was then teaching, Wegner (now at Harvard) decided to replicate Nikólenka's challenge.

A student was seated alone in a laboratory room at a table containing a microphone and a bell, then was asked to speak aloud everything that came to mind. When the time was up, the experimenter came in and asked the student to continue for five more minutes, but to be sure not to think of a white bear. If at any point the creature poked its snout into consciousness, the student was to ring the bell on the desk. Here is an abbreviated transcript of one such episode; each asterisk indicates a bell ring.

> Of course now the only thing I'm going to think about is a white bear. Okay, I mean it's hard to think that I can see a bell* . . . and don't think about a white bear. Ummm, what was I thinking of before? See, if I think about flowers a lot* . . . I'll think about a white bear, it's impossible.* I could ring this bell over and over* and over* and over* and . . . a white bear* . . . and okay . . . so, my fingernails are really bad they . . . ummm . . . they need to be painted because they are . . . ummm . . . they're chipping at the ends. One thing about this is every time that I really want like ummm . . . to talk, think, to not think* about the white bear, then it makes me think about the white bear more so it doesn't work, so I'm going to try harder not to think about the white bear. Okay, it's like I have to force myself to not think* about the white bear. So, I also have this little brown freckle on my finger and I also have little sparklies* all over my hands and neck from Halloween last night 'cause . . .

You get the picture. The average student in the experiment rang the bell more than six times, but this particular student rang fifteen times. If nothing else, the researchers had proven how easy it is to create a synthetic obsession—something that Tolstoy and his brother proved long ago.

Freud, who would have liked this experiment, made a big deal out of the unconscious, but the biggest troublemaker lately in terms of subverting the very idea of self-control may have been the late Benjamin

Libet, a professor at the University of California in San Francisco. Using an electroencephalogram, Libet asked wired volunteers to make random movements, such as flicking a finger. He discovered that the human brain initiates freely made actions a split second *before* conscious awareness of the choice. Libet's general results have been borne out by other researchers. For example, neuroscientist John-Dylan Haynes, at the Bernstein Center for Computational Neuroscience in Berlin, monitored young adults as they watched random letters passing along a screen. Whenever they wanted, the participants could push a button with their left or right hand, but they had to record the letter they saw the instant they made the decision. They did all this inside a functional magnetic resonance imaging machine. From the resulting images, the scientists were soon able to tell when the students had decided to move *several seconds before the students knew it themselves.* Creepier still, about 70 percent of the time researchers were able to predict which button the subjects would push. Haynes called the results "eerie," adding that while such findings don't rule out free will, "it does make it implausible."

The Biology of Influence

The message of all these studies seems to be that you are controlled to a large extent by your environment, which unconsciously triggers actions that consciousness only later tries to rationalize. And of course, this is not just something that goes on in the lab. The world is priming us all the time—we are massively primed, all of us, sometimes intentionally, sometimes not. Other people, advertising, culture—anything at all we perceive, apparently, and even some things we don't consciously perceive—all of it is priming, priming, priming.

Leave aside the tsunami of advertising—present now in elevators, in e-mail messages, and at gasoline pumps—and consider the disinhibiting effect of crowds. Self-awareness and self-control go together, but mobs seem to dissolve both into a form of group identity accountable to no individual conscience. In a frightening study of sixty reported lynchings of black Americans by whites, the psychologist Brian Mullen found the level of atrocity in this inherently atrocious act varied with crowd size: the higher the ratio of lynchers to victims, the greater the cruelty.

Did I mention hormones? One answer to Freud's famous question, "What does woman want?" is that it depends on the time of the month, for ovulation has a big effect on female behavior. Women going to singles bars tend to wear more jewelry and makeup near ovulation, and those who cheat on their partners are likelier to do it around this time. Women's preferences in men also change depending on where in their monthly menstrual cycle they happen to be. And their sensitivity to nicotine varies with the ebb and flow of estrogen in their bodies, as does the pleasure they derive from cocaine and amphetamines. Blokes or smokes, it doesn't matter which; women's choices are strongly influenced by endocrinology.

So are men's. Several studies have correlated testosterone to risk taking in guys. One study, conducted among male securities traders in London, found that morning testosterone levels in a trader predicted the day's profitability. In general, guys with more testosterone are more aggressive, have a higher sex drive, and take more chances—all behaviors that may be inconsistent with delaying or forgoing gratification, but perfectly congruent with, say, becoming governor of New York and then visiting a prostitute at a fancy hotel. In many species (not necessarily excluding ours) these behaviors are rewarded, and among some species, few males besides the alpha get to reproduce. All this suggests a further evolutionary bias against delay of gratification.

Is it surprising, then, that sexy images (like sexy people) distort male decision making? This commonplace was confirmed by a study in which men who were shown photos of hot babes were more likely to choose sooner, smaller rewards over larger, later ones, even though the larger, later ones were unequivocally preferable. (I cannot resist mentioning the title of the resulting paper, which is "Bikinis Instigate Generalized Impatience in Intertemporal Choice.")

Although both sexes are slaves to their hormones, there is no getting around the fact that women have more self-control than men. In every culture, men commit vastly more violence, which is associated with impulsivity. Women the world over are more religious, and being religious is associated with the ability to defer gratification. Men's impulse control is a leading predictor of divorce. Females of every age are more prone to shame and guilt. Boys are much more likely than girls to be diagnosed with attention deficit disorder and hyperactivity. Textile mill and apparel entrepreneurs across time and cultures—from nineteenth-century England to modern China—have preferred female employees, often fresh off the farm, for their diligence and docility. Males take more risks. Females of every age get better grades in school but score about the same on IQ and achievement tests, suggesting the difference may be self-discipline. The list goes on and on. The bottom line: your level of self-control is influenced by whether you have a Y chromosome.

Is it nature or nurture? Certainly environment plays a role; women have traditionally been socialized differently than men, with high expectations for chastity, loyalty, and self-sacrifice, and in general deferring gratification and putting others first. Like Henrietta in Anthony Trollope's *The Way We Live Now*, sooner or later they came to see "that every vice might be forgiven in a man and in a son, though every virtue was expected from a woman." There are good reasons why the historian Laurel Thatcher Ulrich wrote the immortal words that launched a thousand T-shirts: "Well-behaved women seldom make history."

And as legal and social requirements for women change, they seem to be having more problems with self-regulation. Perhaps 20 million American women smoke, for example, up from practically zero a century ago. The health consequences of this change are about what you would expect. And it's not just smoking. In America a quarter of teenage girls are infected with a sexually transmitted disease, and in the United Kingdom more women are being arrested for violent offenses. On both sides of the Atlantic, women are drinking more—and closing the alcoholism gap with men.

Then again, women are biologically more susceptible to booze, generally showing higher blood levels of alcohol than men do at any given dose. So don't sell nature short. In one interesting experiment, scientists suppressed serotonin in a group of men and women (you can do this by administering a specially formulated amino acid drink). The results were surprising: The men responded with increased impulsivity while the women became more cautious. Each sex, it seems, hewed closer to its phenotype.

Yet there are ways in which the biology of self-control is surprising. A brain scan study of fasting men and women who were exposed to favorite foods for forty minutes found that men were better than women at putting their hunger out of mind—in effect, at suppressing the clamor of the obsessional amygdala, the primitive brain structure linked to powerful emotions and implicated in phobias and obsessive-compulsive disorder. (OCD is relatively common—an estimated 2 percent of the population is affected—and interesting with regard to self-control because at first glance it isn't clear whether sufferers have too much control or too little. Once considered prime fodder for psychoanalysts, OCD more recently appears to be a brain disorder involving low serotonin and problems in the communication between part of the frontal cortex and deeper brain structures. Lady Macbeth today would probably be given a prescription.)

Then there is the matter of birth season. Our faults aren't exactly in our stars, but some of them might as well be, because a bevy of studies have correlated birth season with body mass index, left- or right-handedness, mental illness, and even life expectancy. Of relevance here, a study in Britain found that individuals born in April, May, or June were quite a bit more likely to take their own lives than others, especially more likely than those born in October, November, or December. The effect was even more pronounced in women, for whom the increased risk was 30 percent. Researchers differ on why season of birth should have such effects.

Still believe in free will? Then let's go back to heredity for a minute. The short form is: it ain't just about frontal lobes. There is a gene, for instance, that influences nicotine metabolism, which probably plays a role in how easily one can become addicted to tobacco. Family studies have also implicated heredity in obsessive-compulsive disorder. Since genes influence our propensity to put on pounds, maintaining a healthy weight will require a lot more willpower from some people than from others. Genes can also play a role in violent antisocial behavior (findings that some defendants have embraced as a possible shield against culpability). Scientists have also demonstrated a genetic influence on the ability to direct attention, an important element of self-control; in a study of more than two hundred Dutch twins, for instance, researchers identified students with attention problems and came to the conclusion that this characteristic was about 60 percent heritable.

So are we just kidding ourselves with this whole business of self-control? Do we have any freedom at all, or are we really just meaty robots acting out some invisible script? The scientific evidence is somewhat depressing, but perhaps things are not as bleak as they seem.

Free Won't

All actions have causes, and we'd be fooling ourselves if we were to pretend that we know or understand what all of the causes are, even of our own actions. The philosopher Patricia Churchland, who has a strong interest in neuroscience (as perhaps all philosophers should), points out that freedom of choice is to a great extent a matter of degree and falls along a spectrum of possibilities. We have virtually no control over the function of our bone marrow, for example, limited control over breathing, and quite a bit of control over whether we watch a basketball game on television. So many other factors (some of them completely invisible to us) influence action and control, Churchland argues, that we'd be better off focusing less on something as mysterious as free will, with its suggestion that people somehow act without prejudice upon a blank slate, and more on self-control—on using our conscious will to take hold of ourselves to the extent we can. Libet has suggested that what we imagine to be freedom of action is mainly a kind of veto power. In this view we don't have free will as much as a kind of "free won't."

Yet apparently there is free something, because the amount of self-control people muster seems to vary depending on punishments and rewards. Incentives matter. Social tolerance for anger has varied widely across different times and places, as we'll discover in a later chapter, and displays of anger appear to vary accordingly. The rise of no-fault divorce seems to have led many husbands to treat their spouses better for fear that otherwise their wives will walk. In these and many other cases, incentives affect behavior in ways that imply choice. Stephen Morse, a law professor at the University of Pennsylvania, likes to ask audiences to stand up and raise an arm. People invariably comply. Then he asks them to sit down, which they also do. Voilà—free will.

As to heredity, it would be lovely to say that our destiny isn't in our genes any more than it is in our stars, but that wouldn't be strictly true. On the other hand, there is little about us that is truly destined. Our genes are among the factors that determine the realm of possibility for each of us, but that realm is so large, its boundaries so mysterious, that for the most part they are irrelevant.

Thus, the takeaway from all this evidence against free will should not be despair but humility based on awareness. Most of us have less self-control than we might like; against the mighty forces of evolution, heredity, and environment, we should feel very small indeed. We aren't powerless, but we're weak. On the other hand, what we have on our side is this very knowledge, which we can use as a lever against the world's enormous weight. Of the three great forces working against the exercise of conscious will, only one is subject to our influence: you can to a degree control your environment. Want to kick a habit? Eradicate the cues. Want to save your marriage? Avoid the hot new hire in accounting. And vote for politicians who are (within reason) likely to help us reclaim the public realm from the forces of temptation. This doesn't mean a return to Prohibition or prudery; it's just an acknowledgment that in the face of our own conflicting desires, we might prefer some over others, and we desperately need mechanisms for avoiding the unwanted options we might not be able to resist.

Like it or not, life is conducted as if all of us have fairly extensive agency. Your spouse, employer, and bank account manager all expect you to be the master of your actions, just as the legal system does—most of the time. And people have always been of two minds about this stuff. The Greeks were obsessed with self-command, yet also had their gods, whom they regularly blamed for clouded judgment or inflamed passion. In the Middle Ages and Puritan New England, the devil sometimes was detected in people's doings, although even when supernatural forces were at work, their human collaborators often were burned at the stake for the crime of freely going along. There is a certain logic to this; all behavior is caused by something. Does it really matter if it's the devil, bad genes, or an unhappy childhood?

In Aristotle's day, it was understood (by Aristotle, at least) that to be valid, ethical arguments must be useful and helpful in some way. But as with solipsism, another piece of hoary philosophical cleverness, it's hard to find a way in which determinism has much real-world value beyond tempering our hubris a bit and perhaps fostering a little more sympathy. The world depends on the idea that people are responsible for their behavior in the absence of tangible compulsion; we may suspect otherwise, but what society could be organized on that basis? What kind of lives could we live without personal responsibility?

There is evidence that skepticism about free will can be costly. In experiments by Kathleen Vohs and Jonathan Schooler, college students who were asked to read texts opposing free will were reliably more likely to cheat afterward than students who had been given neutral texts to read. The very effectiveness of the priming in this case will not offer much comfort to those who insist on free will. But who cares? The point is that losing faith in self-determination can be dangerous, not to mention impractical. Nobody has complete freedom of action, of course, but in life there is simply no alternative to the assumption that people have substantial control over their conduct.

John Bargh says that, despite his research into priming and human automaticity, he lives pretty much like everyone else—except that he's become more conscious of his environment, and he actually works to improve it. For example, he and his kids like to watch *The Simpsons,* but they turn it off during the parts of the show when the Simpson kids watch *Itchy & Scratchy*, a hideous parody of violent TV cartoons. Bargh also tries to prime himself; on the way somewhere to give a talk, he might listen to Led Zeppelin in the car to get himself charged up. "Change the environment," he said during our interview. "That's the way to do it."

Ultimately, I think, our best bet is to stand pragmatically with William James on this one. James wrestled with the problem of free will at length until finally arriving at a characteristic conclusion. "My first act of free will," he said, "shall be to believe in free will."

Odysseus and the Pigeons

The trouble with an alarm clock is that what seems sensible when you set it seems absurd when it goes off.

—REX STOUT, *THE RODEO MURDER*

B urrhus Frederic Skinner heard the news about Pearl Harbor while listening to a symphony on the radio. Skinner was then a psychologist at the University of Minnesota, not yet famous, and his great subject was "operant conditioning," or the way behavior is modified by its consequences. Skinner's role in the war began in 1940, even before the United States entered the conflict, when he was traveling by train and noticed, through the window, a flock of birds "lifting and wheeling in formation as they flew alongside." Inspired, he got himself some pigeons and set about training them to peck in response to certain visual cues. He knew from experience that pigeons were good subjects for conditioning research; the birds are easy to handle, have good eyesight, and can see colors. Skinner's idea now was to stick one of them into the nose cone of a bomb and have the bird guide it to a target with deadly accuracy.

Training avian suicide bombers sounds as far-fetched today as it did in 1941, when government officials at first rejected the idea. But Skinner was certain he was onto something, and he wasn't the only one bent on using animals to deliver ordnance. Over the years people have experimented with bats, dogs, dolphins, and other creatures for this purpose, to say nothing of the microbes that can be a kind of weaponry in biological warfare. Remember, too, that bombing accuracy in those days was poor and missile-guidance systems primitive. Skinner's arrangement seemed crude—the pigeon was basically thrust into a sock and controlled the projectile by pecking at a steering mechanism attached around its neck—but it was probably better than most of the alternatives, and for a while the U. S. Navy funded his work.

This work, at least by Skinner's account, went exceedingly well. He managed to inculcate an astonishing degree of single-mindedness into his target-finding birds, whose conditioning was so thorough that they were impervious to distraction by velocity, gunshots, flashes simulating antiaircraft fire, heavy vibrations, or massive g-forces. Atmospheric pressure equivalent to that at 10,000 feet—enough, at one point, to blow out a window and knock the psychologist's glasses off—made no difference. After a while Skinner had the birds pecking with the force of a miniature air hammer. They were rewarded for these patriotic feats with hemp seed, the psychologist having read that the birds were "almost fearless" after eating it. (Like so many warriors across the ages, Skinner's pigeons were not just conscripts but had the benefit of intoxicants to undermine their inhibitions in the face of violence.)

Skinner's air force reached something of an apotheosis in the heroic conduct of a single bird, whose job was to demonstrate what the pigeons could do. The performance was to occur in wartime Washington, at a meeting of skeptical officials from the Office of Scientific Research and Development, the government agency overseeing R&D for the war effort. Skinner set things up so that the pigeon would do its job in a darkened box, like all the others, pecking at a target projected onto a small screen in front of it; officials could take turns looking through a narrow tube to see what was going on. But that was considered too time-consuming, and so Skinner was forced to open up the box, flooding it with target-obscuring light and forcing the bird to perform surrounded by the looming faces of the federal scientific apparatus. Yet the bird's performance was flawless. Years later, in a famous paper recalling the episode, Skinner described the upshot: "I will not say that the meeting was marked by unrestrained merriment, for the merriment was restrained. But it was there, and it was obvious that our case was lost."

Pigeons at Harvard

Like so much about the life and work of B. F. Skinner, his exploits training avian bombardiers make for a great story. But they're more than just a source of historical diversion. In his war work with pigeons, we get an early glimpse of Skinner's worldview as a psychologist and philosopher, a worldview that would eventually make him a household name—and an important figure in the science of self-control.

Skinner was a behaviorist, a direct intellectual descendant of John B. Watson, the father of this particular flavor of psychology, which turned its back on the swamp of people's emotions, their inner lives, and the issues they were supposed to have with their mothers or their penises. Behaviorism instead put forth the straightforward idea that organisms respond to reinforcement, which conditions behavior. A behaviorist is agnostic as to what's going on in your mind, or for that matter whether you have a mind. What matters is what you do, and to a radical behaviorist like Skinner, what you do is a result of the outward consequences of your actions. Reality is a feedback system, and each of us is conditioned by a lifetime of reinforcements. If you broke your toe on the sofa last time you walked around barefoot in the dark, next time you'll turn on a light or put on your slippers.

Behaviorists like Skinner had something in common with economists, who also emphasized the role of incentives in people's actions. But the economists for the most part insisted that, no matter what people claimed they'd like or not like to do, their actions reveal their true preferences. Skinner, on the other hand, had strong preferences about preferences and must have believed that other people did, too, which is not the kind of humane notion generally ascribed to him in the popular mind. His wartime pigeon experiments, with their essentially mechanical view of organisms, are more the kind of thing that made him such a notorious figure over the years. Skinner taught pigeons to play Ping-Pong and created a scary-looking box for holding (and conditioning) babies.

The implications seemed pretty creepy. People don't like to think they're nothing more than flesh-and-blood robots, which many concluded that Skinner considered them to be. Worse, Skinner's chillingly grandiose aspirations went far beyond the laboratory. He summed them up in a 1967 interview with *Psychology Today*: "What I really expect to be known for is the application of all this to education, psychotherapy, economics, government, religion and its use in designing a world that will make us into the kind of people we would like to be."

But what Skinner was advocating, on a vast scale, was really just the kind of environmental control that John Bargh urged in the wake of his priming experiments. If our behavior is conditioned, after all, why not set things up so that we're conditioned to be who and what we want to be? Since Skinner saw the frequency of behavior largely as the result of its consequences, it made sense that he should see the problem of self-control in terms of establishing consequences that would produce desired behaviors. Conditioning yourself, then, wasn't any different from conditioning a pigeon or even another human. A person controls himself, Skinner wrote, "precisely as he would control the behavior of anyone else—through the manipulation of variables of which behavior is a function."

Unlike Freud, who dismissed the notion of raising his own children according to his ideas, Skinner avidly practiced what he preached during a lifetime of systematic self-management—and in later years could point to a long life of staggering productivity. "I have studied when I did not feel like studying, taught when I did not want to teach . . . I have met my deadlines for papers and reports . . . In short, I arrange an environment in which what would otherwise be hard work is actually effortless."

He even laid out a taxonomy of self-management techniques in his book *Science and Human Behavior*, including physical restraint (biting your tongue), changing the stimulus, aversive stimulation (perhaps a photo of yourself at your fattest on the fridge), arranging rewards and punishments, and simply finding something else to do in lieu of some unwanted behavior. The list may be useful for self-management, but it can also help us place Skinner in a long and very American tradition of self-improvement, one that goes back to Ben Franklin, at least. Like Franklin, Skinner was an inventor and pragmatically oriented problem solver, and both men employed formal self-management tactics.

Franklin, whose fame as an exemplar of self-control was sealed by the enduring success of his autobiography, reports that as a young man he "conceived the bold and arduous project of arriving at moral perfection," and as an aid in this venture developed a kind of moral spreadsheet, writing the days of the week across the top and listing thirteen virtues along the side. This enabled him to plot his failings by date and category in a grid that would make his performance easy to assess. Temperance is first on the list. Moderation ("avoid extremes") is number nine. Like Bridget Jones, whose fictional diary records not just her romantic misadventures but her encounters with the bathroom scale, Franklin instinctively understood the usefulness of self-monitoring and record keeping in any self-improvement scheme.

In 1948, two big things happened to B. F. Skinner. His novel *Walden Two* was published, giving the world, in fictional form, a more digestible version of his views on human nature than had been available before. And he returned to Harvard, the institution with which he would forever be identified, and from which he had earlier taken his PhD. There, at what had been the institutional home of the great William James, he launched the famous Pigeon Lab in the vast basement of Memorial Hall, where professors and graduate students labored beneath a network of overhead pipes to push back the frontiers of experimental psychology.

The Pigeon Lab, which produced a generation of leading experimental psychologists in the second half of the twentieth century, was really more like a beehive than an aviary, humming with activity. People were always coming and going, the mechanical recording devices were always clacking away, and grad students regularly and noisily debated their work. During the Vietnam years in particular, politics were debated as well. The place bubbled with enthusiasm; every experiment seemed to break new ground. Skinner was a lifelong tinkerer, and to work in this environment it helped to be mechanically inclined. These were the days before the personal computer revolution; experiments were controlled mostly by telephone circuit equipment, and the tall, vertical racks of these relay devices replicated the environment of some other, traditional experimental subjects—the kind with whiskers—by forming a large maze for the lab's human denizens.

By 1967, when a lean young man named George Ainslie appeared at the lab, it had migrated over to Harvard's new William James Hall, where it occupied the seventh floor and, no longer subterranean, enjoyed a lovely view. It was Ainslie's good fortune that by now the brilliant but aloof Skinner had mostly lost interest, and so the place was being run by one of his former students, also brilliant, named Richard Herrnstein.

For much of his career, Herrnstein was almost as controversial as Skinner. In 1971—the same year that Skinner published *Beyond Freedom and Dignity*—Herrnstein became a lightning rod because of an article in the *Atlantic Monthly* in which he emphasized the heritability of intelligence. "Greater wealth, health, freedom, fairness, and educational opportunity," he predicted with dispiriting accuracy, "are not going to give us the egalitarian society of our philosophical heritage. It will instead give us a society sharply graduated, with ever greater innate separation between the top and the bottom."

The article generated intense hostility, and some critics branded him a racist, a charge he would battle for years. Hounded by protesters and death threats, Herrnstein later wrote a book defending his argument (*I.Q. in the Meritocracy*) and then ignited further controversy by expanding on his ideas about intelligence and heritability (with coauthor Charles Murray) in *The Bell Curve*, the much-debated book for which he is perhaps most widely known. Herrnstein died just as it was about to appear.

Among some of his detractors, Herrnstein became known as Pigeon Man, which as an insult probably said more about its source than its target, for Herrnstein's work with pigeons was important in understanding how creatures make choices. It built on Skinner's work, yet departed from it. And it is crucial for understanding the problem of self-control.

Ainslie wasn't a psychologist and by any reasonable standard should have had no spare time to spend in the Pigeon Lab, since he was a full-time student at the Harvard Medical School and married as well. But as an undergraduate at Yale, Ainslie had taken a psychology course in which the professor said that a rat in a maze would run faster to reach a bigger piece of food than a smaller one. In fact, there was a direct relationship (within reason) between how fast the rat would run and how ample the reward. What the professor was describing was something called the "matching law," which had been discovered by none other than Richard Herrnstein.

Basically this law says that animals (including us) acting freely will spend their time doing things in direct proportion to the relative value they get from each. Herrnstein derived this law working with those Harvard pigeons; he discovered that, when offered two different objects to peck, the birds pecked them in proportion to the *rate* of reward delivered by each. Varying the *quantity* of reward—a little grain—had the same effect. And most interesting of all, *preference was proportional to the inverse of delay.* In other words, the later the reward, the less the birds liked it. And the less they would peck.

What the matching law did was to express mathematically the experimental evidence that organisms discount future rewards. Even pigeons, apparently, will weigh larger, later rewards against smaller, sooner ones and, if the larger reward is not sufficiently larger, pick the smaller, sooner one—as if they have some instinct that reminds them that a bird in hand is worth two in the bush. And since self-control is about deciding between now and later (perhaps even infinitely later, a period otherwise known as "never"), the matching law provided something like a formula for self-control.

The problem was that there already was such a formula—and the two conflicted. In the Pigeon Lab, George Ainslie was about to prove which one was right.

Discounting the Future

This problem of deciding between now and later is known to economists as intertemporal choice, and it has bedeviled thoughtful people for an awfully long time—at least since 1834, when the Scottish-born physician and economist John Rae published *The Sociological Theory of Capital.* In it, he explained that different people have different levels of desire for accumulation, desires that depend in significant part on their self-control—"the extent of the intellectual powers, and the consequent prevalence of habits of reflection, and prudence." He recognized, in other words, that self-control and intelligence go together, as psychologists would later prove. He also saw that the desire to accumulate, which involves deferring gratification, was opposed by the desire to consume now, an impulse that (as subsequent research would affirm) gets all fired up by "the actual presence of the immediate object of desire in the mind."

John Stuart Mill, who was influenced by Rae, made similar observations some years later, in 1871: "Men often, from infirmity of character, make their election for the nearer good, though they know it to be the less valuable; and this no less when the choice is between two bodily pleasures than when it is between bodily and mental. They pursue sensual indulgences to the injury of health, though perfectly aware that health is the greater good."

Some saw the faultiness of our trade-offs between now and tomorrow as a failure of imagination. The Austrian economist Eugen von Böhm-Bawerk speculated that "we possess inadequate power to imagine and to abstract, or that we are not willing to put forth the necessary effort, but in any event we limn a more or less incomplete picture of our future wants and especially of the remotely distant ones." Arthur Pigou saw the problem as a kind of myopia, just as Socrates had done in the *Protagoras.* "Our telescopic faculty is defective," wrote Pigou, "and we, therefore, see future pleasures, as it were, on a diminished scale."

Economics over the years has grown relentlessly more quantitative, and in 1937, economists finally came up with a way to reduce the future to a single equation, when Paul Samuelson developed the "discounted utility" model. Samuelson, you'll recall, was the wunderkind who embedded "revealed preference" in modern economics. He later became famous to a generation of undergraduates for his best-selling introductory econ text, and, in fact, he as much as anyone propelled his profession down the mathematical road. "In Samuelson's simplified model," we are told in one history of the subject, "all the psychological concerns discussed over the previous century were compressed into a single parameter, the discount rate."

The formula looks complex, but basically it postulates that *Homo economicus* rationally discounts the future at some consistent rate. What does it mean to discount the future? Imagine that you've won the lottery and you're offered a choice of $150,000 a year for twelve years, or a single lump sum up front. The question is, what is the single sum you would accept to forgo the payments spread over a dozen years? Assume there's no risk the state would fail to pay either way. So think for a minute: How much would you take in lieu of the payment flow?

Would $1 million be enough? How about $750,000? The lower the number you name, the more impatient you are; name a really low number and you might go down in history alongside Esau, who in a moment of hunger traded his birthright for a meal. Let's say you offer to take $1 million. Should the state accept? To get the answer, lottery officials will calculate the interest rate at which the payment flows would be worth the same as the lump sum; financial calculators on the Internet make solving these "time value of money" problems easy. In this case the interest rate exceeds 10 percent—a very good investment for the state, but a bad deal for you, since you can't safely invest $1 million to reliably return 10 percent annually.

This interest rate is also your discount rate, and it is a measure of how much the future matters to you now. The higher it is, the less you're willing to defer gratification. Life is complicated, of course, and it's hard to compute a clear discount rate for many of the now-or-later choices that we make. Nonetheless, under certain circumstances, it's a way to quantify a messy thing like self-control.

These aren't esoteric calculations; hardheaded businesspeople do them every day all over the world, for the most part without knowing that they owe the basic principle to a medieval mathematician named Leonardo of Pisa—a man mostly remembered as Fibonacci. Fibonacci wrote his famous *Liber Abaci* (literally, book of calculation) in 1202, and it earned him lasting renown for what would come to be known as Fibonacci's numbers: 0, 1, 1, 2, 3, 5, 8, and so forth, where each number (after the first two) is the sum of the two preceding. In the twentieth century, the Fibonacci numbers were the subject of great interest, and the sequence has been found all over the natural world.

The significance of this series, alas, has helped obscure the fact that, for the most part, *Liber Abaci* is devoted to the mathematics of commerce—including how to calculate the value today of sums that are scheduled to arrive over time. When we think about the future and grope toward an estimate of the value of, say, a secure retirement or good health in our old age, we're mentally performing something like a present-value calculation, and in doing so our choice of discount rate is crucial.

It turns out that some people labor under consistently higher discount rates than others—meaning they habitually place less value on the future. The poor seem to fall into this category, along with the young, the male, and those who are prone to substance abuse. Older people, females, and those with higher intelligence seem to have a lower discount rate and, by placing a greater value on the future, tend to be more willing to defer gratification. Studies of addicts have found that those hooked on cocaine, heroin, alcohol, gambling, or cigarettes all had a higher discount rate with respect to money (that is, they devalued delayed money more) than did people who weren't addicted. Japanese students were found to discount future sums less than their American or Chinese counterparts. And in general small future sums are discounted more deeply than larger sums.

Animals seem to discount future rewards as well. Feeding studies of pigeons, rats, and various primates rarely elicit patience lasting more than a matter of seconds, although some chimpanzees and bonobos have been able to wait up to two minutes. Yet in their natural environment, some animals show quite modest discount rates. Squirrels stashing away nuts for the winter are deferring consumption more effectively than some humans are capable of doing, yet their behavior appears to be more instinctual than consciously planned. And of course many animals appear to "invest" in the future, as when beavers build dams or chimpanzees pour time and energy into cultivating other chimps in an effort to climb the local hierarchy of dominance.

Before we give our own species too much credit for self-control, we ought to consider just how much humans tend to discount the future. Researchers have studied this question and the scientific answer is, a helluva lot. How do they study such a thing? Basically there are two ways. One is simply to ask people how much money they would demand today to forgo, say, $100 in a year. Researchers can then calculate the discount rate implied by the sums and the delay. Another method is to seize on some real-world examples of human behavior from which a discount rate can be derived.

One study, for instance, looked at the decisions of U.S. military personnel confronted with a cutback in force. The government offered more than 65,000 individuals who were about to be let go a choice between a onetime lump sum and a series of annual payments. The terms depended on rank, but one typical example was $22,283 up front or $3,714 annually for 18 years. These payments were a direct obligation of Uncle Sam, so there was no risk of default—yet the present value of the annual payments compared to the lump sum in this example implied a remarkable discount rate of 18.9 percent. That was fairly typical. So the annual payments were a vastly better deal—so good that even Warren Buffett probably couldn't invest the lump sum any more effectively. What's more, the lump sums would be taxed more harshly. The government went out of its way to explain the choices with pamphlets, counseling, and media. Yet more than half of officers and more than 90 percent of enlisted personnel chose the lump sum. Although this episode reflects badly on people's ability to defer gratification, there is a silver lining: the poor choices by the outbound military personnel saved American taxpayers $1.7 billion, which is how much extra it would have cost if all had chosen the annual payments.

Studies of people's discount rates over the years have produced a range of results, but they all tend to be high. As George Ainslie reports in *Picoeconomics,* his nonpareil account of self-control and the problem of the future, studies of consumer behavior (say, the choice between an air conditioner with a higher price and lower operating costs and a cheaper model that gobbles more power) find implicit discount rates running into the hundreds. Employees surveyed on how much they would accept to forgo a later bonus racked up discount rates from 36 to 122 percent. Even finance students posted median discount rates as high as 60 percent, and at an English university, grad students and staff who were asked how long they would wait for £10 instead of immediately getting £5 gave answers that reflected discount rates of 5,000 percent.

Curves

Ainslie was fascinated by the idea that behavior could be expressed as a mathematical function—a nice, smooth curve that plots our preferences over time. The curve, according to Samuelson's theory, was smooth because we're supposed to discount the future consistently. But Ainslie was also fascinated by the ways in which each of us seems to be in conflict with ourselves. We might have a long-term goal—for instance, saving for retirement or maintaining domestic peace—that is in conflict with our short-term desire for the pleasures that spending or infidelity might bring.

People confront this kind of problem all the time. I could work on this paragraph, contributing in some infinitesimal way to my long-term wealth and happiness, or I could shop for music on the Internet, sharply increasing my short-term happiness. I have two desires. Which should I honor? Although he was young, Ainslie understood the nature of this dilemma. So for his senior thesis at Yale, he built an unusual maze—one that confronted a rat with two paths to separate food-rewards of three pellets each. Both routes were identical except that one offered a tempting shortcut leading to only a single pellet of food. The question was, would the rat realize, after running the course repeatedly, that it should take the path that *didn't* offer the shortcut?

Ainslie got conflicting data from the experiment and graduated before he could press it further. But it was still on his mind when he got to Harvard, and so the medical school's resident behaviorist, Peter Dews, sent him to see Herrnstein. It was there that he learned to translate his rat problem into a pigeon problem.

That was in 1967, the same year Herrnstein and Shin-Ho Chung reported what was perhaps their most interesting finding to date, which was that pigeons weren't only sensitive to quantity and frequency of reward—they were also sensitive to its timing. They would peck a lot more—disproportionately more—for an immediate grain reward than for a delayed one. When Ainslie read about this, he realized something: If these birds value short-term rewards disproportionately over long-term rewards, then those nice, smooth curves depicting their preferences must be wrong. If you plot preferences against time, and preferences rise sharply as time-to-reward gets shorter, than the curve looks different. It takes on the shape of a hyperbola, meaning it is concave, rising sharply as time grows short.

What hyperbolic discounting meant was that the pigeons weren't acting sensibly or consistently with respect to time. And as Ainslie suspected, what was true for the pigeons turns out to be true for the rest of us as well.

To explain hyperbolic discounting, the psychologist Stuart Vyse likes to offer his students two envelopes, one containing $10 and the other $12. Naturally they pick the one with $12. Then he offers $10 now and $12 a week later, at which point most students still pick the larger amount. But when he offers the larger amount two or even three weeks later, things change, and most students say they want the $10 now. That's not the end of the story; once Vyse has established the point at which students switch to the smaller, sooner reward, he freezes this gap and moves both rewards out into the more distant future. For instance: Would the students prefer $10 in twenty-eight weeks or $12 in thirty weeks? At this point, or with the offers somewhere out there in some far-off tomorrow, student preferences switch back again, and most go for the larger, later sum. It's a classic example of time inconsistency; rationally, we should choose the larger, later reward in every instance, because the extra wait for it is unchanging.

Why do we experience this crucial preference reversal? Why is two weeks of delay unacceptable in the near term but not further off in time? The answer is the human tendency to place excessive value on rewards that are nearer in time. David Hume recognized this problem more than 250 years ago: "Tho' we may be fully convinc'd, that the latter object excels the former, we are not able to regulate our actions by this judgment; but yield to the sollicitations of our passions, which always plead in favor of whatever is near and contiguous."

We don't just value near more than far; we value it disproportionately more. The simple fact is that people are made to prefer immediate rewards inordinately. Perhaps instinctively they know the truth of Keynes's famous dictum: "In the long run, we are all dead." In the evolutionary environment, life was uncertain, and without reliable mechanisms for securing or refrigerating precious meat, for example, it may not have selected very effectively for the exceedingly future-minded. The Bible gives creationists some parallel evidence for this aspect of human nature. Adam and Eve weren't thinking very far ahead when they ate of the forbidden fruit, after all, just as their descendant Esau was blind to long-term consequences of the deal he was making.

As it turns out, the notion that the curve of our preferences might not be consistent over time was postulated in 1956 by the economist Robert H. Strotz in a witty but daunting paper breezily entitled "Myopia and Inconsistency in Dynamic Utility Maximization." Strotz also noticed that, when temptation was far off, people with foresight would employ what he creatively dubbed "precommitment" techniques—just like Odysseus when approaching the Sirens—to limit their own choices against the day when temptation grew near. With respect to his own self-control, by the way, Strotz was a sophisticate; this brilliant economist, who would go on to become president of Northwestern University, had his academic employer pay him in twelve monthly installments because he didn't trust himself to save enough of his school-year salary to get through the summer.

Ainslie knew nothing of Strotz, and he notes that the economist never mentioned hyperbolic discounting in his paper. What Ainslie wanted to do was prove in a lab what the matching law implied—that effort is related to reward. His idea was that, if creatures did have a powerful change of preference when confronted by an immediate (albeit inferior) reward—a change in favor of the thing right in front of them *now*, as implied by hyperbolic discounting—then they could be expected to learn how to prevent themselves from making this choice if the means were available. As Ainslie explained, "this prediction would not depend on the existence of 'higher intelligence,' but only on whether the effect of the larger reinforcement was great enough to cause learning of the pre-commitment device at the time the device was available."

The idea, in other words, was to teach an animal to act like Odysseus. To accomplish this, Ainslie worked with white male Carneaux pigeons. (Carneaux were the only breed used at the Pigeon Lab because of their genetic uniformity. Males were used to avoid the estrus cycle.) Kept at just 80 percent of their free-feeding weight, these birds were hungry—and were therefore paying close attention whenever there was the prospect of some grain. For Ainslie's experiments, the birds were put, one at a time, into a soundproof, lightproof box—a Skinner box—that measured about a foot in all dimensions. In this box, the pigeon encountered one or more translucent disks on the wall; these objects are known as keys and can be lighted or dark. The box was connected to the usual Pigeon Lab apparatus for keeping track of what was going on, but it also had a peephole on top so researchers could peer inside.

Managing pigeon experiments by hand would be tedious, so each box was wired to what amounted to an early computer system, except there were no microchips involved. Inside the box, the keys (lit by 7-watt Christmas bulbs) went on and off at intervals in a sequence programmed onto a loop of movie film, which functioned much the way punch cards did in the computers of the day. Holes in the film controlled the opening and closing of electrical circuits, and the pigeons' reactions were recorded by a printer not unlike those which produced cash register receipts.

Ainslie would put a pigeon into the box, and periodically the key on the wall would light up red for 2.5 seconds; if the pigeon pecked it during this time, the food hopper would open up for 1.5 seconds. But if the pigeon *didn't* peck the key while it was red, the food hopper would open up for 4 seconds. The pigeons thus had the chance to gain a lot by exercising a little self-restraint—yet they all pecked the key as soon as it turned red. They just couldn't stop themselves.

So Ainslie tried a different approach. This time, about 11 seconds before the key turned red, it was lit green. Pecking it while it was green prevented the key from turning red and gave the birds 4 seconds' worth of food—eventually, for the interval was the same as if they had merely refrained from pecking red. If the birds didn't peck green but later pecked red, the reward would be just 1.5 seconds of food.

It was a great experiment. Ainslie was giving the birds a chance to emulate wily Odysseus by binding themselves fast against the temptation to come. The green key was a classic precommitment device—the most powerful device in the self-management tool kit. Astonishingly, two pigeons proved themselves capable of precommitment: they learned to peck the green key about 90 percent of the time it was offered.

Sound like a fluke? Ainslie ran a control experiment in which the key would turn red whether or not the birds pecked it while it was green. Sure enough, the Odyssean pigeons stopped pecking the now-useless green key—but persisted in pecking red. There was no doubt about it; the pigeons who had pecked green were making effective use of precommitment, having discovered that they could profitably constrain their own impatience. Howard Rachlin (another leading self-control theorist) and Leonard Green, in a somewhat different experiment, published in 1972, got even more pigeons to precommit, and two years later Ainslie replicated and expanded his own work with some more pigeons.

Getting pigeons to make like Odysseus is pretty cool, but the real significance of Ainslie's work at Harvard was in showing that organisms—whether pigeons or humans—are driven biologically to place inordinate value on immediate rewards. While others had noticed the human tendency to favor today over tomorrow where pleasure is concerned (Saint Augustine: "Give me chastity and continence, but not yet"), it was Ainslie who plotted the shape of our preferences. His experiments—which led to a lifetime of thinking and writing about hyperbolic discounting—demonstrated that conflicting desires are baked into the evolutionary cake—and that when it comes to self-control, humans and pigeons are birds of a feather.

Crimes of Passion

"When husbands and wives start throwing dishes at each other, they do not usually throw the fine china."

— RICHARD HERRNSTEIN

I n a riveting case in New Zealand in 2009, a young man named Clayton Weatherston apparently got into an argument with his girlfriend, a promising economics student named Sophie Elliott. At his trial, Weatherston claimed that Elliott, in a fit of rage, attacked him with a pair of scissors, causing him to lose control of himself and stab her 216 times, including in the eyes, genitals, breasts, face, and neck. Because he lost control, Weatherston contended, he was guilty not of murder, but only manslaughter, which carries a lesser penalty.

This so-called provocation defense is controversial; it relies on the willingness of the law to draw a distinction between premeditated actions and those committed in the heat of passion. The provocation defense had worked before in New Zealand, as it has elsewhere. During Weatherston's trial, in fact, a Hungarian tourist named Ferdinand Ambach admitted to killing his elderly drinking partner in suburban Auckland but said he did so because the victim's advances made him fear being raped; Ambach claimed this fear caused him to lose control of himself—and brutally beat the man with a banjo before ramming the stem down his throat. He was convicted only of manslaughter.

Weatherston's jury wasn't buying; they found him guilty of murder. But the case did set off renewed debate over whether such a defense should even be allowed, and it was soon repealed by New Zealand's parliament. Ironically, at the same time the provocation defense has been on the wane in the English-speaking world, advances in neuroscience are producing evidence of a biological basis for at least some violent criminal behavior—evidence that could easily undermine the accountability that opponents of the provocation defense are demanding.

In the early 1990s, for example, Herbert Weinstein, a sixty-five-year-old advertising executive, strangled his wife and threw her body out the window of their twelfth-floor apartment on Manhattan's Upper East Side, allegedly to make the killing look like suicide. Weinstein's lawyer argued his client wasn't responsible, because he had a brain cyst. After the judge ruled that jurors could be told of the cyst, prosecutors allowed Weinstein to plead guilty to a reduced charge of manslaughter.

During the case, the prosecution brought in a forensic psychologist named Daniel Martell, who testified that brain scanning technologies (which revealed the cyst) were new and untested. Since then, Martell has appeared in literally hundreds of criminal and civil cases, offering neuroscientific evidence on behalf of prosecutors and defense attorneys alike. Martell reports that such evidence has become de rigueur in death penalty cases.

People are still being held accountable for murder, but the rise of what's been called neurolaw isn't helping. There is evidence, after all, that many killers have brains which deviate from what's normal, and that these deviations aren't their fault. Does this mitigate their responsibility, as Weinstein's lawyer claimed in that case? If they inherited these brain abnormalities, should they be absolved altogether?

The question, ultimately, is, how much self-control can society expect from us, and how should it treat us when we lose it?

Crime

In 1990, something like a gale-force wind hit the world of criminology with the publication of *A General Theory of Crime*, by Michael Gottfredson and Travis Hirschi. The "general theory" of the title is that crime is caused by poor self-control, and while this notion has generated some controversy, by and large it has stood the test of time. Most crimes, the authors noticed, take little planning or effort and provide immediate (although quite limited) gratification, since the average financial gain from a mugging or burglary is relatively small. The people who commit one kind of crime often commit another kind as well, and indeed, "the evidence of offender versatility is overwhelming."

Criminals, moreover, are much likelier than others to be involved in noncriminal doings that, while often legal, are nonetheless dubious or harmful. A thief, for instance, is quite a bit more likely than others to engage in smoking, drinking, drug abuse, fighting, or skipping school. This sort of person seems to have a lot of accidents as well, including fires, car crashes, and unwanted pregnancies. Not surprisingly, criminals are likelier than others to die at an early age.

It's not hard to notice the pattern here; as the authors observe, people with strong self-control tend to be more verbal, less physical, more conscious of the future, and better able to apply themselves to projects of a long-term nature. Not so with criminals.

"Criminal acts will tend to be short lived, immediately gratifying, easy, simple, and exciting," Gottfredson and Hirschi wrote, adding that "the properties of criminal acts are closely connected to the characteristics of people likely to engage in them." In some sense, the two authors were following (at least a little) in the giant, muddy footsteps of Freud, who argued that many criminals unconsciously want to be caught so that they can be punished, possibly for masturbation or some other infantile transgression. Gottfredson and Hirschi made no such argument. But when Freud did so, he "tended to recast the entire social problem of crime as one of personal impulse management," in the view of psychologist Robert R. Holt, which is very much like what happens in *A General Theory of Crime.*

For instance: Gottfredson and Hirschi cite the work of the sociologist Lee Robins, who traced the fate of 524 children referred to a guidance clinic in St. Louis. Robins matched these kids to a control group based on gender, IQ, age, and neighborhood. Compared to the control group, the lives of the children referred for guidance were train wrecks. The referred kids were more likely to get arrested and to abuse alcohol. They were less likely to marry, but those who did were more likely to divorce and also more likely to marry someone with behavioral problems. They were more likely to have kids with such problems, too. As to work, they were more likely to be unemployed or change jobs often, and not surprisingly, they were more likely to be on welfare. Socially, they were more isolated. As adults, the referred kids were less likely to be in touch with relatives or attend church, had fewer friends, and were more likely be hospitalized for psychiatric illnesses. Robins described these individuals as having "antisocial personalities," but Gottfredson and Hirschi don't much care for this concept. To them, such disorganized souls are just very low in self-control, and Robins's work is further proof that "the variety of manifestations of low self-control is immense."

Not everyone agrees with Gottfredson and Hirschi; Hirschi himself later wrote that the book was wrong on some points. But he stood by the central thesis, and in a 2004 review of the many things high self-control predicts, the psychologists June Tangney, Roy Baumeister, and Angie Luzio Boone wrote: "In subsequent empirical tests, this theory has held up well." In 2000, the journal *Criminology* published a meta-analysis of twenty-one studies based on seventeen data sources (involving more than forty-nine thousand individuals) and found that, despite differences in how a lack of self-control was measured, it consistently predicted crime and similar behaviors.

Remarkably, a 1998 study of 555 adults found that differences in self-control account for the gender gap that is typically evident in crime. In other words, crime isn't so much committed by males as it's committed by people who lack self-control. It's just that a lot more of those people happen to be male.

Low self-control, by the way, predicts not just criminality but also victimization. In a study published in 2006, Christopher J. Schreck and his coauthors looked at sixth- and seventh-graders in half a dozen U.S. cities and found that those low in self-control were more likely to be the victims of crime over the following years. "Victimization is not a random event," the researchers wrote. "Studies spanning the past 25 years have consistently reported that certain lifestyles and contexts increase the chances of victimization."

Gottfredson and Hirschi blamed bad parenting practices for low self-control in kids. But since their book, research has suggested that impulsivity, hyperactivity, and attention deficit disorder, all of which look and sound a lot like self-control deficits, are strongly heritable. For a long time it was taboo to suggest that criminality or its causes might also be at least partly hereditary, and in certain circles it remains so. Unfortunately, this taboo isn't recognized by the evidence. Advances in brain imaging have bolstered the case for heritability by providing evidence of genetic influence on brain structure—and evidence connecting brain structure with crime. Many studies have found that if one identical twin is a criminal, there's a 50 percent likelihood the other twin will be, too. Criminologist Kevin Beaver, who has explored crime and heredity by studying twins, says that when it comes to self-control, heredity probably accounts for 60 to 75 percent.

Beaver's not arguing that parenting doesn't matter. He acknowledges that parent-child interactions are complex and that environment surely plays a role—but that role is conditioned by individual genotypes. Nevertheless, this is not a message that many people like to hear; culturally we have a strong preference for environmental explanations, and we recoil from anything that smacks of eugenics, blaming the victim, or the suggestion that crime runs in families. Pointing to heredity, Beaver told me in an interview, "is like pissing in the wind in criminology."

But the wind is starting to blow in the other direction, in part thanks to the work of a former juvenile delinquent named Adrian Raine. After a series of scrapes during his boyhood in the United Kingdom, Raine went to Oxford, got a PhD in psychology, and became one of the world's leading neurocriminologists, a discipline he now studies and teaches at the University of Pennsylvania. And what he's found is that there is a whole range of physical differences between criminals and the rest of us.

People with antisocial personality disorder—a group that tends to break the law—turn out to be literally more cold-blooded than the rest of us. They have lower resting heart rates. They even sweat less. A long-term study found that three-year-olds with lower heart rates were more aggressive at age eleven—and likelier to commit crimes by the age of twenty-three. Raine also studied the brains of twenty-one psychopaths in Los Angeles and discovered that their prefrontal cortices (the area he calls the "guardian angel" riding herd over the aggressive impulses that can rise up from the limbic system) were, on average, 11 percent smaller than those in normal brains. In another study, Raine and colleagues found that murderers had significantly lower neural activity in their prefrontal cortices than other people. With less processing power in the reasoning part of the brain, perhaps such people are more likely to explode in violence when they get angry.

Findings like these raise questions about the extent to which such people are capable of enough self-control to be responsible for their actions and in turn how severely they should be punished—or whether they should be punished at all. The alternatives (lifelong internment, perhaps preemptively?) do not seem much more appealing. And it's not clear that even psychopaths are immune to incentives; some number of them may be deterred by the knowledge that they will be held account-able. Studies of anger show that people who have potentially violent impulses do, in fact, respond to punishment and reward.

Passion

According to Aristotle, people lose control and act contrary to reason largely as the result of two things: pleasure and anger. This book has mostly concerned itself with pleasure. But anger presents self-control problems—and insights—as well. (And it, too, undermines control with pleasure, for who can deny that there is at least momentary joy in giving in to ire?)

Like most problems of self-command, anger reveals our dual nature. We are "beside ourselves" with it. It carries us off, yet to some extent we eagerly go along, for there is ample evidence people can control their temper when the incentives or the will are strong enough. Philosophers have conceived it as a kind of madness—"*Ira furor brevis est*," said Horace ("Anger is brief madness")—yet one in which reason plays a role, for how else do we know we've been insulted? "Temper seems to pay some attention to reason," said Aristotle, "but to hear it imperfectly—just as eager servants go darting off before hearing the end of what is said to them, and then mistake their instructions."

Controlling anger can be difficult because provocations can be hard to anticipate, so we are left trying to rein in temper only when it is aroused. At that point we can try delaying tactics, like Donald Duck counting to ten in the cartoon "Self-Control," but as Thomas Schelling points out, "If I am too enraged to mind my behavior, how can I make myself count to ten?"

The law has long recognized this problem, which is why there is a provocation defense. In the United States, Georgia, Texas, and Utah at various times have considered the husband's killing of an adulterous wife's lover a justifiable homicide and therefore not a crime at all. New Mexico even excused killing the wife. "The purpose of the law is not vindictive," that state's Court of Appeals insisted. "It is humane. It recognizes the ungovernable passion which possesses a man when immediately confronted with his wife's dishonor."

This legal allowance for passion usually wasn't available to wives; in Texas, for example, during the 1930s, a woman killed her husband's lover with a pistol and was convicted of murder. The courts rejected her claim of justifiable homicide; the state penal code, after all, stated clearly that "homicide is justifiable when committed by the husband upon one taken in the act of adultery with the wife," and the courts followed the law to the letter.

On the other hand, a passionate defendant of either sex might go free if he or she has a sympathetic judge and jury—or sometimes, a clever defense attorney, like the one played by Katharine Hepburn in *Adam's Rib*. Her distraught client (Judy Holliday) fired a pistol at her husband and his lover but got off as a result of what amounts to jury nullification after a circuslike trial. (Sexist provocation laws notwithstanding, female murder defendants often get more lenient treatment than men, possibly because women rarely kill, and often when they do it's after years of violent abuse at the hands of the male victim. In such murderers, too, we see a violent loss of control, although it's clearly provoked.)

Now, if you're starting to sense we're on a slippery slope here, you're right, although we started down the slope long ago, when we allowed motives and states of mind to play a role in criminal justice (as they inevitably must). But the question before the law is, how much self-control can we expect of one another? And once factors beyond duress are admitted—factors like one's neurological makeup, for example—the slippery slope grows steeper.

Thus the provocation defense became more widely available with the advent of the modern principle that "legally adequate provocation exists if the hypothetical reasonable person in the defendant's shoes would have been provoked into a heat of passion."

No longer was "ocular observation" of an unfaithful spouse necessary. In the eyes of the law, self-control could now be undermined by a whole range of romantic dislocations, making ex-wives, former girlfriends, and their significant others all fair game. In East Windsor, Connecticut, for instance, in the wee hours of February 28, 1987, Mark Chicano went to the home of his ex-girlfriend, Ellen Babbit. Lurking outside the bedroom window, he heard Babbit making love to another man. Then he snuck into the house and hid until the couple were asleep, at which point he beat her lover's brains in with a crowbar. When Babbit's eleven-year-old son came in and started screaming, Chicano strangled him to death—and then beat Babbit to death with the crowbar as well. At his trial, the killer suggested he acted under extreme emotional disturbance—hearing his ex's lovemaking was just too much to take—and the jury convicted him of manslaughter instead of murder.

The tide began to turn against the provocation defense when women began work in large numbers as attorneys, judges, and law professors— and argued that the courts should demand greater self-control from men. Yet the legal scholar Susan Rozelle, who has studied the issue, reports that provocation is still a permissible defense in most states and that the trend in recent years is for courts to leave it up to the jury to decide if the provocation was sufficient to drive a reasonable person around the bend. Rozelle doesn't like it: "The provocation defense nonchalantly asserts . . . that to a certain extent we simply cannot expect people to control themselves when faced with the sight of a faithless spouse. This is not true. We should, and in fact do, have more control over our passions than the defense and the prevailing scholarship assume."

Even in the case of anger, incentives matter, which is why precommitment can work against it. Jon Elster, who has written thoughtfully and at length about self-control, tells of an ancient king who "paid handsomely when some beautiful and ornate tableware was offered to him, but since it was unusually fragile he immediately smashed the lot, ridding himself in time of an easy occasion for anger against his servants." Rabbi Moshe ben Nachman, the thirteenth-century Torah scholar better known as Ramban, again and again cautioned against ire, which he considered to be avoidable even in extremis: "Never lose your temper—even when you are exhausted, drained, disappointed, aggravated, shocked, confused, terrified." Not content with exhortation, he also suggested a strategy: "Set aside a sum of money that you will give away if you allow yourself to be angered. Be sure that the amount you designate is sufficient to force you to think twice before you lose your temper."

If incentives matter, so does culture. Murder rates vary widely around the world, as does social tolerance for anger. In Japan, for example, one is, by and large, expected to stifle it. The psychologist Carol Tavris, in her excellent book *Anger: The Misunderstood Emotion*, observes that small, cooperative societies are intolerant of anger, in contrast with the way Americans actually seem to value it. In our culture it's a sign of authenticity, even health, and thanks in part to Freud, many Americans have come to adopt a hydraulic view of the emotions, which places great emphasis on venting. If we don't let out emotions, the theory goes, they will build up dangerously, or turn on us and consume us. Tavris reports that most American adults endorse this view of anger and that even experts such as Bruno Bettelheim believed in it. Depression has been described as anger turned inward, and anger was believed to be the cause of ulcers.

The problem is that it's all wrong. Depression isn't anger turned inward, and bacteria (not anger) causes ulcers. Venting anger seems only to escalate the emotion. In fact, since facial expressions and body language generally work in both directions, the physical manifestations of an emotion can magnify it, as recent studies have demonstrated. Both Charles Darwin and William James suspected as much all along. "The free expression by outward signs of an emotion intensifies it," Darwin quite rightly observed. "On the other hand, the repression, as far as this is possible, of all outward signs softens our emotions."

Everyone gets angry. But most of the time we have quite a bit of control over how we react to our anger. Some proof of this comes from Malaysia, with its tradition of the *pengamok*, or one who runs amok. Pengamok mayhem often involves bloodshed. Although traditionally regarded as a form of madness, there is much about running amok that appears voluntary, if not premeditated. One study in the 1970s of pengamoks who had committed murder and were incarcerated at a mental hospital found that all of them used traditional Malay weapons rather than whatever was at hand, and "almost all of the victims were known to the amok and were sources of criticism, frustration, or provocation."

Some pengamoks showed consistent patterns in their choice of victims, and sometimes a high level of purpose—all suggesting quite a bit of forethought. One pengamok made his way to three separate coffee houses in the process of singling out five ethnic Chinese victims. Most telling of all, when Malaysian society shifted from tolerance to Draconian punishment—pengamoks for a time could be drawn and quartered—the incidence of these supposedly uncontrollable outbursts declined dramatically.

Evidently, pengamoks do not so much lose control as abandon it.

16

Addiction, Compulsion, and Choice

The Greeks gave full recognition to pleasures in themselves. We, on the other hand, are tending more and more to ascribe lack of self-control over appetites to some agent of compulsion within the object consumed, or to some disguised psychical damage sustained in childhood, babyhood or even in the womb. The Greek notion of addiction may have been too innocent, but by denying that people consume too much of something because they enjoy it, we are also making a mistake.

—JAMES DAVIDSON, *COURTESANS AND FISHCAKES:*
THE CONSUMING PASSIONS OF CLASSICAL ATHENS

It's really not that difficult to overcome these seemingly ghastly problems . . . What's hard is to decide.

—ROBERT DOWNEY JR.

D iseases come and go. In the decades following the Civil War, all the best people had neurasthenia, a vague nervous disorder said to afflict sensitive souls in the face of modernity. For a while homosexuality was considered a disease, until it wasn't. It's also worth noting that diseases can be quite profitable; Geritol lucratively promised to alleviate "iron-poor blood," and more recently such newfangled ailments as social anxiety disorder and attention deficit disorder have been quite rewarding for drug companies who publicize these illnesses and their treatments.

Perhaps the most egregious of today's socially constructed diseases is the burgeoning category of addiction. For the notion that at least one type of addiction is a disease, we mainly have to thank not a physician or scientist but a public relations man by the name of Dwight Anderson. A recovered alcoholic himself, Anderson was recruited during World War II by a medical group called the Research Council on Problems of Alcohol in its quest to claim jurisdiction over the problem of chronic excessive drinking.

Anderson's canny advice, published in a seminal article in 1942, was to recast the alcoholic as a sick man. "Sickness implies the possibility of treatment. It also implies that, to some extent at least, the individual is not responsible for his condition . . . it follows from all this that the problem is a responsibility of the medical profession, of the constituted health authorities, and of the public in general."

Of course, Anderson didn't invent the disease of alcoholism, although he did popularize it. As long ago as the seventeenth century, British clergymen warned their parishioners about the "disease" of alcoholism, which one called "so epidemical" that "all the Physicians in England know not how to stop it." In the eighteenth century, the great Philadelphian Benjamin Rush, a signer of the Declaration of Independence, was among the physicians who took up the issue, writing that "drunkenness resembles certain hereditary, family, and contagious diseases."

But the concept never fully took hold until Anderson came along. By now the disease model is well established, and a whole range of self-destructive behaviors that were once considered self-control problems have been medicalized. Nor does addiction any longer require a substance. People are now considered to be helpless against a panoply of "impulse disorders" routinely treated by health care professionals and in popular culture. The American Psychiatric Association's *Diagnostic and Statistical Manual of Mental Disorders* (DSM-IV) sanctifies several, including pathological gambling and kleptomania. The larger culture has invented countless others, including addictions to shopping, sex, food, work, video games, TV, the Internet, and your no-good ex. Whether to include any of these in the next edition of the manual has been the subject of debate, but it's hard to see how they can all be kept out, for when you read the diagnostic criteria for pathological gambling in the current edition, it's easy to imagine drawing up very similar standards for any of the others.

There is an important reason why it's so difficult to draw a bright line between addictions involving substances that act chemically on the body and the more recent kind, which involve activities such as shopping or sex. The reason is that, as the philosopher Gary Watson has put it, "addictions are continuous with ordinary appetites." Seen in this way, addictions can help us understand the problem of self-control, for there is no more stark illustration of the conflict between short-term and long-term preferences—a conflict often present when our appetites are engaged.

There are good grounds for regarding an addiction as just an unusually durable form of desire. All humans seek pleasure; whether these pleasures are from drugs or behaviors, they act on us in similar biochemical ways. And people who are vulnerable to one kind of addiction often are vulnerable to others as well, suggesting the issue is desire rather than any particular addictive item.

What do we mean by addiction? A repetitive harmful action that persists even though you know it's bad for you. It typically involves spending a lot of time using, using more than intended, trying to cut back without success, sacrificing social or professional activities to the abused substance, and suffering withdrawal symptoms upon stopping.

In polite company, nobody doubts that this syndrome is an illness, but I will confess to agnosticism as to whether addiction is a disease. An addict's behavior, it seems clear, can be influenced by incentives, while the symptoms of cystic fibrosis cannot. And what we call addiction is just an unhealthy pattern of behavior rather than something apparent on an X-ray or a blood test. So how can addiction be a disease?

On the other hand, lots of diseases are socially constructed. And lots of problems that are indisputably diseases arise from a pattern of behavior. Lung cancer results largely from smoking, as smokers well know. Heart disease, diabetes, cirrhosis, hypertension, HIV, and many other ailments could mostly be prevented by different behavior, just like drug or alcohol abuse, yet nobody doubts that they are genuine diseases.

Addiction in particular can teach us something about compulsion. We call neat people compulsive, praise movies and books as compelling, and say that addicts are compelled in some way. But the behavior of most addicts shows that they are not truly compelled. For example: most people who become addicted to opiates—which are quite addictive—somehow manage to quit without professional help, usually by the age of around thirty. In one celebrated series of studies that began to appear in 1974, Lee Robins found that only 12 percent of heroin-addicted Vietnam veterans remained hooked three years after returning to the United States. When the stresses of duty in Southeast Asia ended, so did most of the heroin use—typically without professional intervention. Indeed, treatment seems to be the resort of the most intractable addicts, which is probably why it so often fails. The actor Robert Downey Jr.'s many publicized treatment lapses may give the impression that addiction is always compulsive, but what it really illustrates is that addicts who seek treatment are far from typical.

It's worth noting as well that rates of addiction vary widely in different times and places, suggesting that drug abuse, like other appetitive behaviors, is more subject to custom than compulsion. Americans born after World War II have drug addiction rates many times higher than those of Americans born before the war, a difference that far exceeds age-cohort differences for other psychiatric disorders. The high-stress, big-money, self-absorbed culture of Hollywood seems particularly conducive to substance dependence (just ask Mel Gibson, Lindsay Lohan, Kelsey Grammer, Charlie Sheen, Liza Minnelli and countless others). When it comes to addiction, apparently, culture matters, just as it does with respect to eating, shopping, venting anger, or any other form of gratification.

History also suggests that social pressure, intelligent use of law, and other such factors can be an effective antidote. In 1790, the average American consumed about 2.5 gallons of alcohol per year—not much more than we do today. But in the first three decades of the nineteenth century, consumption rose sharply, so that by around 1830 annual average intake had reached 7 gallons of pure alcohol, leading one historian to call ours "the alcoholic republic." It was not a pretty picture; saloons sprang up everywhere, violence flourished, and for many women and children, home life grew chaotic and brutal.

Then the culture changed. A wave of Protestant revivalism, which brought self-control back into the realm of God, spawned a nationwide temperance movement. "Evangelical preachers," the historian Jackson Lears tells us, "became a key force for popularizing a culture of control, a force that put human choice at the center of the spiritual order." Predestination was out, in other words, and free will was in. The result was that Americans cleaned up their act. By 1845 per capita alcohol consumption had fallen to less than 2 gallons a year. (All these figures vary depending on the source, but the magnitude and direction of the change are unmistakable.) Localities slashed the number of tavern licenses and many storekeepers stopped stocking booze. Gambling, racing, and such blood sports as cockfighting, all of which went hand in hand with drinking, receded as well.

The fact that addicts respond to incentives further argues against their helplessness. For instance: it turns out that treatment for drug addiction has a relatively poor track record *except* with pilots and physicians, who afterward face random drug testing and potential loss of their licenses and careers. For these two groups of professionals, scared straight by the knowledge of catastrophic consequences if they relapse, treatment has a high success rate. Nor are threats of Draconian punishment the only things that work; programs that offer relatively modest rewards such as movie tickets also have had some success.

Price also affects consumption, even when the price isn't as high as early death. The economists Philip Cook and George Tauchen found that higher liquor taxes significantly reduce the incidence of cirrhosis of the liver, a reliable proxy for chronic heavy drinking. The main argument against legalizing substances such as marijuana and cocaine—that more people will abuse them—implies that laws and penalties make a difference in whether they are abused and therefore that addiction is far from invariably compulsory.

Incentives probably matter to *most* addicts; it's a fair bet that, offered $1 million to abstain for a month, most will manage to stay clean long enough to collect. Or recall the case of John Cheever, who described himself as "a weak man, a man without character" because he couldn't stop himself from drinking. On one level, Cheever was too hard on himself, since alcoholism was considered a disease even as he wrote those words and, like many self-regulatory disorders, has a significant hereditary component. (Years later, his daughter Susan Cheever would write about her own struggles with addiction.) On the other hand, his reference to character suggests some sense of his own acquiescence when he gives in. Is it possible, at the moment when he took the drink, that he literally didn't want to? If so, did he have a sudden bout of alien hand syndrome (an actual medical condition in which the sufferer's hand, like Dr. Strangelove's, seems to have a mind of its own)? Unlikely, unless he happened to have the hemispheres of his brain surgically separated.

Imagine for a moment that Cheever's long-suffering wife held a gun to his head and said, "Don't blink or I'll shoot!" Because the autonomic nervous system is immune to such threats, we can predict with certainty that eventually he would blink, proving he had no choice in the matter. But imagine now a different scenario, a more realistic one in which she credibly said, "Don't *drink* or I'll shoot," perhaps after a night of raging and tears so that she seemed persuasively distraught. The odds are that there would be no drinking—which makes us wonder if Cheever's drinking really was compulsory, hard as it may have been for him to stop. A gun pointed at the head, after all, will not banish the symptoms of Alzheimer's disease or multiple sclerosis.

At this juncture it may be helpful to consider what we mean by compulsion, a notion that has been stretched so far in recent decades that it's hard to recognize. If you are in your car, stopped at a light, and a tornado carries it off with you in it, this is surely compulsion—you didn't want this to happen, yet you were powerless against the forces of nature. But does this model apply to addiction? For if the addict is compelled, how do so many manage to quit? Compulsion implies that the addict is acting against his will, but what stops him from taking steps—seeking treatment, giving away his drugs and money, turning himself over to the police—to *enforce* his will while desire is satiated?

Addiction, it seems, is at least to some extent voluntary—like so many other behaviors. In general, we might say with the psychologist Gene M. Heyman that "the degree to which an activity is voluntary is the degree to which it systematically varies as a function of its consequences." And we know that addiction varies with consequences. Addiction is not good for job performance, family finances, or spousal relations. It impairs health. It can put the addict at risk of robbery or worse in the hunt for illegal drugs. These consequences carry less weight for people in their late teens or early twenties, a period of risk taking when most drug addicts start using. But by their late twenties, these same addicts stop or cut way back. (Not every addiction ends with a dish of cold turkey.) It's possible their maturing brains can produce greater self-regulatory resources at that point. It's also possible that in their late twenties they begin to realize that adult responsibilities aren't going away, and keeping a family intact or holding on to a job is incentive enough.

There is a further sense in which addiction is voluntary, and that has to do with knowledge. Many users of addictive substances know from the very first hit that addiction is a risk they run. They probably also know that the longer they use, the more likely addiction becomes. And if they don't know, it's reasonable to think they should, just as a person who fires an arrow in a crowded city park is expected to know that someone will likely be hurt. The role of knowledge is evident when it comes to tobacco. Nicotine is highly addictive, but millions of people have quit smoking—unassisted—since word got out that tobacco kills, suggesting that they were not truly compelled to smoke in the first place.

Now, clearly something physical is at work with addiction—as it is with any appetite. Some have said that the addict's compulsion comes from changes in the brain caused by the abused substance. Others cite heredity; genes clearly play a role in addiction and in self-control generally. Like criminals, addicts often have broader self-control problems; one researcher found that "smokers, alcoholics, drug dependent patients and pathological gamblers all suffer from abnormalities in motor impulsivity and delay discounting problems and . . . these abnormalities are associated with hypoactivity of the prefrontal cortex." In other words, addicts have difficulties inhibiting their actions—in a game of Simon Says, for example—and they place a lower value on the future than others do. The problems of addicts in this department are not unlike those of people who have damage to the forebrain, the area where self-control functions are thought to reside. In short, addicts are worse than the average person at managing desire.

Yet neither biochemistry nor genes can fully remove addiction from the realm of voluntary behavior. Heyman has noted that just about everything changes the brain; plasticity is its essence, yet this doesn't lead to what we consider a loss of choice. Nor do genetics imply compulsion, since all behavior is genetically influenced, yet this doesn't make people unfree. Even the manifest self-destructiveness of addicted behavior doesn't necessarily imply compulsion; people make bad choices all the time without anyone's calling into question the voluntary nature of their choices.

This is *not* to say that behavior never comes close to being compulsive; people with anorexia nervosa and obsessive-compulsive disorder, among other such ailments, seem to suffer from a disorder of the will, almost as if alien invaders somehow abolished their autonomy and made them shun life-giving calories or check the gas for the hundredth time—as if these people were puppets on a string. Some addicts seem like this as well—people whose will has been hijacked or is otherwise defective, who often have additional psychological problems, and who will persist in drinking or shooting up even to the death.

It may be reasonable to say that these people have a disease, and perhaps we should reserve the term "addicted" for these refractory cases rather than the millions of smokers and coffee drinkers and Internet surfers and cocaine users who, when they stand up to their own cravings, can change their behavior for good. Too many behaviors, over the years, have been shifted from the voluntary part of the spectrum to the involuntary part, as if we could no more stop shopping than we could stop breathing. But every time we move something into this involuntary category, we chip away at our humanity.

Maybe it would be better to acknowledge, like the Greeks, that a lot of the behavior we call addiction is really a love of pleasure that carries the force of habit. We become addicted mostly because of the central issue in all self-control problems, which is the disproportionate value we place on short-term rewards. An addict who's using drugs or who's headed for the craps table is meliorating—choosing one more line of coke or throw of the dice as if each choice were made in a vacuum. Behavioral economists call this the peanuts effect, because one more of almost anything is just, well, peanuts in the grand scheme of things.

But our choices add up; each one influences others, and cumulatively a series of delightful short-term choices can leave us much worse off in the long run. This is the addict's dilemma, and this may be why addictions of all kinds appear to be proliferating—because technology has enabled the production of vastly more seductive pleasures, such as crack cocaine and video games, and because the cultural and practical barriers to short-term pleasures are a lot lower than they used to be.

Tomorrow Is Another Day

Everyone puts things off, but nobody is better at it than I am. Drawing on talent and experience and employing a vast repertoire of delaying tactics, I can find a way to postpone almost any work indefinitely.

Sometimes, for example, I organize my office. Other times I tell myself I can't concentrate unless I pay some bill, talk to some plumber, or otherwise distract myself with pseudo-productive administrivia. The Internet, of course, is always ready to get in the way of true accomplishment. Nutrition is frequently available as an issue; like the desire some people have for a cigarette after sex, I long for a snack before work. And then there's the "ripeness" story that I'm so fond of telling myself—the story about how something isn't quite "ready." The idea is that I can't write whatever it is I'm supposed to write until the shape of it *comes* to me, bobbing up suddenly from the depths of my unconscious like a bloated corpse.

Procrastination, like masturbation, is among the guiltiest of pleasures. It's something people do for themselves, it's never quite as satisfying as the thing for which it substitutes, and it is almost never done in public. Yet whole societies have been known to procrastinate. New York has put off the much-needed Second Avenue subway for years rather than face the expense and disruption. In car-oriented cities, it's easier to build a costly rail system that hardly anybody will ride than to impose hefty taxes on gasoline and parking to discourage driving. Borrowing postpones pain and building trains to nowhere gives the appearance of doing something, both classic features of procrastination wherever it is found.

And rest assured, procrastinators are found everywhere. Joseph Ferrari, a DePaul University psychologist who has practically made a career of studying the subject, has surveyed people in the United States, Australia, Peru, Spain, Turkey, and the United Kingdom and found no meaningful difference in their procrastination scores. Even some animals procrastinate. As with so many issues relating to self-control, dopamine appears to play a role.

In one study, at the National Institute of Mental Health (NIMH), monkeys were transformed into workaholics by a preparation that temporarily knocked out certain dopamine receptors for several weeks. When, set to work once again on the simple lever-release task for which they had been trained, "the monkeys became extreme workaholics, as evidenced by a sustained low rate of errors in performing the experimental task, irrespective of how distant the reward might be," said NIMH scientist Barry Richmond. "This was conspicuously out of character for these animals. Like people, they tend to procrastinate when they know they will have to do more work before getting a reward."

Procrastination is an ancient affliction, coming to us from the Latin verb *procrastinare,* which means, roughly, "push forward until tomorrow." Hesiod, that most ancient of Greek poets, warned against it around 800 BCE; "do no put off your work till tomorrow," he urged, declaring that a man who does so "is always at hand-grips with ruin." Later, among the Romans, Cicero argued that "in the conduct of almost every affair slowness and procrastination are hateful." But some commentators have suggested that it was never really considered much of a problem until around 1750, with the advent of the Industrial Revolution and the need to regulate human behavior more closely for the purpose of coordinating production. Samuel Johnson described procrastination in 1751 as "one of the general weaknesses, which, in spite of the instruction of moralists and the remonstrances of reason, prevail to a greater or less degree in every mind." It was Philip Stanhope, a contemporary of Johnson's, who advised, "Never put off till tomorrow what you can do today."

For this brief history we can thank Piers Steel, a University of Calgary psychologist who has made a specialty of the subject, and who reports that prevalence appears to be growing, at least according to some researchers. Studying procrastination is not always easy. Students of the literature evidently have to cope with endless pranks, including a fake history that cites the authors Stilton and Edam for a report on the use of cheese in a study of procrastination in mice. Steel, however, takes the subject seriously and has even developed an impressive-looking formula that supposedly captures such factors as the desirability of a task and a person's sensitivity to delay. Steel also has a procrastination Web site—but then again, aren't they all?—which offers an eighty-one-question quiz to help you measure your procrastinating tendencies, although one would think merely taking such a quiz would answer any doubts. (Google it if you must.)

Procrastination is a classic self-control failure because procrastinators almost always have a strong second-order preference *not* to procrastinate. The job won't go away, after all, and putting it off won't make it any easier. Procrastination is also associated with other self-control shortcomings. In studies, procrastinators score low on self-control questionnaires and also score low for the specific personality trait known to psychologists as conscientiousness. Expressed in terms the Greeks would have used, procrastination is an example of the type of akrasia Aristotle called *astheneia,* or sheer weakness, in that we want to get to the task at hand, we know we should, and if we could utter an incantation to make it so, we would. But somehow we just can't muster the strength of will.

Procrastination Is a Drug

People procrastinate in order to put off things that are unpleasant or wearisome—dreaded confrontations, burdensome homework assignments, cleaning out the garage. Jobs that are intimidatingly difficult are especially likely to inspire delaying actions. Long delays to reward—a doctoral degree six years away, for example, with no guarantee of employment afterward—also make us procrastination-prone.

But procrastination is not just about putting off some deed—it's also about the doer. And my own theory, based on what is surely unparalleled personal experience, is that procrastinators use distraction to self-medicate when they're feeling bad about themselves, much like what Tolstoy said about why people smoke and drink: "simply and solely in order to drown the warning voice of conscience."

Think of procrastination as a kind of drug: mood altering, mildly addictive, harmful in quantity, and leading to a kind of altered consciousness—the unique state of dithering into which it dispatches us. Seen in this light, procrastination can proudly claim its place in the mainstream of self-control problems, so many of which feature self-medication as a central element. Drug and alcohol addiction are obvious examples, but even obsessive-compulsive disorder involves unhealthy patterns of behavior undertaken to reduce anxiety, however momentarily. The need to lock the door or check the faucet one more time is like an itch, and it feels good to scratch.

It makes a certain sense to self-medicate when the task at hand makes us anxious or depressed. So procrastination is a mood-management technique, albeit (like eating or taking drugs) a shortsighted one. But we're most prone to it when we think it will actually help. In an interesting study by the psychologist Roy Baumeister, one of America's leading scholars of self-control, and two coauthors, eighty-eight college students were told they were taking part in an experiment to see how aromatherapy and mood affected color matching. They were also told they would be given an intelligence test involving math, and that taking 10 to 15 minutes to practice beforehand was a proven score enhancer. But they could use the practice time as they pleased—in a room that contained what the instructor called "time wasters."

Now, some students had access only to boring time wasters (preschool puzzles and outdated technical journals) while others were given fun ones (a video game, a challenging plastic puzzle, and some popular current magazines). The students were then asked to read passages designed to put them in good or bad moods. And some students were asked to smell a candle that, they were assured, would temporarily fix their mood. Remember, this was supposed to be an aromatherapy study.

So what did all this effort produce? Well, far and away the most procrastination occurred among the bad-mood students who believed their mood could be changed *and* who had access to fun distractions. This group spent nearly 14 of their 15 minutes of prep time goofing off! Students who believed their bad mood was frozen (those who were not given a supposedly mood-lifting candle) spent less than 6 minutes goofing off. (Even the good-mood students procrastinated slightly more if they believed their mood could be altered.)

So we seem to think procrastination will make us feel better. Yet the cure is worse than the disease, because putting off the job usually makes us even more anxious and depressed. The existence of procrastination is further evidence that self-destructive behaviors can be voluntary. Think of yourself at work: You freely decide to check your e-mail, seducing yourself with the balm of distraction for an instant's relief. You're not leaving your desk, after all; you're still at your keyboard! Yet how willingly you jump through any escape hatch that presents itself, and how much better it feels just now to be reading an article in the *Financial Times* or looking for bargains on eBay. The great psychologist Alfred Adler, who gave us the inferiority complex, saw neurosis "not as unconscious repression but as a deliberate ruse whereby one evades some overwhelming task," and by this standard procrastination is neurotic indeed.

Procrastination as Theater

Procrastination is a ruse. We know what's really going on, but we want badly to be fooled. For instance, people chronically underestimate the amount of time and effort a task will take even though they know better. "Scientists and writers, for example, are notoriously prone to underestimate the time required to complete a project," according to the psychologists Daniel Kahneman and Amos Tversky, "even when they have considerable experience of past failures to live up to planned schedules."

Kahneman and Tversky called this the planning fallacy, and it crops up all over the place, particularly when we're facing an onerous task; repeated experiments have shown that people consistently predict they can get a job done faster than the time it ultimately takes. This excessive optimism isn't just American; it's been demonstrated in Japan and Canada as well. Some people even suggest that the benefits of underestimating the time required by a task—and therefore putting off work on it—can outweigh the costs associated with poor planning. Self-deception may be necessary lest the true magnitude of the job scare us away altogether. And the period of good feelings we enjoy while believing the job is smaller than it is may help us get the work done later on.

The planning fallacy looks to be voluntary; it persists despite people's experience to the contrary, after all, and appears subject to incentives. In one interesting experiment, undergraduates who were asked to solve anagram puzzles were able to predict their time to completion much more accurately when they were paid for accurate predictions. The students took about the same time to solve the puzzles as a control group, so they weren't adjusting their performance to match their prediction. The prospect of payment just seemed to wash away their excessive optimism—they actually finished the puzzles in this case *faster* than they had predicted.

We also deceive ourselves with the diverting tasks we perform instead of the job we're so busily putting off. Household chores suddenly become pressing, for example. When asked how to write a novel, Hemingway supposedly told people that first you clean the refrigerator. Or we linger at the first stages of a task: one of my sons, who is supposed to practice the saxophone nightly, can spend an amazingly long time unpacking his instrument and moistening the reed before he plays a note. Delays of this kind, carried to extremes, might qualify as pathology; "primary obsessional slowness" is said to occur when people with obsessive-compulsive disorder take a really, really long time to do almost anything, including getting dressed or preparing to go out.

The psychologists John Sabini and Maury Silver are especially insightful about the things we do when we procrastinate instead of working—contingent, ephemeral sorts of things, often, which are laden nonetheless with symbolic value. Serious procrastinators do not just go off with friends and have a party, except perhaps when time is ample and the deadline seems vanishingly small. But when that deadline really begins to loom, we drag ourselves to our desks—there to discover that almost anything will capture and hold our rapt attention. Sometimes we'll spend the entire time dithering and at the end of the evening have no progress to show for it. We might as well have gone out with friends and at least had a good time, instead of guiltily playing solitaire on the computer.

But there is an important element of theater about procrastination. We have a need to dramatize our commitment to working, not only to others but to ourselves, which is why someone writing a term paper doesn't go and do something worthwhile. Instead, he sits down to work, gets stuck, and decides to take a little peek at Facebook, just to see what's going on. Or perhaps he lets his attention be captured by a golf story on Yahoo or in the out-of-town newspaper that was used to wrap the new Freud figurine on his desk (the one he ordered on eBay during a prior bout of procrastination). This particular student cares not a whit about golf, but his looming paper is stressful to contemplate, and he can't just go off and do something else. An article about golf is just the thing, especially because it doesn't give too much pleasure (which would make him feel too guilty). It's a welcome anesthetic, however bitter the taste of relief. Most important, Sabini and Silver remind us, by staying at his desk the student can avoid *committing* to his distractions: "We might say these irrationalities of procrastination are attempts to maintain oneself in readiness to work, in what might be called a 'procrastination field.'"

Giving in to procrastination feels bad even while it feels good, like eating too many potato chips. And it's exhausting; it takes a lot of concentration sometimes to avoid doing what you know you're going to have to do sooner or later (and perhaps with greater difficulty). Attention has to be kept off the business that should be at hand, and attention control of any kind takes energy. What a shame to waste so much of it fending off the only thing—tackling the avoided work—that could put an end to the situation.

Procrastination is irrational by definition—any reasonable delay just wouldn't be procrastination—but from a certain myopic perspective, procrastination can look rational. Sabini and Silver give this example: imagine you have some weeks to write a paper, but meanwhile you have to decide what to do with your next five minutes. Playing pinball will have no measurable impact on the paper and is far more pleasurable, so you play. The same decision applies, with only the slightest change, to the next five minutes. And so on, for most of the minutes available before the paper is due. We have a type of melioration at work here, akin to what we see in addicts of all kinds, and the authors are having none of it. "One of the ways of being irrational and procrastinating," they observe, "is to act on rational calculations for intervals that are irrationally short."

Procrastination, Guilt, and Shame

For humans, procrastination is a guilty pleasure, but it appears to be more closely associated with shame—which is something altogether different. Unfortunately, guilt and shame have been tarred by the same brush.

Guilt is the good one of the pair. The focus of guilt is on our actions, for which we might feel remorse and regret. Someone who feels guilty about something may want to apologize or somehow erase or correct the deed from which guilt arises.

But if guilt means feeling bad about what you do, shame means feeling bad about what you are. Feeling shame means feeling unworthy; instead of seeing what you did as horrible, what you see as horrible is yourself. Guilt focuses on changing some action or behavior, while shame focuses on changing some part of the self. This "soul-stifling shame," as Coleridge called it, is a sad thing indeed, with sufferers finding it harder to describe and more painful than guilt. Shame is associated with feeling small and inferior, and with the feeling of being watched disapprovingly by others. Guilt wants to make amends, but shame just wants to hide.

When the psychologist June Tangney, in a study with Ronda L. Fee (later Dearing), used questionnaires to assess eighty-six college students on measures of shame, guilt, perfectionism, conscientiousness, and other factors, they found that the tendency to procrastinate was related to their subjects' proneness to shame—but not to guilt.

Shame is associated with other self-control problems as well. In a study of 380 children (and their parents and grandparents), Tangney and her colleagues found that, "Shame-proneness assessed in the fifth grade predicted later high school suspension, drug use of various kinds (amphetamines, depressants, hallucinogens, heroin), and suicide attempts. Relative to their less shame-prone peers, shame-prone children were less likely to apply to college or engage in community service."

This was all quite a contrast to the kids more given to guilt (and these findings remained even when researchers controlled for socioeconomic status). "Relative to less guilt-prone children, guilt-prone fifth graders were more likely to later apply to college and do community service. They were less likely to make suicide attempts, to use heroin, and to drive under the influence of alcohol or drugs, and they began drinking at a later age. Guilt-prone fifth graders were less likely to be arrested, convicted, and incarcerated. In adolescence they had fewer sexual partners and were more likely to practice 'safe sex' and use birth control."

Shame, it seems, is something like guilt's evil twin. With its focus on behavior and responsibility, guilt promotes self-control across the board—and empathy as well. But shame appears almost wholly destructive, inspiring sufferers to lash out not just at others but at themselves—it's a well-known trigger for suicide, and study after study has linked it with substance abuse. The ugliness of shame, with its sense of furtiveness and impairment of the self, was captured by Erving Goffman in the title of his classic *Stigma: Notes on the Management of Spoiled Identity.*

"In our Longitudinal Family Study," Tangney and Dearing report, "no apparent benefit was derived from the pain of shame. There was no evidence that shame inhibits problematic behaviors. Shame does not deter young people from engaging in criminal activities; it does not deter them from unsafe sex practices; it does not foster responsible driving habits; and in fact it seems to inhibit constructive involvement in community service. Guilt, on the other hand, seems to be a powerful moral emotional factor."

The closer you look, the more shame comes to look like a disease, and as with so many diseases, this one looks at least partially genetic, or at least significantly more so than guilt. A 1995 study of 160 twins found this very thing. Guilt seemed more influenced by environment.

One thing shame and guilt have in common is that they can inspire procrastination as a way of avoiding bad feelings. And they can result from procrastination, which in itself is likely to make us feel bad. Procrastination is thus both cause and effect, escape and exacerbater. And while it is usually in our power to stop our dillydallying, our propensity to procrastinate in itself seems to have a hereditary component. Yet another study of twins, genes, and personality implied that roughly 22 percent of the variance in procrastination is genetic.

The War on Motivation

One reason procrastination may be increasing is the changing nature of work. Thanks to technology (one of our great self-control bugbears,

remember) the things we do for a living are changing in ways that promote dithering.

If you work on an assembly line, for example, you have little opportunity to procrastinate. Remember the episode of *I Love Lucy* in which
Lucy and Ethel get a job in a chocolate factory? But if you work at a desk,
as so many of us do nowadays, performing some task that is almost
impossible to measure on a daily basis, procrastination seems almost
inevitable. (Some organizations are even going along. At the headquar-
ters of Best Buy, for instance, they've tried something called ROWE,
for Results Only Work Environment, which measures performance by
output rather than an input like time invested.)

The trouble is that today the very same fruits of technology which
have helped make us so productive also promote procrastination. For
many of us, in fact, the main tool of our work—an Internet-connected
computer—is our primary temptation *not* to work, continually subverting our attention with e-mail, chat invitations, and the siren song,
acutely audible to those with tasks to complete, of a million Web sites
bent on our diversion. The result is that today's "knowledge workers"
don't seem to spend all that much time working, even if they claim to be
on the job day and night.

Distraction has always been a problem. "His days were consumed
by nervous pedantry," Thomas Mann writes of Thomas Buddenbrook,
his fictional 1870s business executive. "Harassed by a thousand details,
all of them unimportant, he was too weak-willed to arrive at a reasonable and fruitful arrangement of his time."

Yet it's hard to deny that the challenge of distraction is at least somewhat worse today. We live now in what's been called a toxic motivational environment in which concentration is continually undermined
by phone calls, e-mails, instant messages, and importuning or alluring
colleagues. The market economy feeds our desire for a constant flow
of novelty, so that the ocean in which we swim every day is rich with
the new, flitting past in all directions. The result is a standing invitation
to procrastinate. As Piers Steel has said, it's like "trying to diet with a
magic floating spoon of ice cream following you around."

The contrast between work that inspires procrastination and work that stifles it is especially stark in my own household. My wife, a dentist, must find opportunities to procrastinate at home because she has none on the job. Her day is tightly scheduled, and anxious patients are always staring her in the face. The effect of all this is galvanizing; even when she's tired, on the job she is wired.

A writer, on the other hand, often seems to do nothing but procrastinate.

I'll Write Tomorrow

Someday, perhaps, roving bands of burly men will roam taverns, pressing civilians into the writing trade at the point of a musket. Until then, we have to assume that most writers are volunteers rather than conscripts. So presumably, they want to write. Why, therefore, are they so notorious for procrastination?

One reason, I think, is that writing involves abstract thinking rather than visible, concrete tasks—abstract thinking, in fact, that will be rewarded only far into the future or perhaps never at all. Abstract thinking that nowadays is done in front of an Internet-connected computer. Can you imagine any scenario more likely to inspire procrastination?

If you analyze your own dilatory tendencies you may find that you tend to procrastinate most aggressively when disturbing thoughts and memories set in. The reason has to do with self-awareness. Thinking abstractly can open the door to an awful lot of it, and in some sense Samuel Johnson spoke for all of us when he said, "My life is one long escape from myself."

Roy Baumeister envisions a hierarchy of processes at work within us, with the higher ones involving longer time spans, more elaborate meaning, and more abstract goals. Self-regulation fails when the higher ones fail to override the lower ones. Procrastination is the example par excellence.

So imagine that you are sitting at your desk, staring at a blank screen, struggling to find a way to synthesize an avalanche of complex material into something palatable and coherent. Then you start thinking of some recent embarrassment or transgression—perhaps of the previous day, spent dithering instead of working. These kinds of thoughts are likely to make self-awareness painful—and send us scurrying back down the hierarchy to the kind of lower satisfactions (the Internet, the refrigerator) so familiar to procrastinators everywhere.

Writing offers an escape of sorts, yet the solitary, self-motivating context of the trade, along with the abstract nature of the work, mean that postponement is an ever present temptation. Writing is really about thinking—something almost everyone is always willing to put off—and apparently always has been. Joshua Reynolds observed in the eighteenth century that "there is no expedient to which a man will not resort to avoid the real labor of thinking."

This may be why writers, who know how susceptible they are to jumping off the abstract plane, often work so hard to track their output or take other measures to keep themselves at work. Scribblers as diverse as Anthony Trollope, Irving Wallace, and Ernest Hemingway have kept elaborate data on their progress, and Anne Fadiman reports that when the writing was going badly for John McPhee, he would tie himself to his office chair with his bathrobe sash. The famously prolific Trollope required of himself not just a set number of daily pages but specified how many words—250—should be on each. Of course, Trollope, who produced sixty-three books, was nothing compared with his mother, Frances, who wrote 114 novels, starting at the age of fifty. "Nothing surely is as potent as a law that may not be disobeyed," he wrote sensibly enough. "It has the force of the water-drop that hollows the stone. A small daily task, if it be really daily, will beat the labours of a spasmodic Hercules."

Émile Zola—another of those prolific nineteenth-century novelists—must have known this when he had his mantelpiece inscribed with the words NULLA DIES SINE LINEA, which means "no day without a line."

No one tracked his own writing efforts more ruthlessly than the economist Joseph Schumpeter, who gave himself numerical grades as if

he were one of his own students at Harvard. He proved a stern taskmas-
ter. "In grading his daily performances," wrote his biographer, Thomas
McCraw, "he gave himself numerical credit for writing and research—
including his endless effort to master mathematics—but seldom for
teaching, counseling students, or any other duty. He enjoyed reading
Latin and Greek texts, as well as European novels and biographies . . .
Sometimes he indulged himself with Ellery Queen and other detec-
tive novelists. He loved to dine out and to attend art exhibitions and
classical music concerts. But he regarded most of these activities as
unseemly distractions. The only thing that really counted was work.
On that dimension Schumpeter held himself to unattainable standards
and wrestled constantly with his conscience."

Tracking your own output, while as useful in its way as monitoring
your weight, is a less radical step than enlisting someone to make you
write when you mightn't altogether wish to. Sometimes, of course, you
can enlist yourself; Demosthenes is said to have embarrassed himself
into seclusion for three months by intentionally shaving half his head.
Unwilling to be seen in public until it grew back, he used the time to
work on his rhetorical skills.

Jeffrey J. Sallaz, a sociologist at the University of Arizona, overcame
procrastination by posting an embarrassing picture of himself on Facebook, which he resolved to leave there until he finished reviewing copy-
edits on a manuscript he'd produced. He later asserted that while those
who work in manufacturing may daydream about working on their
own, "professionals fantasize about being tethered to an assembly line
and supervised. We are damned to be free, to quote Sartre."

Often, though, it's better to enlist someone else to enforce output.
Victor Hugo, you'll recall, had his valet confiscate his clothes, forcing
the great novelist to remain at work—an approach validated by subsequent research. At least one study of blocked writers has found that
they were more productive and more creative when they were essentially forced to write instead of scribbling only when the mood struck
them. The historian Georg Lukacs would certainly agree; when George
Steiner visited and remarked on his host's remarkable output, "Lukacs

was amused and explained, 'You want to know how one gets work done? House arrest, Steiner, house arrest!'"

One of the best literary attempts to grapple with procrastination comes from Geoff Dyer, who chronicles his own elaborate putting off (which involves extensive travel) in *Out of Sheer Rage: Wrestling With D. H. Lawrence.* Dyer was supposed to be writing a book about Lawrence, but kept putting it off. In the end, he came away with a book about procrastination.

18

Cutting Loose

There never has been, and cannot be, a good life without self-control.

—LEO TOLSTOY

Resist the temptation to resist the temptation.

—ADVERTISEMENT IN *THE NEW YORKER*

In the modern world, self-control buys a good life indeed. Having self-control to spare is rare enough nowadays that the marketplace lavishes huge rewards on society's scary new self-control elite, those lords of discipline who not only withstood all that boring stuff in graduate school, but keep themselves thin by carefully regulating what they eat after flogging themselves off to the gym at the crack of dawn.

We all know who these people are; they're the ones who schedule their children's perfectly calibrated mix of mental and physical exertions with minute-by-minute precision, plotting little Taylor's path from preschool to Harvard. It's easy to make fun of them, but these folks don't seem to be doing badly to me, at least compared to us weak-willed hoi polloi frantically rolling over our credit card balances and ordering the fried cheesecake whenever we see it on a menu. On the contrary, America's aristocracy of self-control seems ideally adapted to the world in which we find ourselves, blast their steely backbones. It's as if they got the news ahead of the rest of us—no doubt by waking up

earlier—that self-control may well be the most important personal trait
of the twenty-first century.

For the rest of us Americans, a people conditioned by the popular
belief that suppressing our innermost desires is the surest path to misery, this may come as a bitter pill. Happiness, after all, is often pur-
ported to require loosening the bonds of self-control—letting go, giving
in, indulging—rather than remaining fearfully in thrall to those terrible
inhibitions by which we thwart our own fun.

Yet many people, including, no doubt, many of these self-regulatory
superstars, do in fact need to cut loose, for *over*-control can be as
much of a problem as *under*-control. Science to the rescue: A number
of studies have been published lately about hyperopia, or excessive
farsightedness—another name for the problem of over-control. Unfor-
tunates thus afflicted apparently yearn to emulate the witty columnist
Don Marquis who, after a month of abstention, finally marches up to
the bar, explaining: "I've conquered that god-damn willpower of mine.
Gimme a double scotch."

Over-control rarely causes the horrible symptoms (neuroses, regret,
Freudian slips) that are popularly attributed to it, but there are costs
nonetheless. Perhaps the best way to understand them is to imagine
that you've received a present of some rare and delicious tea, which you
naturally save for a special occasion—and save, and save, until finally
it goes stale and ends up in the compost. Your exercise in deferred
gratification has left you poorer rather than richer. "Wisdom has its
excesses," Montaigne reminds us, "and has no less need of moderation
than does folly."

So we drink bourbon, smoke marijuana, undergo primal scream
therapy, ask our lovers to tie us up, all to free ourselves from . . .
ourselves. "We long for a holiday from our frontal lobes, a Dionysiac
fiesta of sense and impulse," writes Oliver Sacks, referring to the part
of our brains where self-control is said to reside. "That this is a need
of our constrained, civilized, hyperfrontal nature has been recognized
in every time and culture."

Committing to Cutting Loose

As you might expect, much of the vast literature on our internal divisions is concerned with how the deliberative self can enforce its will on its frustratingly impulsive sibling—a problem familiar to all of us who've tried to lose weight or stop surfing the Internet and get down to work. But a few economists, perhaps in the spirit of Oscar Wilde ("The only way to get rid of temptation is to yield to it"), have taken the opposite tack, arguing that people often make themselves unhappy as a result of under-indulgence.

Tyler Cowen, who posits a "rule-oriented self" and an "impulsive self," argues that we tend to give the latter short shrift despite all the wonderful things he can do for us. At the very least, Cowen suggests, the two selves ought to cooperate; for example, stimulating the impulsive self may be rational for the rule-oriented self, which is the more future-oriented of the two. The rule-oriented self may understand the value of novelty and surprise and so may work to cultivate opportunities for his impulsive sibling to engage in spontaneous indulgence.

God knows many of us are all too ready to diagnose under-indulgence in ourselves—what better pretext for another beer?—but some people really are over-controlled, and they sometimes put their rational, planning-oriented selves to work in order to commit to their own impulses. The classic method is having a drink. Alcohol is a tried and true disinhibitor, one often consumed in full knowledge of its effects for this very purpose; people willingly "put an enemy in their mouths to steal away their brains," as Cassio says in *Othello*. Soldiers throughout history have been prepared for killing—and dying—with alcohol. In the Spanish Civil War, men serving on firing squads were given generous portions of brandy despite the early morning hour, and during World War II, the French army was provided with large quantities of wine in the brief period before its collapse.

Imbibing isn't the only way to influence our choices in the direction of cutting loose. Another good technique is to choose rewards that will promote indulgence. There's a great example in George Bernard Shaw's *Pygmalion*, when Eliza Doolittle's ne'er-do-well father, Alfred (the Doolittle in the following passage), explains it all to Henry Higgins and Colonel Pickering.

> **Higgins:** I suppose we must give him a fiver.
>
> **Pickering:** He'll make a bad use of it, I'm afraid.
>
> **Doolittle:** Not me, Governor, so help me I won't. Don't you be afraid that I'll save it and spare it and live idle on it. There won't be a penny of it left by Monday: I'll have to go to work same as if I'd never had it. It won't pauperize me, you bet. Just one good spree for myself and the missus, giving pleasure to ourselves and employment to others, and satisfaction to you to think it's not been throwed away. You couldn't spend it better.
>
> **Higgins:** This is irresistible. Let's give him ten. [*He offers two notes to the dustman.*]
>
> **Doolittle:** No, Governor. She wouldn't have the heart to spend ten; and perhaps I shouldn't neither. Ten pounds is a lot of money: it makes a man feel prudent like; and then goodbye to happiness. You give me what I ask you, Governor: not a penny more, and not a penny less.

Along these lines, it's not unheard of (or irrational) for the conscientious, when they win a contest, to pick the sports car or expensive vacation as a prize instead of cash precisely because they would never allow themselves such a luxury under any other circumstances. Like Alfred Doolittle, these winners fear that if they took the money, they would save it or use it to pay household bills, never experiencing that dream vacation to Bali. It's a form of commitment against excessive or unwanted prudence (and yes, it does take prudence to ward off too much prudence).

In 2002, marketing professors Ran Kivetz and Itamar Simonson ran a series of fascinating experiments demonstrating this very thing.

In one, 124 female travelers were given a hypothetical choice between $85 in cash or a spa package worth just $80. Easy choice, right? Wrong. Forty of the travelers chose the spa package, even though they could have taken the money, bought the same package, and had $5 left over. All the women were asked to explain their choices in writing, and the vast majority of the spa choosers did so in terms of committing themselves to indulgence. A typical answer: "That way I'd have to pamper myself and not spend the money on something like groceries."

The need to cut loose, paradoxically enough, may account for the enjoyment some people derive from sexual masochism, the practice of which seems to hold special appeal for society's most self-controlled individuals. Roy Baumeister has suggested that masochism, like alcohol and spirituality, is a way of escaping self-consciousness, of putting down, however briefly, the immense burden of ego that so many of us bear in the modern world. If you like to be handcuffed and spanked, in this view, well, then maybe Atlas just needs a break.

Bound for Release

Our friend Odysseus bore just such a burden of ego, and the episode of the Sirens can be seen as a dramatization of his desire both to uphold and break free of his *enkrateia*, or self-command, which was aimed above all else at returning to his wife and throne. Think of that whole business again in light of the need to cut loose: in a flurry of homoerotic solidarity, our hero orders his men to bind him to the vessel's giant phallus— its mast, of course, but perhaps also his own patriarchal outlook—lest a pack of treacherously irresistible females seduce him away from his own ethos and dissolve his potency in the vast maternal ocean. Like all alpha males, he enjoys this bondage, which was after all voluntary, and when the Sirens flog him with their songs, he is helpless to succumb or withdraw.

In this scene, Odysseus has to give up his powers for a while in order to retain them, and perhaps something similar is at work in garden-variety sexual masochism. The term covers a bunch of risqué practices, but what most of them have in common is that they dramatize the desire to lose control. Getting your lover to tie you up, in particular, implies enacting a certain commitment to cutting loose, since the helpless "victim" can't very well resist.

But in asking to be constrained against the harmful impulses that lie ahead, those who "submit" to bondage differ from Odysseus in that the unwanted impulses beckon not to some fatal ecstasy but to the dreaded mantle of propriety. For the over-controlled, bondage thus represents a form of freedom, and "slavery" a way of enlisting for the guilty pleasure that is the masochist's true preference. The notion that bondage could equal freedom sounds Orwellian but makes sense if you bear in mind a single crucial fact: those who want to be subjugated in this way have asked for it. Even the most ardent embracers of sadomasochistic sex emphasize that the practice must be consensual. The masochist, like Odysseus, is bound at his own request by people who are in some sense his subordinates inasmuch as they carry out his wishes.

In the case of Odysseus there is a temporary but genuine transfer of authority—while those Sirens are singing, our hero's demands for freedom are not to be obeyed. The average masochist, by contrast, hands off only a sham kind of power, remaining in control throughout by means of such measures as a previously agreed on "safeword" whose utterance will bring the proceedings screeching to a halt. Bondage, in other words, is not a truly binding form of commitment; yet like the flimsy-seeming constraints we place on ourselves in other walks of life, it may be just binding enough for the masochist, who remains, as the psychoanalyst Jessica Benjamin has observed, "the hidden director of the experience."

The strange dynamic of S and M was dramatized quite vividly nearly three hundred years ago by John Cleland in the novel *Fanny Hill*, when Fanny's client Barville pays her to give him a ritualized flogging. First he puts on "some little show of reluctance, for form's sake," after which his own garters are used as "ceremonial" bonds to tie him down for a flogging. Fanny describes Barville as "enslaved to such a taste," which seems to fill him with self-loathing, and, in fact, psychologists consider sexual masochism, like sexual sadism, to be an illness if it causes distress or impairment.

In all likelihood, the recent mainstreaming of S and M will gradually diminish the stigma its adherents have felt. Nowadays S and M themes crop up regularly in popular culture; bondage-wear has influenced fashion, for example, as is obvious from a glance at the expensive leather women's shoes advertised in the *New York Times*. In the real world, masochism may be too harmless, too widespread—even too normal—to be considered truly pathological. Research (however dubious) indicates that around 5 to 10 percent of Americans engage in S and M play, and no doubt many more have such fantasies.

What's interesting, for students of self-control, is who these people are and what it is they like. Most seem to prefer the submissive, or masochist's, role—which is in keeping with the idea that modern life makes this especially appealing. Successful, individualistic people prefer this role especially, and, in fact, sexual masochism is found mainly in successful, individualistic societies—in other words, in the West. While most sexual practices are as old as, well, sex, masochism apparently emerged only in the period from 1500 to 1800, a time when individuality flourished.

In his *Confessions*, first published late in the eighteenth century, Rousseau frankly confesses a lifelong desire to be spanked and dominated by women. "To fall on my knees before a masterful mistress, to obey her commands, to have to beg for her forgiveness, have been to me the most delicate of pleasures," he reports in both embarrassment and relief, explaining, "It is the ridiculous and the shameful, not one's criminal actions, that it is hardest to confess."

All this said, it's perhaps not surprising that men apparently like S and M more than women do, and their prevailing taste for submission, given traditional sex roles and the difference in physical size between men and women, looks a lot like willful gender reversal. For men, it seems, sexual submission is a chance to play at abdicating control over themselves and those around them.

There is also evidence that this is a taste of powerful men—men like Max Mosley, the former British overseer of grand prix motor racing, who,

while he was president of the Formula One governing body, made headlines after he was videotaped in a sadomasochistic sex scene. According
to the *New York Times*, Mosley was bound naked and lashed more than
twenty times on camera. He might have consoled himself after the scandal with the knowledge that his masochistic tendencies were more embarrassing than rare, especially for men of his social class. Roy Baumeister
reports that prostitutes get most of their masochistic requests from rich
and powerful men; one study found that call girls in Washington, D.C.,
were asked for quite a bit of S and M—and that requests for M outnum-
bered the opposite eight to one. "The bigger the burden of the ego," Baumeister writes, "the more likely people seem to be to turn to masochism."

Surely part of its appeal is that the masochist remains, ultimately,
in charge, although there are ways for him to commit to his own subjugation for a period longer than he may later prefer. Even mainstream retailers, such as Cartier, for example, sell jewelry that cannot
be removed without a tool or key—on the premise, I assume, that the
means of release will be given to one's lover, who will at times be absent
or unavailable or even, potentially, uncooperative.

Chastity belts carry this idea further. If the belt makers are to be
believed—and their numbers evidently have been increasing—sales of
these devices have been on an upward trajectory for the past decade or so,
thanks perhaps to the Internet, where anybody can find anything without a
lot of embarrassment. The more expensive devices boast of being inescap-
able without a key, which presumably is never in the wearer's possession.
This suggests something like the temporary (and temporarily irrevocable)
transfer of authority carried out by Odysseus when faced with the Sirens.
Speaking of sirens, you can now buy serious chastity devices made of
high-tech plastic guaranteed not to set off airport security alarms.

"Live all you can; it's a mistake not to."

So said Henry James. Unfortunately there are no patients rights organizations for the victims of excessive farsightedness, no fund-raising 5K runs

or colored wristbands, or emotionally greedy magazine ads from which the cautious eyes of the excessively prudent stare out at us, pleading mutely for rescue. No, the tragic plight of these quiet victims of virtue is ignored by virtually everyone—everyone except the novelists.

Novelists love the subject. Remember Macon Leary, in *The Accidental Tourist*, who travels with a flask of sherry in case of a sleepless night? The trouble, for a guy like Leary, is when to use it: "He's gone on saving it for some occasion even worse than whatever the current one was, something that never quite arrived . . . In fact its metal lid had grown rusty inside, as he discovered when he unscrewed it." Until the selfless Leary finally makes like a Saint Bernard—he opens the flask for a stranger who is terrified of flying—his hoarding of this emergency hooch looks like an example of what one economist calls "the paradox of the indefinitely postponed splurge."

Novels weren't always this concerned with over-control. In the nineteenth century, women such as Hester Prynne, Anna Karenina, and Madame Bovary paid dearly for their inability to resist temptation—but so did such unfortunate men as R. R. Raskolnikov, whose terrible crime led inexorably to punishment; Michael Henchard, the alcoholic mayor of Casterbridge who was excess personified; and hapless George Hurstwood, the embezzler who came to such a bad end even as Sister Carrie was bound for stardom. Then there was *McTeague,* in which immoderate temper and greed claim the lives of men and women alike.

Robert Louis Stevenson gives us perhaps the frankest and most sophisticated treatment of this theme in *The Strange Case of Dr. Jekyll and Mr. Hyde*, a wonderfully complex metaphor for the interaction of self-command, addiction, and technology, all in the ethically murky context of Victorian London. The good Dr. Jekyll, eager to taste the forbidden fruit growing on the foggy streets all around him, first needs to invent a potion in order to cut loose. Then he needs a potion to regain control of himself—a potion that grows less and less effective in the face of his habitual indulgence of Mr. Hyde. Jekyll learns to his rue that we can't separate ourselves from our sins—and, for that matter, that when our planning selves work with our impulsive selves, they can make quite a morally dangerous duo.

At some point, though, the emphasis seems to have shifted from the wages of sin to the high price of suppression. Lambert Strether (in Henry James's *The Ambassadors,* published just a few years after *Sister Carrie* and *McTeague*) and George Babbitt (the eponymous character in the 1922 novel by Sinclair Lewis) suffered the sharp pain of regret for their inhibitions. And what could be sadder, in a more recent example, than the pathetic butler Stevens, in Kazuo Ishiguro's *The Remains of the Day,* who is so repressed that he can't even tell, until years after the fact, that he's been in love?

The need for the uptight to cut loose is a stock plot element in Hollywood as well. In *The Philadelphia Story* (1940), Katharine Hepburn is Tracy Lord, a Main Line heiress whose ex-husband (Cary Grant) is a drunken, wife-abusing lout and whose father jeopardizes the family's reputation with his scandalous womanizing. Both men naturally assail Lord as an icy and unforgiving prig; her father even seems to blame her for his own transgressions. In fact, she is just the kind of accomplished, self-respecting, independent-minded person anyone ought to admire, except perhaps for her taste in men. But in the film, Lord achieves true personhood only by getting herself stinking drunk. The cutting-loose theme has been especially prevalent in romances and buddy films; Leo Bloom even offers an extenuating version to the judge in his courtroom speech at the end of *The Producers* (1968) as part of an effort to win leniency for the incorrigible Max Bialystock.

Yet in real life, the costs of repression are often dubious. Who knows what regrets Lambert Strether might have had from leading a more devil-may-care life? Exercising self-restraint can be depleting, yet it can also be ennobling, as it might have been for Newland Archer, who gives up his great love in order to stay with his pregnant wife in *The Age of Innocence.* Today we see mainly the cost of Archer's restraint and the sticky power of the social web that held him—without much valuing the benefits of these things to his children, his community, or even to Archer himself.

This brave new emphasis on cutting loose is reflected across the arts in the very shape of new works, which in the twentieth century were constrained by fewer of the formal requirements that once prevailed in, say, poetry and painting. Jon Elster, who wrestles with self-constraint and its advantages in such books as *Ulysses Unbound*, cites Henri Peyre's observation that "after a long century of individualism, many of our contemporaries seem to be overweighted by their absolute artistic freedom which has rendered any revolt insipid."

In the commercial arts, on the other hand, form seems to be everything. Hollywood movies are as formulaic as medieval religious painting, yet those oppressed by the constant exertion of self-control can find vicarious release in what Peter Stearns has called a "fantasy culture of excess." An example: the garish spectacle of professional football, in which players rage, exult, attack one another, and embrace teammates freely. Other popular compensating outlets might include rap music (for white middle-class boys), or TV shows such as *Family Guy* or *Married with Children*, in which people are blatantly awful or lacking in self-control. As one of Aristotle's dreary temperate men, I always get a kick out of Homer Simpson; when he makes himself his famous moon waffles (caramels, batter, and liquid smoke cooked on a waffle iron, then wrapped around a stick of butter and eaten burrito-style), I know that in some sense he's eating them for us.

Collective Hyperopia

Not surprisingly, hyperopia can afflict groups as well as individuals. Freud speculated that the Jews might have a hyperactive superego, and the historian Jerry Z. Muller, who is learned in Jewish tradition and intellectual history, once told me that "the Jews are a people of self-restraint." What better system of precommitment than Jewish law?

But it's hard to pin hyperopia on this particular tribe, much as Philip Roth has tried. On the contrary, the Jews' success in the modern world may well be the result of their extraordinary tradition of self-control, a tradition in which Freud (and many of his Jewish patients) fully participated. American Jews drink less, get more education, achieve greater affluence, and engage in less violence than other groups. There is a stereotype—of the New York Jew, for instance—that Jews can be impatient, but if that's true, it's only in the service of a longer-range plan. (Perhaps, like the Puritans, they have bigger fish to fry.) Anyway, I suspect that Jewish impatience, like so many stereotypes, is a canard; who on earth is more patient than a people still waiting for the Messiah, after all this time and all this trouble?

China, on the other hand, may be an example of an entire country beset by hyperopia—possibly as the result of national policy. The profitable counterweight to America's frenzied, present-oriented overconsumption in recent years has been China's determined delay of gratification, the better to invest in the factories and equipment needed to produce the exports America wanted—and to fund those exports with Chinese loans, in the form of Treasury securities. The Chinese savings rate was so high that, by using their mountains of dollars to bid up Treasuries, the Chinese helped suppress U.S. interest rates, which in turn fueled the bubble that led to the boom that ultimately went pop. Everyone—including the Chinese—probably would have been better off if people over there had saved less and consumed more.

But can we really characterize whole cultures with respect to their ability to defer gratification? Are some societies more future-oriented than others? In the course of a multiyear study of seventeen thousand middle managers in sixty-one societies, business scholar Mansour Javidan tried to find out. He discovered that when it comes to delaying gratification, investing, and planning, cultures differ widely. He found that Singapore was the most future-oriented, followed by Switzerland, the Netherlands, Malaysia, and Austria. Japan also did pretty well. Russia was the biggest loser, followed by Argentina, Poland, Colombia, and Venezuela. The United States did quite well, given that size and diversity were not otherwise correlated with a high score. It was future-oriented all right, but not enough to be described (as Singapore could be) as hyperopic.

19

Government and
Self-government

We must give up the insane illusion that a conscious self, however virtuous and however intelligent, can do its work single-handed and without assistance.

—ALDOUS HUXLEY

If self-mastery is such a problem, should we demand that government do more to protect us from ourselves? And is it really capable of doing so?

The answers are yes and maybe. Governments operate under many disabilities, including, to name just a couple, the politicians and the electorate. And Americans have a long tradition of not wanting a great deal of government. That people are freer here—even if we are freer to commit financial hara-kiri—is a source of our strength, I think, and uniqueness. Besides, there are always good reasons to be wary of the power of the state—and to be skeptical that someone in officialdom really knows what is better for each of us than we do. John Stuart Mill expressed the position succinctly in *On Liberty*: "The only purpose for which power may be rightfully exercised over any member of a civilized community, against his will, is to prevent harm to others. His own good, either physical or moral, is not a sufficient warrant."

Ah, but there is evidence that, left completely to his own devices, he *will* harm others—for example, by running up debts that will later need to be socialized. And recall that few of us can live up to our second-order preferences without some outside assistance. The problem isn't just weakness; we're also ignorant, and by this I mean something other than unschooled. I'm talking here about the impenetrable complexity of modern life, the limits of time, energy, and rationality, and our inability to sort everything out for ourselves. How many of us really want government to abolish medical licensing and allow anyone to set up shop as a surgeon? Do we really believe we have the ability to judge basic competence in this realm? How many of us want government to do away with auto safety regulation? Or allow swimming in treacherous waters, with their hidden currents and depths, when the lifeguards are off duty? "I suggest we think of the imposition of paternalistic interferences in situations of this kind," the philosopher Gerald Dworkin writes, "as being a kind of insurance policy which we take out against making decisions which are far reaching, potentially dangerous, and irreversible."

Our ignorance, moreover, makes it hard for us to guard against weakness. When people exercise, for example, they often end up overeating; ignorant of the actual number, they overestimate how many calories they've burned by exercising and feel entitled to eat a lot more. And then there is the problem of protecting ourselves from the weakness of others. Isn't gun control a way of enlisting government to guard against the passions of our neighbors? As Adam Smith puts it in *The Theory of Moral Sentiments,* "There are some situations which bear so hard upon human nature that the greatest degree of self-government . . . is not able to stifle, altogether, the voice of human weakness, or reduce the violence of the passions."

One way the government might protect us, paradoxically, is to expose us fully to the consequences of our actions, no matter how terrible. If societies let people starve, for example, they would be a lot more careful with their money. If hospitals didn't have to treat the uninsured, more people would get insurance. A few horror stories might scare many more citizens into cleaning up their act. But we are not prepared to let people die in the streets, thankfully, and we do not want to live in a society that would. Some people are merely victims of misfortune, after all, and most of us believe they deserve help. The problem is that once we take up this burden, however reluctantly and inconsistently, we become all the more invested in one another's choices.

Questions about the role of government have been asked with renewed insistence since the financial crisis, which laid bare the inadequate regulation of major players such as Citicorp and AIG, whom the taxpayers had to bail out in order to save the financial system. The crisis also made clear the inability of average citizens to properly assess complicated and risky financial products, never mind their own ability to repay what they borrow, leading too many of us to take on too much debt from too many greedy or myopic lenders. It's wonderful to give everyone access to powerful financial tools, but in retrospect even the experts couldn't use many of them safely. Perhaps it's not so very cruel to keep monkeys away from dynamite and matches.

In the modern world, with its weak family ties and strong temptations, it's inevitable that some part of this job should fall to government. One reason we have a government is that individuals cannot adequately regulate themselves. David Hume is good on this point; in his view, our response to intertemporal choice—our preference for lesser, sooner objects over larger, later ones—will lead us to pursue our own short-run interests in ways that are damaging to ourselves and our society. Even those who are not inclined to act in this way would be forced to do so by the stampede of the rest to grab what they can today without regard for tomorrow. The prudent would suffer right along with the imprudent— as is happening today.

Hume's answer was a government that, with the consent of the governed, will constrain some behavior for the good of all. This government would be a kind of precommitment device by means of which people would give up some authority over themselves so as to counteract their natural myopia. In this way, people might "acquire a security against each other's weakness and passion, as well as against their own."

There is a potentially slippery slope problem here—give the government enough authority and you have North Korea. Nonetheless, I think government can and should do more—at the very least, it needs to step in where informational asymmetries or dangerous appetites make people easy marks for amoral profit seekers. It needs to shape the public realm in ways that promote healthy choices. And most of all, it needs to provide strong weapons of precommitment to those who would use them.

It won't be easy.

The Difficulty with Democracy

Democracy presents problems because it depends on individuals who might not be good at controlling themselves nonetheless voting for others to do the job for them. It needs people to have some second-order preferences—and a willingness to let someone else enforce them. There is the added problem, in any government, that it must consist of human beings—all of them subject to the same temptations as the rest of us, and in addition, to the unique temptations of power.

Alexis de Tocqueville, the uncannily observant Frenchman who discovered practically everything we would ever need to know about America, recognized long ago that self-control can pose problems for a democracy. Here is his devastating diagnosis, no less accurate today than the day he made it:

> The difficulty experienced by democracy in conquering the passions and silencing the desires of the passing moment in the interest of the future can be observed in the United States in the most trivial of things. The people, surrounded by flatterers, find it difficult to master themselves. Every time they are asked to impose some privation or discomfort even for an aim their reason approves, they almost start by refusing.

Not just at first, either. Ever since the 1973 Arab oil embargo sparked gasoline lines all across the country, Americans have known that we have an energy problem. Subsequent oil shocks, the increasing realization that oil imports were funding some of the world's worst regimes, and a growing consensus that burning fossil fuels is warming the planet, possibly catastrophically, still haven't prompted any significant change in behavior. Not only is there a complete absence of political will for meaningful new energy taxes, but when oil prices go up some politicians demand that energy taxes be cut to help people cope. When it comes to oil, as with so many things, we are unable to overcome our inclinations.

Why do we lack the political will to make a change? First, as Tocqueville observed, it's hard for elected representatives to ask the voters to do anything unpleasant. Democracy, at least as practiced in America, is the opposite of paternalism. Uncle Sam is a kind of Dutch uncle, easygoing and indulgent, who doesn't even try to make us take our medicine—and anyway doesn't want to buy it for us (unless we're old). Can you blame him? The electorate would surely turn out anyone who, for example, attempted to raise gas taxes or reduce Social Security benefits, no matter what the consequences of inaction. Democracy is good at promising people things, and sometimes even delivering. It's less good at taxing people to pay for them, which is why it excels at borrowing money.

Many of the strengths and weaknesses of our American system are a reflection of the founders' embrace of precommitment in the form of our Constitution. National constitutions often serve this function, especially constitutions as difficult to change as ours. These documents are a way to confine current and future citizens and leaders to a particular path and are adopted in full knowledge that folks might later think differently about things. That's the whole point, I suppose. "Constitutions," in the words of the nineteenth-century politico John Potter Stockton, "are chains with which men bind themselves in their sane moments that they may not die by a suicidal hand in the day of their frenzy."

That kind of constraint is necessarily somewhat inflexible; our Constitution has helped safeguard essential freedoms but has made it difficult for the national government of a large, complex nation to deal with large, complex problems, absent some dire emergency.

It's also hard for democratic governments to put the proper empha-sis on the future because today's voters are the ones casting ballots, and those voters care less about the voters of tomorrow than they care about themselves. So democratic governments tend to overpromise and undertax, relying on budget-balancing gimmicks and excessively rosy projections of future revenue. Thus, at the end of 2008, public pen-sions in this country had $3 trillion in liabilities but only $2 trillion in assets. These huge obligations arise due to the willingness of politicians to promise costly pension benefits to public employees. The promises bring immediate benefits—mollified workers, campaign contributions, employee support at the polls, and perhaps even lower cash wages for public employees, which helps keep taxes down. All the immediate beneficiaries, including the electorate, have reason to rejoice, since the costs have been deferred to their later selves or to future generations. These payers-to-come would be entitled to shout, "Taxation without representation!" if only they were around to make themselves heard. It's like the high hotel taxes you see in many cities; they exist because visitors don't vote.

Democracy suffers from an essential contradiction concerning self-control, which it depends upon, reinforces, and undermines all at the same time; in this way it is much like capitalism, which both breeds and undermines the restraint and calculation on which it relies. Yet the very idea of democracy implies some form of self-regulation on the part of the citizenry—and theoretically, a democratically elected gov-ernment ought to be a means of helping people commit to their best interests. Make no mistake: any vacuum left by individual willpower will tend to be filled by the state and its proxies. Even the citizens of well-established democracies will accept the infringement of civil liber-ties when freedom is not accompanied by self-command.

Thus in England, a place once known for self-restraint as much as it is for liberty, an Orwellian crop of more than four million public surveil-lance cameras—flowers of evil watered by crime—captures each Briton on camera many times daily. It's as if the United Kingdom decided to turn itself into a giant version of Jeremy Bentham's Panopticon, a round prison designed so that invisible jailers could watch any inmate at any time—creating a climate of constant surveillance whether anyone was watching or not. In the United States, meanwhile, employers demand not just résumés but urine to test prospective workers for drugs. In both cases, bad public policies would seem to be at work, yet these policies do not spring up in a vacuum, and it's fair to say that civil liberties were compromised at least partly as the result of crime and drug abuse—of lapses, in other words, of self-regulation. "Men are qualified for civil liberty," Edmund Burke wrote in 1791, "in exact proportion to their disposition to put moral chains upon their own appetites.

Our own government presents us with many good examples of how mechanisms of control can fail, including most famously Prohibition and its equally ugly latter-day correlate, the war on drugs. Even before Prohibition, elected leaders had taken to adding repulsive chemicals to cheap industrial alcohol (a project later ramped up to include lethal poisons) so that people wouldn't drink it. This form of collective pre-commitment, echoing what individuals can do with Antabuse and the like, evidently proved fatal to thousands of Americans.

Control measures sometimes also backfire by encouraging abandon. Federal deposit insurance is an example. Think back to the thrift crisis of the 1980s; savers had every incentive to park their money with the riskiest institutions—which paid the highest interest rates—because they knew that if that thrift failed, Washington would pay them back. When thrifts started to fail in large numbers, the insurance magnified the scope of the disaster—and left taxpayers in the position of reimbursing depositors who had reaped extra gains because they were indifferent to the risk involved in investing with dodgier institutions. It's possible that the rise of the modern welfare state has undermined the private safety nets once provided by individual savings, family ties, fraternal organizations, and other powerful nongovernmental social institutions.

Yet there's no point pretending government has no place in protecting us from ourselves—or that its successes are few. Thalidomide was kept off the market in this country by a vigilant federal official, Dr.

Frances Oldham Kelsey. Seat belt laws have saved lives, as have workplace safety regulations and government funding for science, which
helps underwrite medical advances. And thanks partly to public education and government policies that include higher taxes on tobacco, the
prevalence of smoking in the United States today is roughly half what
it was in the 1950s. Indeed, we cut per capita cigarette consumption
more than any other nation from 1970 to 2000 (although that probably
accounts in part for why we've also gained more weight than people in
other countries).

How Government Can Help

It seems to me that the first step in determining what government's
role should be is to acknowledge that the government already exercises quite a bit of influence over behavior and always will. Through
the tax code, for example, Uncle Sam encourages people to buy bigger houses than they need, diverts resources to home construction, and
makes home ownership more appealing than renting. Some changes in
the government's own behavior, in fact, could have a big economic pay-
off by saving us just a little from ourselves. Taxing consumption rather
than earnings would probably bolster savings and reduce consumer
indebtedness even while increasing productivity. A consumption tax
could be quite progressive and vastly simpler than the income tax system we have now, although, of course, even Einstein's theory of relativity is easier to understand than the American tax code.

The second step is to acknowledge that any time government limits
our choices for our own protection, it levies a kind of tax on those most
capable of taking care of themselves (the wealthy, the well educated,
the highly conscientious), who suffer some loss of advantage. But the
advantage isn't altogether lost; for the most part, it's just transferred—
to those least able to control their impulses (the poor, the underedu-
cated, the marginalized). I am willing to admit, in other words, that
greater paternalism will have a price, and I am willing to pay it. I doubt

I will have a choice because, short of allowing people to perish as the result of their improvidence, I'm going to pay one way or another, just as the prudent are now forced to pay for the financial profligacy of others. The global financial system will always be too big to fail, and when governments rescue it now and again, responsible taxpayers must pick up the tab. So yes, it would have been better for all of us if it weren't possible to buy a house with no money down and if we opted instead to require higher capital requirements for all borrowers, from Citibank to Joe and Mary Sixpack. As even Mill acknowledges, "it is a proper office of public authority to guard against accidents."

Just as individuals have to recognize the limits of willpower, societies recognize that private action can go only so far to constrain unwanted choices. Rare is the community whose laws protect us only against the actions of others, even if there isn't much rhyme or reason to these constraints. In the United States, some intoxicants (like cocaine) are prohibited, while others (like bourbon) are allowed. Gambling was once mostly off-limits; nowadays it's not. Suicide is against the law, but certain slow forms of suicide are actively encouraged, at least by the commercial interests that stand to gain from the consumption of tobacco or other less egregiously harmful products. Over the years, our government has sought to protect us at various times from drinking beer, owning gold, engaging in certain sex acts with other consenting adults, buying or selling a spare kidney, aborting a pregnancy, marrying a partner of another race, and eating some imported deli meats. The historical record is enough to make a libertarian out of almost anybody.

In many ways I am one, but libertarianism, too, has its limits. To a libertarian, the conceit shared by liberals and conservatives is that they know what is best for everybody. But libertarians also suffer from a harmful conceit—the belief that each of us knows what is best for himself *and* can enact these judgments. In reality, however, while most of us have some general idea of our own best interests we have only a limited ability to act accordingly in the face of human nature and temptation.

So what is to be done? Banning what people want doesn't work, as we should have learned by now from Prohibition and the drug war.

Higher sumptuary taxes on unhealthy items might help but would run into practical problems (is candy more harmful than cheese?) while penalizing those who eat and imbibe in moderation. A little alcohol, for example, is said to be good for you. So should booze taxes be higher or lower?

One easy answer is more and better education. You can't graduate from most colleges without studying a foreign language, but you can (and probably did) emerge ignorant of financial management and nutrition. Even if a national campaign to educate people on these matters had little effect on those who suffer weakness of will, it could at least bring around some of the thoughtless by raising their consciousness. Some of these impetuous akratics, as Aristotle called them, might be persuaded to form healthy second-order preferences and (God willing) adhere to them.

But what people really need are binding ways to commit themselves to their enduring preferences. As I mentioned earlier, several states and countries offer self-exclusion programs so that problem gamblers can have themselves barred from casinos for a fixed period. The programs are hard to enforce, and some self-banned gamblers have even sued casinos for letting them in. Nonetheless, these do seem to help; an evaluation of 161 participants published in 2007 in the *Journal of Gambling Studies* found a reduction in gambling problems as well as in the urge to bet.

Why stop with gambling? One can imagine all kinds of equally voluntary analogues; people could agree to be taxed for excessive weight or blood pressure, for example, as they already are by life insurers, who demand higher premiums from those with such risk indicators. Perhaps we could allow people to make voluntary additional contributions to the Social Security system—contributions that couldn't be withdrawn until retirement. And surely the notion of covenant marriage, which is harder to dissolve than the regular kind, is worth some additional experimentation. Couples might even be given a tax break every time they reach some marital milestone—a project that could give new meaning to the term "golden wedding anniversary."

Carrying this further, maybe purchases of cigarettes or alcohol could require a driver's license or official photo ID—and we could have the right to request a "no alcohol" or "no tobacco" label that couldn't be removed, at least until the next renewal. Several states (including, when I last looked, California, Texas, and Florida) had carried this precommitment concept quite a bit further with their castration laws for sex offenders. Although defendants can be sentenced to a period of mandatory chemical castration (a temporary measure that relies on medication), the laws also allow convicts to request chemical or even surgical castration. The Texas law was passed in 1997, inspired by a serial offender who begged to be surgically castrated before he harmed another child, and by 2005, three men had chosen to have the surgery. Said Bill Winslade, a University of Texas medical ethicist: "The three people who underwent the procedure, to my knowledge, have expressed no regrets and felt it contributed to their ability to exercise self-control."

All the warnings plastered all over everything are largely a waste, but any reasonable self-paternalist should welcome informational disclosures. Requiring freshness dates and nutritional information on foods surely helps—as does banning trans fats, which are invisible, poisonous, and without many redeeming advantages. There is every reason for government to acknowledge the power of automaticity in our choices and, by use of incentives, psychological "framing," and other techniques, to guide people toward what most of us would agree is best for us in the long run. The costs of not doing so are steep indeed, and as Locke reminds us, "that ill deserves the name of confinement which hedges us in only from bogs and precipices."

Since people who have poor self-control often have lower income and inadequate education as well, it might help to work harder on those things, even if we're not sure whether low income causes poor self-control or vice versa. Reducing income inequality (as national health insurance is likely to do) and improving the public schools (perhaps by ending their monopoly on public funding) would seem obvious measures that might help with self-control.

Voters often recognize their self-control problems. As noted earlier, this may explain widespread support for the Social Security system from an electorate that suspects it wouldn't save for its own retirement. In the United Kingdom, similarly, people more or less willingly pay a TV tax to fund the BBC, which helps to insulate the audience from its own worst instincts. In effect, U.K. voters have chosen to make themselves pay for the healthy media diet they know they should consume rather than the junk food they would likely choose on their own. (The tax, by the way, is quite a bit less than Americans pay for cable.)

The Anglo-Israeli economist Avner Offer has suggested that this is precisely why the public sector is so large in Western democracies, consuming roughly 30 to 55 percent of gross domestic product. In his view, people are sophisticated enough to know that the package of benefits provided by the state—a package they have to pay for—will do more for their well-being than they could accomplish if they were left to spend their money on their own. Taxes, in this way of thinking, are just a costly precommitment device by means of which the electorate makes itself forgo unsatisfying profligacy in favor of insurance against age, illness, and destitution.

But everything has its limits, including public spending and the patience of taxpayers, who are not so sure, over here at least, that the government can use their money more effectively than they can. There's an old saying about socialism: sooner or later, you run out of other people's money. The funny thing is that after the financial crisis of 2008, the same could be said of capitalism. Somewhere along the line, somebody has to exercise some self-control, as Burke reminds us: "Society cannot exist unless a controlling power upon will and appetite be placed somewhere, and the less of it there is within, the more there must be without."

20

Being Your Own Godfather

"We're not supposed to deny our nature."

"It's natural to deny our nature. . . It's the whole point
of being different from animals."

"But that's crazy."

"It's the only way to survive," I said from her breasts.

—DON DELILLO, *WHITE NOISE*

As graduate students at MIT about a decade ago, Dean Karlan and John Romalis didn't just feast on food for thought. That's why, as they completed their studies in economics, they found themselves getting fat.

Neither of them was terribly happy about this, but unlike the rest of us mere mortals who might buy a diet book or join Weight Watchers, these pudgy scholars were getting fat at one of the world's leading centers of economic thought. Karlan and Romalis knew a little something about incentives, so they struck a deal: each would have to lose 38 pounds in six months or forfeit half his annual income to the other. If both failed, the one who lost less would forfeit a quarter of his income.

It sounded great—who could pig out on Twinkies at those prices?— but for a while, nothing much happened, so they just extended the deadline until they both had to admit that they were getting nowhere. The possibility of extensions was undermining the discipline they had hoped to derive from their scheme, so they decided to get serious. The new rule was that if either tried to renegotiate even one more time, that would be the basis of immediate forfeiture.

I learned all this from Karlan years later on a sunny afternoon in New Haven, where I'd gone in my quest to find out just why self-control is so hard and what we can possibly do about it. Karlan is a stocky, low-key Yale professor nowadays, known for his work on Third World development. He told me he'd always struggled with his weight. It's a familial propensity; his mother battled obesity for years until finally she had stomach-reduction surgery.

But back to graduate school, where Karlan and Romalis found that the new agreement worked. By 2002, both men had lost the weight, and as long as the stakes remained serious and nonnegotiable, they mostly kept it off. At one point, Romalis's weight popped back up over the limit and Karlan actually collected $15,000 from his friend. He felt he had no choice. He had to take the money to maintain the credibility of their system—without which they'd both get fat.

For a while, when they were living in different cities, they kept things going by means of surprise weigh-ins; either had the right to demand one on short notice. But eventually they went their separate ways, and when I talked to them, both were struggling separately with their weight. Romalis, now at the University of Chicago, told me in 2008 that after ending his agreement with Karlan, he'd piled on the pounds. Karlan, too, gained weight in the absence of a financial penalty for doing so—until he set up a similar contract with his friend Ian Ayres, a Yale law professor. Karlan has kept his weight under control this way for years, at one point risking $50,000 on it.

Why must these disciplined intellectuals subject themselves to a Damoclean legal agreement just to control their eating? As Karlan explains it, the contracts work by counteracting the natural human tendency to prize short-term rewards—the taste of pistachio Häagen-Dazs *right now*—over such longer-term goals as a healthy body weight and reasonable cholesterol level. We can all make rules for ourselves; Karlan's weight-loss contracts raise the cost of breaking them. Could he have lost the weight without a contract? Over a nice, healthy salad one sunny afternoon, he answered without hesitation: "No."

Precommitment works, which is why Karlan set out to make it available to the world via his Web site, stickK.com, which might be thought of as the Internet's precommitment superstore. Karlan's venture, formed in partnership with Ayres, enables any of us to contractually control our own actions or, if we violate the agreement, to face a penalty we've chosen. Theoretically, it could make a Trollope of the most recalcitrant writer, allowing him to impose on himself the wanted law that cannot be disobeyed. Despite its nerdy origins, the site has a cleverly rakish motto: "Put a contract out on yourself!"

The concept is fiendishly simple. stickK.com (the second K is from the legal abbreviation for *contract*, although baseball fans will detect a more discouraging connotation) lets you enter into one of several ready-made binding agreements to lose weight, quit smoking, or exercise regularly, among other things. You can also create your own agreement, which many of its 45,000 registered users have done. You specify the terms (say, a loss of one pound per week for twenty weeks), put up some money, and provide the name of a referee if you want one to verify your results. Whenever you fail, stickK.com gives some of your money to a charity you've chosen. Whether you fail or succeed, stickK.com never keeps your money for itself.

If you want a sharper incentive, you can even pick what stickK.com calls "an anti-charity." Democrats, for instance, might find it especially motivating to know that if they fail to live up to a binding personal commitment on stickK.com, some of their hard-earned money will go to the George W. Bush Presidential Library. Anti-charities apparently are highly motivating; stickK.com says they have an 85 percent success rate. "All stickK is doing," Karlan told me, "is raising the price of bad behavior—or lowering the cost of good behavior."

(It should be noted that stickK.com didn't invent the anti-charity. In a 1984 book called *The Blackmail Diet*, author John Bear suggested people could force themselves to lose weight by committing to some hideous consequence if they didn't. Bear himself slimmed down by pledging to donate $5,000 to the American Nazi Party if he failed.)

You might jog for exercise this afternoon because of some vaguely hoped-for health benefit, but if failing to jog cost you $1,000, you would probably get out there regardless of the weather, your workload, or your sore ankle. And unlike Coleridge or Mr. Krabs, who in the heat of desire could all too easily countermand the orders they gave in the cool of reflection, people who sign a contract with stickK.com can't back out. Rest assured, says Ayres, that "these are legally binding contracts. I'm a contracts professor."

People use stickK.com to make commitments small and large. A number of users have committed to write a novel, while at least one has pledged to bring a brown-bag lunch to work. Many affirmatively commit to do something, such as pray daily or floss regularly, while others pledge to stop doing something (including at least one who vows to gradually lay off masturbating). A lot of the pledges are aimed at what might be called compulsive behavior, including nail-biting and "self-injury." Some, like the commitment to "stop calling my ex," are even poignant.

People on stickK.com do seem to be conscious of incentives. One user vowed to give up sugar, for instance, and pay $10 for any week in which she failed. One day she reported a transgression in her "commitment journal": "I ate gingerbread on April 9th. I knew I was hungry, but I had company and wanted to serve fresh baked goods. I thought I could resist it, but I did not. I only had a little bit, though. But now I'm feeling that since it cost me $10, I should have had a bigger piece."

Precommitment and the Poor

Dean Karlan had spent a good deal of time thinking about precommitment before launching stickK.com, especially in conjunction with his other great interest, Third World finance. A few years back, he and colleagues from Harvard and Princeton set out to investigate whether people would freely choose a precommitment device to help them save, and if so, whether it would make much of a difference.

They designed an elegant experiment that produced fascinating results, which they recorded in a paper entitled "Tying Odysseus to the Mast: Evidence from a Commitment Savings Product in the Philippines." They carried out their project on Mindanao, in partnership with a rural financial institution there known as the Green Bank. The professors first surveyed 1,777 current or former customers of the bank to assess how good they were at deferring gratification. The surveys asked such questions as, "Would you prefer to receive 200 pesos guaranteed today, or 300 guaranteed in one month?" And, equally important: "Would you prefer to receive 200 pesos guaranteed in six months, or 300 guaranteed in seven months?"

Customers who chose the sooner, smaller reward in answer to the first question but the larger, later reward in response to the second were deemed likely to have self-control problems. The researchers offered 710 of these individuals a new kind of savings account called Save, Earn, Enjoy Deposits, or SEED. These special accounts offered the standard 4 percent interest, with a single catch: withdrawals weren't allowed until either an agreed-upon date or sum was reached. (Almost all the savers chose a date rather than a sum, since failing to accumulate the latter could mean their savings were locked away indefinitely.)

Some 202 self-aware individuals, or 28 percent of those receiving the SEED account offer, accepted—a group that skewed somewhat female. And 83 percent of SEED enrollees also bought a *gananSiya* box from the bank. This is like a piggy bank with a lock—except that the bank holds the key. It's a way for savers to accumulate small sums by putting a peso or two into a box. The boxes are, of course, a poor man's precommitment device, in this case one that echoes, on a small scale, the design of the SEED accounts.

Karlan and his colleagues found that, for the participants, SEED worked. After just a year, SEED account holders had increased their savings by a remarkable 81 percent. It was a modest experiment, but it showed that giving people the opportunity to precommit can help them rapidly accumulate capital, even if they don't have much income.

The experiment also showed that lots of people with self-control problems know they have them. The SEED account participants mostly knew themselves well enough to purchase *ganansiya* boxes. This kind of self-knowledge isn't uncommon among the Third World poor. Researchers who studied poor South Africans found that they often relied on money guards—"a neighbor or relative or friend that you trust and say, 'Hold this, and don't let me touch it,' " one researcher explains. "Sometimes the same money guard asks you to hold their money, and so when someone comes to borrow money, you say, 'It's not my money.' It works."

Back in the 1990s, when it was suggested that early-withdrawal penalties might be discouraging Americans from saving more in retirement accounts, a survey found that 60 percent of us wanted to maintain the restrictions; only 36 percent favored making it easier to tap retirement savings early. Why such a lopsided result? I think it's because people understood how susceptible they would be to the temptation to crack open their own nest eggs—and they wanted the barrier left in place to keep themselves away.

I'm not surprised. I remember my mother, in the 1960s, dutifully making regular deposits into a Christmas club account at the local bank. On the surface, Christmas clubs make no sense; you have to make regular deposits—I seem to recall my mother having something like the kind of payment book you might get with a car loan—and receive little or no interest. Most amazing of all, the bank won't let you have your money back until December. But, of course, this was the reason my mother signed up; the arrangement forced you to save, and it kept your savings out of your hands.

I did something similar when I worked at a big newspaper and I signed up for automatic payroll deductions into my credit union savings account. Then, every time I got a raise, I raised the savings deduction by the same amount. My lifestyle never expanded with my income, but I did build up a pile of cash. I had colleagues who used the government's withholding of income taxes the same way. Those unfamiliar with this technique may not know that you have some discretion about how much Uncle Sam withholds from your paycheck; if you have a mortgage, kids, and other significant deductions, you should reduce the withholding to match what you'll ultimately owe, since the government won't pay you interest while it has your overpayments. On the other hand, you can't access the withheld money until you file your taxes—after which you'll get a nice, big refund. Think of the lost interest as a modest service charge, well worth it to people who know they might not save any other way.

Self-control sophisticates use the tools that happen to be at hand, as is apparent from the urban numbers racket. If you know how the lottery works, you understand the numbers game, except that the latter offers better odds.

I grew up around people who played the numbers. They'd wager twenty-five or fifty cents with a bookie on some three-digit number based on a dream or a birthday or some other likely premise, and if the number came in, they'd win. The daily number was always taken from some objective source that was ostensibly beyond manipulation; it might have been the last three digits of the day's take at Aqueduct, for example, or of the trading volume on the New York Stock Exchange. Like many people who buy lottery tickets, many numbers players play for entertainment.

But back in the 1970s, the sociologist Ivan Light looked at numbers gambling in Harlem and saw not a diversion or even "a tax on stupidity" (the term derisive economists use for state-run lotteries) but a functioning financial system—and an effective precommitment device to help people save. What outsiders didn't seem to understand was that Harlem residents didn't trust—and weren't well served by—banks. The so-called numbers racket, illegal though it may have been, partially filled this vacuum.

First, remember that the winning number is always just three digits, 000 through 999, so the odds of winning are a far-from-astronomical 1 in 1,000. And while the pot never contains millions, a winner who

bet $1 might clear $500 after the customary 10 percent tip to the run-
ner, who carries the loot back and forth. (No taxes are paid, of course.)
How did this add up to a savings plan for gamblers in Harlem? Well,
survey data showed that the lottery players were persistent, with nearly
75 percent playing two or three times a week and 42 percent playing daily, for years on end. In other words, they acted something like
long-term investors. And they were likely to get back $500 for every
thousand bets of $1 each. That may not seem like much of a return on
investment, but bear in mind that many players bet with quarters, a
sum that even among the poor tends to vanish unaccountably. They
got some hope. They couldn't raid their "savings" until they won. And
their money also bought convenience—numbers runners made house-
calls, and these visits no doubt helped people keep playing. In some
poor neighborhoods of India, "deposit collectors" perform the same
function. The collector gives a would-be saver a card imprinted with a
grid of 220 cells, and the customer commits to handing over, say, five
rupees for each cell each day. At the end, the saver would get back 1,100
rupees, less 100 rupees for the collector's fee. Savers are happy to live
with this negative interest rate in exchange for the convenience—and
the commitment device.

In Harlem, numbers players also knew that their money was sup-
porting black enterprise, local jobs, and a certain amount of neighborhood investment. But most of all, sooner or later you had a large sum of
money to look forward to—and no control over when it would arrive.

"Most gamblers understand their numbers betting as a means of
personal saving," Light reported, adding: "The bettor's justification
for this seemingly preposterous misconception arises from unsatisfac-
tory experiences with depository savings techniques. Once a numbers
collector has a man's quarter, they aver, there is no getting it back in a
moment of weakness. If, on the other hand, the quarter were stashed at
home, a saver would have to live with the continuing clamor of unmet
needs. In a moment of weakness, he might spend the quarter. Therefore, in the bettor's view, the most providential employment of small
change is to bet it on a number."

Precommitment and Paternalism

Perhaps not coincidentally, stickK.com has come along at a time of renewed interest in paternalism, a word that was once right up there with eugenics as a politically incorrect taboo. But lately a number of smart people, most prominently the economist Richard Thaler and the legal scholar Cass Sunstein, have suggested that the time is right for institutions to help people make better choices, by means of more thoughtful "choice architecture." The global financial crisis, with its accompanying borderless recession, has added impetus to these ideas. At company cafeterias, for instance, the fruits and vegetables might be displayed more prominently and priced more attractively than desserts so that people will be more likely to pick healthier items. The idea is not to mandate behavior but to present choices so that the indisputably better option is more likely to be selected. It's all about "soft paternalism."

The classic example is the movement in business to automatically enroll employees in a 401(k) plan, with the right to opt out. This is the opposite of the traditional approach, which relies on employees to opt in. It turns out that humans have a strong status quo bias, which is a fancy way of saying inertia is a powerful force in people's lives. In a study published in 2001, for instance, Brigitte Madrian and Dennis Shea found at one company that sign-ups among new hires rose to 86 percent from 49 percent after automatic enrollment was adopted. Reversing the default condition, which cost nothing and constrained nobody, thus significantly boosted the retirement prospects of a great many employees.

StickK.com lets people do this sort of thing for themselves. It's a place where they can act of their own volition to make themselves adhere to their second-order preferences—their preferences about preferences. You may like to smoke a cigar, for example, but you may also prefer not to have that preference. And your rational allegiance is to your second preference—the one that lets you avoid lung cancer and the other problems of smoking. The beauty of stickK.com is that it lets people decide for themselves which longer-term goals they embrace, in effect by becoming their own paternalists. And it gives them the means to enforce their own second-order desires, just as people do when they have their stomachs stapled or their jaws wired to constrain their eating. As Vito Corleone might have put it, stickK.com wants you to make yourself an offer you can't refuse. And what could be better than for each of us to be our own godfather?

21

Carpe Diem

. . . you and your crew may still reach home
suffering all the way, if you only have the power
to curb their wild desire and curb your own

—THE ODYSSEY

S o how can each of us be our own godfather? The answer is to shuck
the naïveté of the untutored in favor of a more sophisticated
approach to ourselves and our intentions. That means, first, relying
as little as possible on willpower in the face of temptation. It's much better,
like Odysseus, to row right past the cattle of the sun god than to count on
controlling the hunger that could lead to a fatal barbecue. It also means ac-
knowledging how much we are influenced by our surroundings—and taking command of our environment so that it influences us in ways we prefer.

Most important of all, a more sophisticated approach means recognizing that we cannot honor our best intentions by ourselves. If we are
to take control of our own destiny in a world of such unprecedented
freedom and abundance, we have no choice but to enlist the help of
others—not just family, but friends, colleagues, and community. The
only hope, in short, is to do all that we can to have ourselves tied to the
mast of our own intentions. Just like Betsy Keller.

Keller is a dietitian and mother in Greenwich, Connecticut, who likes to keep active, but in 2005 she tore a knee ligament in a skiing accident and found herself in a leg brace. Unable to burn up calories by exercising, she ruthlessly took matters in hand. After giving snacks to her kids, she put on slow-drying nail polish so she wouldn't be able to stick her hand into the snack bag and get some for herself. She served her own food on smaller plates to make the portions look bigger. She brushed and flossed her teeth after meals to ward off noshing during cleanup. And, when served dessert, she promptly covered half with salt, rendering that portion inedible (a tactic she learned from her mother, who maintains a healthy weight despite her advanced age). Keller told me that she did these things for a simple reason: "Those tricks work!"

People like Keller have to cope with the ambiguous signals that their tactics sometimes broadcast. She will strike most of us as exceptionally self-disciplined, yet there are times when we might conclude that someone so dependent on precommitment actually *lacks* self-control. A fat person who has his jaws wired shut in order to slim down, for example, signals to all that he couldn't control his eating without resort to artifice. Jon Elster has observed that, when it comes to booze, many societies have norms against drunkenness *and* abstinence. Sydney Greenstreet, pouring a drink in *The Maltese Falcon*, puts the point neatly: "I distrust a man who says 'when.' If he's got to be careful not to drink too much, it's because he's not to be trusted when he does."

By now it should be obvious that, regardless of the signals it sends, committing yourself—irrevocably, if you can—to your best intentions is the most powerful weapon available in the war for self-command. If there are options ahead that you'd prefer not to choose, foreclose them any way you can. The one mistake you shouldn't make is to think you can rely on willpower to do the job when the time comes.

On the Unreliability of Willpower

Willpower is usefully thought of as a muscle. You can build it up in the long run, but in the short run, like any muscle, it's prone to exhaustion.

Research has shown again and again that when our self-control is taxed, we are less resistant to temptation. Some people even think this is our essential problem: modern life imposes such a heavy self-control burden, in some quarters at least, that we're depleted much of the time. As Michel de Montaigne said of the soul, exercising it "must be done with some respite and with moderation; it goes mad if it is too continually tense."

Studies of what some have called ego depletion are quite straightforward. Researchers ask people to exert some self-control—perhaps by resisting a plate of chocolate chip cookies—after which a second task is presented requiring more self-control still. The depleted almost always perform worse on this second task than a control group whose members hadn't been depleted by any preliminary exercise designed to sap self-control. People who were told to avoid thinking about a white bear subsequently found it harder to stifle their mirth while watching a funny video. People who first had to resist chocolate then gave up sooner in solving difficult problems. Depleted individuals choose crappier entertainment and foods. Depleted dieters eat more.

In one interesting study, people were asked "to read aloud a series of boring historical biographies" while theatrically exaggerating their emotions with gestures and facial expressions. A second group of people were asked to read the same material aloud without changing their reading style. Afterward all were allowed to purchase common household items at a discount. Is it any surprise that the emotionally depleted folks spent more money? By the way, depleted individuals are also willing to pay higher prices.

It's not clear what biological processes are at work when our self-control becomes depleted, or how it gains strength over time from being exercised. Perhaps the relevant areas of the brain get better at utilizing glucose, or maybe exercising self-regulation increases the flow of key neurotransmitters. Interestingly, both self-control and decision making seem to draw on the same mysterious energy resources; perhaps we go around in a constant state of depletion as the result of all the choices we face in the modern world.

Glucose appears to play a role. In one study, people had their blood glucose measured before and after completing a self-control task. Sure enough, the level was significantly lower afterward. And the lower the glucose level after such a task, the worse the performance on a second such task. A glass of lemonade sweetened with sugar (but not Splenda) seemed to help. Think of the implications for dieters, whose struggle against food may be undermined by their own self-denial. "Willpower is more than a metaphor," Roy Baumeister has said. "Being our better selves is biologically costly."

What can we conclude? It would probably be hard to quit smoking at the same time you struggle to complete your master's thesis. A chocolate bar or a bottle of Gatorade might well be a useful restorative if your will is feeling depleted, although I won't argue with experts who recommend a diet of complex carbohydrates and lean proteins. It helps to get enough sleep, too.

And you might as well tell the truth, because it seems that lying taxes the same mental precincts as self-control. Using brain scans, psychologists at Harvard's Moral Cognition Lab have found that "individuals who behaved dishonestly exhibited increased activity in control-related regions of prefrontal cortex." The implication here is that lying depletes psychic resources you might need for resisting temptation.

Consistent with the notion that willpower is a muscle, there is evidence that it can be made stronger by exercising it. Maybe this is the reason so many religions require that followers periodically enact rituals of self-denial, such as fasting. Religious people do seem to have more self-control, but so do others who simply work at it. In one study, college students who were given two weeks of self-control exercises (improving their posture, stamping out negative moods) showed significant improvement compared to a control group in how long they could squeeze a handgrip before giving up.

The results of this experiment (led by psychologist Mark Muraven, who has pioneered research into willpower-as-muscle) would not have surprised William James, who exhorted us with characteristic nineteenth-century brio to keep the faculty of effort alive in you by a little gratuitous exercise every day. That is, be systematically heroic in little unnecessary points, do every day or two something for no other reason than its difficulty, so that, when the hour of dire need draws nigh, it may find you not unnerved or untrained to stand the test. Asceticism of this sort is like the insurance which a man pays on his house and goods. The tax does him no good at the time, and possibly may never bring him a return. But if the fire does come, his having paid it will be his salvation from ruin. So with the man who has daily inured himself to habits of concentrated attention, energetic volition, and self-denial in unnecessary things. He will stand like a tower when everything rocks around him, and his softer fellow-mortals are winnowed like chaff in the blast.

Yet every muscle has its limitations; even bodybuilders can't do push-ups forever. So while it's a good idea to follow James's advice, it would be foolish—or rather, in self-control terms, naïve—to abandon all the tactics in the sophisticate's self-management tool bag. If you want to avoid speeding in your car, for instance, use cruise control. If you're thinking of having a second drink before getting into the car, recite to yourself the names of your children, and call to mind their faces, perhaps clouded by grief. Better yet, take out a picture of them before you sit down at the bar. Powerful emotions about your attachments, like laughter and good feelings generally, are known boosters of willpower. Besides, guilt is your friend, and enlisting friends is always helpful—as long as they are the right friends.

Hell Is Not Other People

Inhibition so often begins with the sense that somebody is watching; experiments have demonstrated that simply installing a mirror makes people behave more honestly when, for example, they pick up a newspaper and are supposed to leave their money on the honor system. Mirrors also seem to diminish stereotyping, promote hard work, and discourage cheating. In one study of children, the mere presence of a mirror reduced the stealing of Halloween candy by more than 70 percent.

You can think of other people as human mirrors. "Our friends and relatives," Howard Rachlin writes, "are essential mirrors of the patterns of our behavior over long periods—mirrors of our souls. They are the magic 'mirrors on the wall' who can tell us whether this drink, this cigarette, this ice cream sundae, this line of cocaine, is more likely to be part of a new future or an old past. We dispense with these individuals at a terrible risk to our self-control."

Human relationships are vital in many ways, but in the self-control arena we are as dependent on them as Odysseus was on his crew, for we simply cannot bind ourselves to our own wills without other people. Participants in some twelve-step programs have sponsors they can call upon when the will weakens, and even stickK.com, the Internet precommitment enterprise, encourages users to name a referee who can attest to whether you've met your goals.

We've seen that loneliness subverts self-control, but community can promote it in a variety of ways, not least by minimizing social isolation and establishing norms. Communities are also social information systems, and being known in one is surely a moderating force, because reputations are valuable. Communities can reward with esteem and punish by turning a cold shoulder. You can use this knowledge against yourself. If you make New Year's resolutions, for example, you're much better off telling everyone about them—even putting them on a blog. Once this is done, you'll be much more likely to uphold them, since your reputation will be at stake.

Enlisting others in upholding one's own best intentions is a well-worn technique ("For God's sake, don't let me order any dessert tonight!") for a very good reason, and everyone ought to make use of it. The potential approval or disapproval of friends amounts to a free reward system you can turn to advantage, but the lack of such a system is a self-control disaster for many people. I think the single worst consequence of modern life is the erosion of its communal dimension.

People relocate much too lightly, abandoning the web of friends, relations, neighbors, and colleagues that was the source of their happiness
just for a little more money or sunshine or simply to try something new.
The end of a marriage often has similar consequences, tearing apart
networks of kinship and friendship. If we really want to take control of
our desires, we should reconsider this frantic flight from one another.

Friendship in particular is overlooked, but it may be our only prospect of filling the yawning chasm opened by the decline of family.
Friends are important, as Aristotle well knew, and should be chosen
carefully. There is such a thing as peer pressure, after all, which influences many of the things we do—and therefore it is wise to exercise care
in choosing the peers who will inevitably pressure you. "If you want
to change and maintain behavior over time," says David Holtgrave,
chairman of the Health, Behavior and Society Department at the Johns
Hopkins public health school, "you need people who are going to be
supportive of those changes."

You can also hire a friend by going to a therapist, but while Freud
may dominate our attitudes about self-control, you're better off avoiding psychoanalysis, the expensive and slow form of therapy practiced
today by Freud's heirs. You might instead look to Albert Ellis.

The sickly offspring of emotionally distant parents in the Bronx,
Ellis overcame shyness as a nineteen-year-old by setting himself the
task of speaking to every woman he found sitting by herself in the New
York Botanical Garden. Eventually he spoke to about 130 of them, and
although he only got one date, "nobody vomited and ran away. Nobody
called the cops," he told the *New York Times* years later. "I completely
got over my shyness by thinking differently, feeling differently and, in
particular, acting differently."

Ellis eventually became a writer and then a Freudian therapist,
but soon broke away from analytic orthodoxy to launch what is now
known as cognitive behavioral therapy. Unlike psychoanalysis, which
takes years and focuses on past relationships and traumas, cognitive
behavioral therapy seeks to quickly change the way you think about
your problems. The idea is to stop complaining, look at your situation

without emotional distortions, and take the steps necessary to straighten out. It's like Mrs. Pilletti says in the movie *Marty*, in the face of her sister's histrionics, "Don't make an opera outta this."

Cognitive behavioral therapists owe a debt to the Stoics, who emphasized human agency and a focus on the things you can control— such as your own reaction to circumstances and events. Ellis and the Stoics both saw emotions as largely voluntary states to which we can assent or not, as we see fit. Ellis, who wrote books on dealing with alcohol, anger, procrastination, and mood regulation, stressed changing the way you think about your problems. Self-deception, "catastrophizing," and other harmful mental activities are to be rooted out and subjected, along with other bad habits, to the merciless scrutiny of the prefrontal cortex. The idea is to acquire accurate knowledge about yourself and your environment and put it to use. Cognitive behavioral therapy is even something you can practice on yourself. Is it rational to eat just because something is bothering you? If not, then find a way to cut it out.

Use Your Environment

Don't be naïve: your environment acts on you in ways you can't begin to realize. So why not structure your environment to get the desired responses? All you have to do is make the default conditions of your life—the things that happen as a result of inertia—consistent with your second-order preferences. Better things are likely to happen, and you won't waste cognitive resources on a lot of unnecessary choices. Decide in advance to row right past the cattle of the sun god.

One of the best areas for investment in environment control is attention management. Remove distractions from your desk. If you want to spend less time on the Internet, use software to block access—or at the very least, turn off e-mail and disconnect chat programs for a while. Unplug the phone, resort to earplugs the way Odysseus's sailors did—anything to remove unwanted diversions. If you can't remove distractions and temptations, try changing the way you think about them. Avoid focusing on their most seductive properties and think about who you really want to be.

With regard to your home environment, don't buy the things you need to avoid. Shop when you aren't hungry. Order online, far away from the sights and smells that are so tempting in a store. Take your credit cards out of your wallet and leave them at home in a drawer. Imagine about how much you have to earn pretax to pay for whatever it is you're thinking of buying.

Another useful way of using your environment to bolster self-command is to make sure you have some exposure to nature. It pains me to write this, since the only nature that interests me is human, yet studies demonstrate that urban life, with its stress and anonymity, poses a threat to self-control. Cities are stimulating but also cognitively demanding; even a short walk in a city can undermine attention and memory. Children with attention deficit disorder suffer fewer symptoms in a more natural setting. A study of inner-city girls found that a view of green space accounted for 20 percent of variance in self-discipline scores. In a public housing project in Chicago, women whose apartments overlooked a grassy courtyard were better able to focus their attention and cope with major life challenges than neighbors lacking such views—and there was less domestic violence in the "green" apartments as well. Apparently Bruce Springsteen was onto something when he sang, "It's so hard to be a saint in the city."

If you're serious about living up to your second-order preferences—and you've taken the trouble to formulate some, as people often do when they make New Year's resolutions—then the truly radical approach is to treat yourself like one of B. F. Skinner's pigeons. People often do so instinctively by promising themselves a certain reward—opening the good wine, buying a new dress, taking a vacation in Hawaii—when a certain goal is met. But self-rewards can be tricky without appointing someone else to bestow or withhold the prize. If you don't mind treating yourself like a lab rat—and let's face it, we're not all that different—then friends and family members can be a big help. If I had told my wife not to let me take a drink in the evenings unless I could show her three new pages from the day's work, this book might have been in your hands months sooner. If she had withheld sex, it would have been done in 2007.

If you want to make a difficult but enduring change, announce it (to yourself and others) well in advance; an engagement period is always useful in getting one's intended to the altar. It's not by chance that the military allows enlistees a period of time between signing and induction. One study of charitable giving found that it rose when a delay was permitted between pledging and giving. Another study found that the longer in advance people ordered groceries, the less they spent—and the healthier their choices.

On the other hand, since speed and proximity kill self-control, it pays to keep a buffer of time and space between you and the most dubious gratifications. Scott Jaffa, for example, a systems administrator in suburban Washington, D.C., "destroyed the online access code for his 401(k) so he could no longer have instant access to his retirement accounts. His goal was to make it 'significantly harder' and to require 'human interaction' before he could trade on his own emotions." This act of precommitment helped him watch some stomach-churning stock market declines without taking any harmful action.

Writing a book is a great metaphor for the nature of modern work, which is unstructured, mental rather than physical, and often involves tenuous and far-off rewards. If you find yourself in this situation, the best bet is to set concrete goals, make sure they are reasonable, and monitor your performance, preferably in writing. (In keeping with the essentially adversarial nature of our relationship with ourselves, we should follow the Cold War maxim "trust, but verify.")

Controlling your environment means structuring your work in a way that makes it easier to do. Break big projects down into well-defined "proximal goals," which are easier to swallow and provide a daily sense of accomplishment. Your goal for today, for example, is not to write your book but just to produce two pages. Write them and you get to feel good about yourself even though the book isn't done. It's like melioration, except healthy; you get to choose short-term rewards, yet with each one you move closer to completion.

Controlling your food environment is especially important. Brian Wansink, the Cornell food-priming expert, suggests that you never eat cookies or anything fattening directly from the package; instead, put a handful on a plate. Serve vegetables family-style, in bowls on the table, but put small amounts of the fattening stuff on people's plates in the kitchen. If you're in a group, start eating last. At an all-you-can-eat buffet—and what on earth are you doing there?—establish a policy of taking only two items at a time.

One of the paradoxes about self-control is that it seems to take some to get some. Physical exercise, for instance, improves self-control. Exercise has been shown to diminish age-related shrinkage of the frontal cortex, reduce the risk of dementia, and in rodents, produce a variety of other brain benefits. But for most of us, who have much more sedentary occupations than our forebears, getting exercise requires an investment of self-control. Here, too, a certain amount of sophistication can help—for instance, if you can, live someplace that makes walking unavoidable. Or enlist a workout partner who can "force" you to show up at the gym.

One way exercise may boost self-control is by raising your serotonin level. Bright light seems to help with this as well, although eating turkey and other supposed serotonin enhancers apparently does not. Serotonin affects mood, but mood apparently also affects serotonin. (Actors, it turns out, can change their serotonin levels by "doing" different moods.) If you're in a bad mood, get out and do something active in the light of day. But leave your credit cards home.

The Advantages of Automation

Maybe the best way to uphold one's desired desires is to form a habit. A habit is a behavior that we repeat over and over more or less on autopilot, like Dr. Evil's habit, in the Austin Powers films, of coyly holding his pinky to the corner of his mouth. These behaviors may require conscious effort at first, but through repetition they become virtually automatic in the face of certain triggers. We all have them, because consciousness is a limited resource and human beings evolved to husband it. Thus, the conscious mind will off-load nearly anything it possibly can to the brain's more automated precincts, moving repeated activities from the prefrontal cortex into the much deeper basal ganglia and thereby saving processing power for more important things—and perhaps reducing the chance of error. "Civilization," said Alfred North Whitehead, "advances by extending the number of operations which we can perform without thinking about them. Operations of thought are like cavalry charges in a battle—they are strictly limited in number, they require fresh horses, and must only be made at decisive moments."

In fact, many of the things we do best we do without thinking. Remember your white-knuckle grip on the wheel when you first learned to drive? Operating the family car required every ounce of attention you could muster, yet evolved over time into something you could do unthinkingly while mulling a problem from work or listening to your kids bickering in the back. I can tie a necktie while talking to my sons, but if I focus on it I get confused. My wife can knit a sweater while watching a movie or commiserating with her friends about their boring husbands.

So habits aren't necessarily bad. What habits are is sticky. Bad ones, which seem to travel in packs, are the hardest to break because they are built from our most instinctual urges. Good ones are to be cherished; self-command can be achieved, Aristotle tell us, when "obedience to reason becomes habitual." William James devoted an entire chapter to habit in his monumental *The Principles of Psychology*, observing (with his own ardent italics) that "the great thing, then, in all education, is to *make our nervous system our ally instead of our enemy*. It is to fund and capitalize our acquisitions, and live at ease upon the interest of the fund. *For this we must make automatic and habitual, as early as possible, as many useful actions as we can,* and guard against the growing into ways that are likely to be disadvantageous to us, as we should guard against the plague."

James was right about the ethical significance of habits. And we seem to know that we are what we habitually do; as Mark Leary reports, "once formed, people's self-concepts provide an important source of input to their decisions. Our behavior is often affected by our beliefs about the kind of person we are—what characteristics and abilities we possess, for example. We sometimes do certain things because we see ourselves as the kind of person who does that sort of thing, and we resist doing other things because we're 'not that kind of person.'"

So our likelihood of following through on our intentions is a function of the extent to which we habitually do so. Thomas Mann understood this when he described Thomas Buddenbrook's struggling with exercise and smoking in middle age: "His will-power had grown flabby in these years of idleness or petty activity. He slept late in the morning, though every evening he made an angry resolve to rise early and take the prescribed walk before breakfast. Only two or three times did he actually carry out the resolve; and it was the same with everything else. And the constant effort to spur on his will, with the constant failure to do so, consumed his self-respect and made him a prey to despair. He never even tried to give up his cigarettes; he could not do without them . . ."

On the other hand, when we exercise self-control on a given occasion, we win for ourselves a little credibility we can rely on the next time around. Pretty soon we develop a reputation to ourselves that we want badly to uphold. With each test that we meet, our resolve gains momentum, fueled by the fear that we may succumb and establish a damaging precedent for our own weakness. How we spin our transgressions matters, too; if we see them as exceptions, or rationalize them as somehow intentional, they may be safely quarantined in memory without posing any danger to our resolve going forward. Pile up enough instances of intention and action and pretty soon you might push matters beyond the anxious realm of willpower into the clear skies of habit, where the autopilot can do the work. That's an accomplishment. "Habits," John Dewey rightly observed, "are arts."

If you want to avoid bad habits and cultivate good ones, it's worth bearing in mind that most depend heavily on environmental signals such as a specific time or place, certain people, a particular mood, or some actions you might repeatedly take. Behavior such as starting and driving your car along the familiar route to the office might once have been motivated by goals (getting to work) but soon becomes motivated by cues (morning, coffee, garage, etc.). We're not just dogs, we're Pavlovian dogs. "Habits are formed when the memory associates specific actions with specific places or moods," says USC psychologist Wendy Wood. "If you regularly eat chips while sitting on the couch, after a while, seeing the couch will automatically prompt you to reach for the Doritos. These associations are sometimes so strong that you have to replace the couch with a wooden chair for a diet to succeed."

If bad habits are a problem, good ones are precious because they lower the psychic cost of doing the right thing, and by eliminating the need for a conscious decision, they lower the risk that the right thing won't get done. "Be eager to fulfill the smallest duty and flee from transgression," the Talmud enjoins, "for one duty induces another and one transgression induces another transgression."

Homer and Ned

In America, it sometimes seems, you are either Homer Simpson or Ned Flanders. Homer is a slave to his appetites most of the time, although his fat-clogged heart is in the right place, while Ned (his Homer and Ned Christian neighbor) is a paragon of self-control, never letting his temper get the better of him even for a moment—but only because he's in thrall to a cultlike evangelism. Both men seem to be missing a fully functioning will.

I go back and forth when I think about which I'd rather be. Homer is selfish, shortsighted, flabby, and dumb, finding consolation in a bucket of fried chicken with extra skin; Ned is nicer, handsomer, has better-behaved kids, and runs his own business, yet there is something awful about him, too. The basis of his good life seems contrived, even prefabricated, and his relationship to choice efficient but somehow stunted.

The challenge, it seems to me, is to avoid the fate of both Homer and Ned by deciding for ourselves which of our preferences we like and then defending them against the importuning of those we do not. In Harry Frankfurt's formulation, this is what makes you a person; the alternatives are submitting blindly to impulse, like Homer, or submitting blindly to some power outside yourself, like Ned.

Faced with these options, we find ourselves once again in the position of Odysseus, who must navigate between Scylla and Charybdis as part of his long and difficult journey home. Fortunately, the nature of his heroism means that it is available to everyone, for while we don't have much say over the desires that we have, we certainly can decide which we prefer—and then search for ways to act on that basis.

The crux of our problem with self-control is the future and how much regard we have for it. Today the future looks scary, in part because we are so lax—about warming the planet, increasing our indebtedness, and eating ourselves into obesity. We can do better, both individually and collectively. But we should also remember that things could be much worse. If technology helped get us into this mess, it may well have the power to get us out. Can the time be far off when pills permit us to eat almost anything without gaining weight? What about when we're finally able to manipulate the genes of our offspring? Will some of us engineer superhuman self-control? Will the law require that we do so, the way it requires immunizations and schooling?

These questions will have to wait for another day, and another book. Meanwhile, let's look on the bright side. That self-control is the biggest problem faced by many of the world's people is a blessing in not much of a disguise. Self-regulation will always be a challenge, but if somebody's going to be in charge, it might as well be me.

Acknowledgments

I never could have mustered the self-discipline to write this book without the help of a great many wonderful people. Fortunately, expressing my gratitude is a pleasure rather than a chore, so procrastination won't get in the way.

This would have been a very different (and very much poorer) book had it not been for my friends at Bard College, in particular Jamie Romm, who patiently helped me avoid countless missteps in dealing with the Greeks. Jim Brudvig and Jeff Katz generously arranged library privileges, and Betsy Cawley cheerfully smoothed away library problems. Dimitri Papadimitriou provided a haven at the Levy Economics Institute where I could focus on revisions in a climate of serenity conducive to intellectual endeavor.

This would also be a poorer book had it not been for my friends away from Bard. Tyler Cowen, Eric Felten, Gary Goldring, Charles R. Morris, Lauren Weber, and Susan Wieler kindly read various drafts of the manuscript, offering encouragement and constructive suggestions when I needed them most. I especially benefited from Susan's copy, which came back redolent of suntan lotion. This tantalizing hint of life outside my office proved a motivating form of aromatherapy for an author already too long in solitary confinement.

There would probably be no book at all had it not been for the great Steve Lagerfeld and his crew at the *Wilson Quarterly*, which for years has provided a platform for my maunderings (and a safety net for my failings). WQ was where I first published on this topic, and it was thanks to Steve that the piece made any sense at all. Bits and pieces of this book originally appeared in his relentlessly nonhysterical publication, whose reputation somehow remains untarnished in spite of me.

Thanks also to the staff of the Woodrow Wilson International Center in Washington, D.C., where I spent a productive and joyous semester mulling the role government might play in saving us from ourselves. My colleagues—scholars, politicians, diplomats, journalists, and no doubt one or two retired spies—could not have been more stimulating and helpful. Special thanks go to the philosopher Nancy Sherman, whom I met at WWIC, and who cheerfully steered an ignorant scribe toward the relevant Aristotelian texts and away from misinterpretations of them.

While I was writing this book, three superb editors—Erich Eichman, Naomi Riley, and Nick Schulz—assigned me essays and reviews that helped clarify my thinking as well as pay the bills. Helpful scholars and writers include John Bargh, Kevin Beaver, Martha Finnemore, David George, Jeremy Gray, Gene Heyman, Dean Karlan, George Loewenstein, Mark Muraven, Susan Rozelle, Betsey Stevenson, Bruce Thornton, and Justin Wolfers. George Ainslie was especially generous with his time and his insights.

Someday all publishing may be self-publishing, but until that dark hour it remains a team sport. I was lucky to have a bunch of all-stars on my side, including Vanessa Mobley, Jane Fleming, and Virginia Smith at Penguin Press. Patty Fernandez, my copyeditor, is a wizard of the grease pen. I am especially grateful to my agent, Sloan Harris, and his staff at ICM. Nobody is more future-oriented than Sloan, which is why he makes so many good things happen in the present.

Ultimately, of course, it was all for Louise, David, and Nick. Just like everything else.

Notes

PREFACE

xiii **other than writing:** Tyler Cowen, "Self-Constraint Versus Self-Liberation," *Ethics 101*, no. 2 (January 1991): 360–73.

CHAPTER 1: A DEMOCRACY OF EXCESS

3 **who made it up:** David Marquand, "Accidental Hero," *New Statesman*, December 2007; http://www.newstatesman.com/books/2007/12/mill-british-john-intellectual.

5 **believe that 'anything goes':** Gary Alan Fine, "Everybody's Business," *Wilson Quarterly*, Winter 2008, 92.

6 **half of all U.S. deaths:** Daniel Akst, "Losing Control," *Wall Street Journal*, May 15, 2009.

6 **age, gender, and education level:** Robert S. Wilson et al., "Conscientiousness and the Incidence of Alzheimer's Disease and Mild Cognitive Impairment," *Archives of General Psychiatry* 64, no. 10 (October 1, 2007): 1204–12.

8 **overseas was a debt culture:** Mark Pittman, "Evil Wall Street Exports Boomed with 'Fools' Born to Buy Debt," Bloomberg.com, October 27, 2008.

11 **obtrude virtues noticeably upon others:** John Dewey, *Human Nature and Conduct: An Introduction to Social Psychology,* (Modern Library, 1957), 5.

13 **no different from an animal:** Harry G. Frankfurt, *The Importance of What We Care About: Philosophical Essays* (Cambridge University Press, 1988), 18.

13 **has no character:** John Stuart Mill, *On Liberty and the Subjection of Women*, ed. Alan Ryan (Penguin, 2007), 69.

13 **source of all liberty:** Daniel M. Wegner, *White Bears and Other Unwanted Thoughts: Suppression, Obsession, and the Psychology of Mental Control* (Viking, 1989), 19.

14 **comforts of the moment:** Anthony Trollope, *The Way We Live Now* (Wordsworth, 2004), 16.

15 **smaller when at a distance:** Plato, *The Dialogues of Plato*, trans. Benjamin Jowett (Random House, 1937), 124.

CHAPTER 2: SICKENING EXCESS

18   **inactivity and a lousy diet:** Jonathan M. Samet, J. Michael McGinnis, and Michael A. Stoto, *Estimating the Contributions of Lifestyle-Related Factors to Preventable Death: A Workshop Summary* (National Academies Press, 2005), 5.

19   **of course, some overlap:** Gene M. Heyman, *Addiction: A Disorder of Choice* (Harvard University Press, 2009), 14.

19   **middle-income countries:** Alan D. Lopez et al., "Global and Regional Burden of Disease and Risk Factors, 2001: Systematic Analysis of Population Health Data," *Lancet* 367, no. 9524 (May 27, 2006): 1751.

19   **86 percent of deaths:** "Largely Preventable Chronic Diseases Cause 86% of Deaths in Europe," September 16, 2006, http://www.medicalnewstoday.com/articles/52025.php.

20   **contrary to them:** Quoted in David George, *Preference Pollution: How Markets Create the Desires We Dislike. Economics, Cognition, and Society* (Ann Arbor: University of Michigan Press, 2001), 25.

22   **preceding twelve months:** "Smoking 101 Fact Sheet," American Lung Association; http://www.healthymissouri.net/cdrom/lesson3b/smoking%20Fact%20Sheet.pdf.

22   **white-knuckle it:** Julia Hansen, *A Life in Smoke: A Memoir* (Free Press, 2006), 39.

22   **global warming or self-control:** Juliet Eilperin, "Climate Shift Tied to 150,000 Fatalities," *Washington Post*, November 17, 2005; "WHO | Tobacco Key Facts," n.d.; http://www.who .int/topics/tobacco/facts/en/index.html.

26   **soared to 49 gallons:** Jane Allshouse, "Indicators: In the Long Run—April 2004," *Amber Waves: The Economics of Food, Farming, Natural Resources, and Rural America*, April 2004, U.S. Department of Agriculture, http://www.ers.usda.gov/AmberWaves/April04/ Indicators/inthelongrun.htm.

26   **fullest capacity for self-control:** Deirdre Barrett, *Supernormal Stimuli: How Primal Urges Overran Their Evolutionary Purpose* (W. W. Norton & Company, 2010), 52–53.

26   **diet or exercise:** Quoted in Linda A. Johnson, "Study: Over Half of Americans on Chronic Medicines," Associated Press, May 14, 2008, as published on signonsandiego.com.

27   **diabetes and cardiovascular disease:** Earl S. Ford, Wayne H. Giles, and Ali H. Mokdad, "Increasing Prevalence of the Metabolic Syndrome Among U.S. Adults," *Diabetes Care* 27, no. 10 (October 2004): 2444–49.

27   **perilously close to ours:** "Number of Persons with Diagnosed Diabetes, United States, 1980–2007," Centers for Disease Control and Prevention, n.d.; Margie Mason, "China's Diabetes Epidemic," *Time*, March 25, 2010.

28   **another form of self-control:** B. F. Skinner, *Science and Human Behavior* (Free Press, 1953), 232.

28   **suicide by other means:** "Guns and Death," Harvard Injury Control Research Center; http://www.hsph.harvard.edu/research/hicrc/firearms-research/guns-and-death/index. html.

29   **idea of suicide on its owner:** Quoted in Andrew Solomon, *The Noonday Demon: An Atlas of Depression* (Scribner, 2001), 255.

29   **on the Taft remained unchanged:** Scott Anderson, "The Urge to End It All," *New York Times*, July 6, 2008.

30   **you'll take your own life:** Aurelie Raust et al., "Prefrontal Cortex Dysfunction in Patients with Suicidal Behavior," *Psychological Medicine* 37, no. 3 (March 2007): 411–19.

30   **more cocaine and alcohol:** Dani Brunner and Rene Hen, "Insights into the Neurobiology of Impulsive Behavior from Serotonin Receptor Knockout Mice," *Annals of the New York Academy of Sciences* 836, no. 1 (December 1997): 81–105.

30   **pathological gambling, and kleptomania:** Richard M. Restak, *Brainscapes: An Introduction to What Neuroscience Has Learned About the Structure, Function, and Abilities of the Brain* (Hyperion Books, 1996), 117.

CHAPTER 3: ON HAVING YOURSELF COMMITTED

33   **to go against his orders:** "Krusty Love," *SpongeBob SquarePants*, September 6, 2002, reported in Internet Movie Database; www.imdb.com/title/tt206512/episodes.

33   **basis of a TV show,** *The Cleaner:* Mandy Stadtmiller, "Nixed Drink," *New York Post*, December 16, 2008.

34   **not to give it back to you:** Solomon, *The Noonday Demon*, 275.

35   **man without character:** Quoted in Janet Landman, *Regret: The Persistence of the Possible* (Oxford University Press, 1993), 172.

36   **immediately to his boss by GPS:** Tyler Cowen, *Discover Your Inner Economist: Use Incentives to Fall in Love, Survive Your Next Meeting, and Motivate Your Dentist* (Dutton, 2007), 170.

37   **she knew the combination all along:** Michael Shnayerson, "Something Happened at Anne's!" *Vanity Fair*, August 2007, 128.

37   **eat every last crumb:** Arnold Lobel, *Frog and Toad Together* (Harper & Row, 1972).

38   **in any shape or form:** Quoted in Ray Monk, *Ludwig Wittgenstein: The Duty of Genius* (Penguin, 1991), 171.

38   **clean dress means an unclean soul:** Katherine Ashenburg, *The Dirt on Clean: An Unsanitized History* (North Point Press, 2007), 59.

39   **no safety for us except in victory:** Thomas C. Schelling, *Strategies of Commitment and Other Essays* (Harvard University Press, 2006), 1.

40   **strong anti-Reform statement:** Quoted in Adam Gopnik, "Man of Fetters: Dr. Johnson and Mrs. Thrale," *New Yorker*, December 8, 2008.

41   **even for a moment a debt:** Rebecca West, *The Fountain Overflows* (New York Review of Books Classics, 2002), 21.

41   **Buffon wrote:** Richard Conniff, "Cultured Traveler: Seeking the Comte de Buffon— Forgotten, Yes. But Happy Birthday Anyway," *New York Times*, December 30, 2007.

43   **but was later edited:** Whitney Matheson, "A true tale of tattoo envy," *USA Today*, July 30, 2003.

44   **100,000 of them removed annually:** Natasha Singer, "Erasing Tattoos, Out of Regret or for a New Canvas," *New York Times*, June 17, 2007.

CHAPTER 4: THE COST OF GOOD INVENTIONS

46   **amounts of effort:** Thomas K. McCraw, *Prophet of Innovation: Joseph Schumpeter and Creative Destruction* (Harvard University Press, 2007), 9.

49   **adults considered themselves addicted to TV:** Robert Kubey and Mihaly Csikszentmihalyi, "Television Addiction Is No Mere Metaphor," *Scientific American*, February 2002.

49   **long-term malaise:** Quoted in Neil Tickner, "Unhappy People Watch TV; Happy People Read/Socialize," press release, University of Maryland, November 14, 2008.

49   **rocketed to 62 million:** Brink Lindsey, *The Age of Abundance: How Prosperity Transformed America's Politics and Culture* (Collins, 2007), 34.

51   **two hours is all people owned up to:** "Americans Waste More Than 2 Hours a Day at Work," salary.com, July 11, 2005; http://www.salary.com/sitesearch/layoutscripts/sisl_display.asp?filename-&path-destinationsearch/par485_body.html.

CHAPTER 5: THE PERILS OF PROSPERITY

55   **devoured the mother:** Quoted in Stephen Innes, *Creating the Commonwealth: The Economic Culture of Puritan New England* (W. W. Norton & Company, 1995), 26.

55   **Before he was laid off:** Douglas Belkin, "A Bank Run Teaches the 'Plain People' about the Risks of Modernity." *Wall Street Journal*, July 1, 2009; http://online.wsj.com/article/SB124640811360577075.html#printMode.

56   **wanted their money back:** Ibid.

57   **sixfold increase in just five years:** Mark Landler, "Outside U.S., Credit Cards Tighten Grip," *New York Times*, August 10, 2008.

58   **callous 'cash payment':** Karl Marx and Friedrich Engels, *The Communist Manifesto*, ed. Gareth Stedman Jones, trans. Samuel Moore (Penguin Classics, 2002), 222.

60   **effect of an age of individualism:** William Leach, *Land of Desire: Merchants, Power, and the Rise of a New American Culture* (Pantheon Books, 1993), 3.

60   **America of the 1880s and 1890s:** Charles R. Morris, *The Tycoons: How Andrew Carnegie, John D. Rockefeller, Jay Gould, and J. P. Morgan Invented the American Supereconomy* (Times Books, 2005), 177.

62   **dedicated to gluttony and vice:** Daniel M. Fox, *The Discovery of Abundance: Simon N. Patten and the Transformation of Social Theory* (Cornell University Press, 1967), 93.

62   **with a hoard of mobilized wealth:** Quoted in Leach, *Land of Desire*, 235.

64   **little un-American:** Quoted in Brink, *The Age of Abundance*, 73.

64   **feverish and unquenchable desire:** Ibid., 61.

66   **romantic impatient with the status quo:** John Patrick Diggins, *Ronald Reagan: Fate, Freedom, and the Making of History* (W. W. Norton & Company, 2007), xvii.

66   **led America into temptation:** Ibid., 5.

66   **a million in 2008 alone:** Data from *New York Times*, July 20, 2008, A15; Christian E. Weller. "Drowning in Debt: America's Middle Class Falls Deeper in Debt as Income Growth Slows and Costs Climb," *Center for American Progress*, May 2006.

67   **reckless mortgages:** Edmund L.Andrews,"My Personal Credit Crisis," *The New York Times Magazine*, May 17, 2009.

68   **the other to the 'lottery class':** Barbara Dafoe Whitehead, "A Nation in Debt," *American Interest*, August 2008.

CHAPTER 6: SELF-CONTROL AND SOCIAL CHANGE

71   **we rarely encountered women:** Tony Judt, blog entry, http://www.nybooks.com/blogs/nyrblog/2010/mar/11/girls-girls-girls.

71   **lifestyles and individual self-expression:** Lindsey Brink, *The Age of Abundance*, 5.

72   **his private interests:** Quoted in Jonathan Haidt, *The Happiness Hypothesis: Finding Modern Truth in Ancient Wisdom* (Basic Books, 2005), 133.

73   **new orientation to personal life:** Eli Zaretsky, *Secrets of the Soul: A Social and Cultural History of Psychoanalysis* (Knopf, 2004), 9.

74   **cohabiting unions:** Andrew J. Cherlin, "American Marriage in the Early Twenty-First Century," *The Future of Children* 15, no. 2 (fall 2005), 46.

76   **because they could lose them:** Quoted in Jon Elster, *Ulysses Unbound: Studies in Rationality, Precommitment, and Constraints* (Cambridge University Press, 2000), 14.

77   **his or her assets:** Mary Pilon, "Should I Get a Prenup?" The Juggle, WSJ.com, July 6, 2010; http://blogs.wsj.com/juggle/2010/07/06/to-prenup-or-not-to-prenup.

77   **and sleep less efficiently:** John T. Cacioppo and William Patrick, *Loneliness: Human Nature and the Need for Social Connection* (W.W. Norton & Company, 2008).

78   **resist harmful foods and intoxicants:** Ibid.

78   **frightfully alone:** Thomas Mann, *Buddenbrooks*, trans. H. T. Lowe-Porter (Vintage Books, 1961), 508.

78   **better and happier life:** Darrin M. McMahon, "The Pursuit of Happiness in Perspective," Cato.org, April 8, 2007; http://www.cato-unbound.org/2007/04/08/darrin-m-mcmahon/the-pursuit-of-happiness-in-perspective.

80   **society functions so differently:** Quoted in Sarah Bronson, "No Sex in the City," *Jewish Week*, August 3, 2001.

CHAPTER 7: THE GREEK WAY

83   **a slave instead of a free person:** Quoted in John J. Winkler, *The Constraints of Desire: The Anthropology of Sex and Gender in Ancient Greece* (Routledge, 1990), 50.

83 **either his appetites or his passions:** George William Cox, *Tales from Greek Mythology* (Longman, Green, Longman, Roberts & Green, 1863), 117.

84 **control should be exercised:** Helen North, *Sophrosyne: Self-Knowledge and Self-Restraint in Greek Literature* (Cornell University Press, 1966), 176.

84 **individualism and self-assertion:** Ibid., 258.

84 **sometimes rendered as "self-discipline":** Plato, *The Republic*, trans. Desmond Lee (Penguin Classics, 2003), 134ff.

84 **across the whole scale:** Ibid., 136.

85 **obedience to their rulers:** Ibid., 81.

85 **desires to wax to the uttermost:** Plato, *The Dialogues of Plato*, trans. Benjamin Jowett (Random House, 1937), 551.

85 **symbolizes their innermost aspirations:** North, *Sophrosyne*, 14–15.

86 **and most everything was:** James N. Davidson, *Courtesans and Fishcakes: The Consuming Passions of Classical Athens* (St. Martin's Press, 1998), 213–18.

86 **much greater exercise of restraint:** North, *Sophrosyne*, 12.

87 **during which he was not in love:** Eva Cantarella, *Bisexuality in the Ancient World*, trans. Cormac O Cuilleanain (Yale University Press, 2002), 55.

87 **frequently dragged about by desire:** E. J. Lemmon, "Moral Dilemmas," *Philosophical Review* 71, no. 2 (April 1962): 139–58.

88 **the physical and the moral question:** Dewey, *Human Nature and Conduct*, 19.

89 **not an act but a habit:** Will Durant, *The Story of Philosophy: The Lives and Opinions of the Greater Philosophers* (Simon & Schuster, 1961), 98.

89 **victory over self:** William S. Walsh, *International Encyclopedia of Prose and Poetical Quotations from the Literature of the World* (John C. Winston, 1908); attributes this line to Aristotle via Srobaeus.

90 **erroneous than the other:** Aristotle, *The Nicomachean Ethics*, trans. J. A. K. Thomson (Penguin Classics, 2004), 48.

91 **neither does one day:** Ibid., 16.

91 **voluntary:** Ibid., 61.

91 **contributes nothing to it:** Ibid., 50.

92 **they acted more in keeping with it:** Juliano Laran, "Choosing Your Future: Temporal Distance and the Balance between Self-Control and Indulgence," *Journal of Consumer Research*, April 2010.

92 **fits of madness:** Aristotle, *The Nicomachean Ethics*, trans. David Ross (Oxford University Press, 2009), 122.

93 **responsible for our dispositions:** Aristotle, *The Nicomachean Ethics*, trans. Thomson, 65.

93 **care for their appearance:** Ibid., 63.

94 **all the evil instincts taken together:** Jennifer L. Geddes, "Blueberries, Accordions, and Auschwitz: The Evil of Thoughtlessness," *Culture*, Fall 2008.

95 **mouthful more bread than meat:** Davidson, *Courtesans and Fishcakes*, 314.

CHAPTER 8: THE MARSHMALLOW TEST

97 **my Manhattan apartment:** Walter Mischel, *A History of Psychology in Autobiography*, eds. G. Lindzey and W. M. Runyan (American Psychological Association, 2007), 231.

97 **rum bottles passing:** Ibid., 240.

97 **without ever enjoying today:** Ibid.

98 **found no clear pattern:** W. Curtis Banks et al., "Delayed Gratification in Blacks: A Critical Review," *Journal of Black Psychology* 9, no. 2 (February 1, 1983): 43–56.

98 **by the experimenter's race:** Bonnie R. Strickland, "Delay of Gratification as a Function of Race of the Experimenter," *Journal of Personality and Social Psychology* 22, no. 1 (1972): 108–12.

100 **interacting and changing each other:** "Mischel's Marshmallows," Radiolab, WNYC, March 9, 2009.

100 **waited longest before chiseling:** Walter Mischel and Carol Gilligan, "Delay of Gratification, Motivation for the Prohibited Gratification, and Responses to Temptation," *Journal of Abnormal and Social Psychology* 69, no. 4 (October 1964): 411–17.

100 **concurrent associations are extensive:** Walter Mischel, Yuichi Shoda, and Monica Rodriguez, "Delay of Gratification in Children," *Science* 244, no. 4907 (May 1989): 934.

101 **arrive in the department mail:** Mischel, *A History of Psychology in Autobiography*, 243.

101 **I still put into quotes:** Ibid., 246.

103 **deployed during the delay interval:** Ibid., 247.

103 **instant responses to stimuli:** Walter Mischel and Ozlem Ayduk, "Willpower in a Cognitive-Affective Processing System: The Dynamics of Delay of Gratification," in Roy F. Baumeister and Kathleen D. Vohs, eds., *Handbook of Self-Regulation: Research, Theory, and Applications* (Guilford Press, 2004), 109.

103 **cloud floating in the sky:** Carey Goldberg, "Marshmallow Temptations, Brain Scans Could Yield Vital Lessons in Self-Control," *Boston Globe*, October 22, 2008.

104 **when they applied to college:** Mischel, Shoda, and Rodriguez, "Delay of Gratification in Children," 934.

105 **less than nine minutes:** Yuichi Shoda, Walter Mischel, and Philip K. Peake, "Predicting Adolescent Cognitive and Self-Regulatory Competencies from Preschool Delay of Gratification: Identifying Diagnostic Conditions," *Developmental Psychology* 26, no. 6 (November 1990): 980.

106 **road to building academic achievement:** Angela L. Duckworth and Martin E. P. Seligman, "Self-Discipline Outdoes IQ in Predicting Academic Performance of Adolescents," *Psychological Science* 16, no. 12 (December 2005): 939–44.

106 **than to achievement or aptitude tests:** Angela Lee Duckworth and Martin E. P. Seligman, "Self-Discipline Gives Girls the Edge: Gender in Self-Discipline, Grades, and Achievement Test Scores," *Journal of Educational Psychology* 98, no. 1 (February 2006): 198–208.

107 **used in college admissions decisions:** Raymond N. Wolfe and Scott D. Johnson, "Personality as a Predictor of College Performance," *Educational and Psychological Measurement* 55, no. 2 (April 1, 1995): 177–85.

107 **risk of aggressive behavior and delinquency:** Catrin Finkenauer, Rutger Engels, and Roy Baumeister, "Parenting Behaviour and Adolescent Behavioural and Emotional Problems: The Role of Self-Control," *International Journal of Behavioral Development* 29, no. 1 (January 2005): 59.

107 **smoking tobacco, and smoking marijuana:** Baumeister and Vohs, eds., *Handbook of Self-Regulation*, 548.

109 **how to exercise self-control:** Alex Spiegel, "Creative Play Makes for Kids in Control," National Public Radio, February 28, 2008.

CHAPTER 9: THE SEESAW STRUGGLE

110 **is always true:** Quoted in John Carey, *The Intellectuals and the Masses: Pride and Prejudice Among the Literary Intelligentsia, 1880–1939* (St. Martin's Press, 1993), 75.

110 **and that's not good:** Quoted in Tyler Kepner, "Rivera's a Closer with an Open Heart," *New York Times*, March 9, 2008.

112 **his polished surface:** Horace and Persius, *Horace: Satires and Epistles; Persius: Satires*, trans. Niall Rudd (Penguin Classics, 2005), 120.

113 **ethically rationalized pattern of life:** Max Weber, *Economy and Society: An Outline of Interpretive Sociology*, eds. Guenther Roth and Claus Wittich (University of California Press, 1978), 561.

114 **in a society of Puritans:** Dewey, *Human Nature and Conduct*, 5.

115 **individual and collective well-being:** Innes, *Creating the Commonwealth*, 30; on Puritan literacy, see Daniels, 27ff.

116 **libels against the best government:** Innes, *Creating the Commonwealth*, 159.

116 **something approaching four to one:** Ibid., 145.

117 **minimize the former:** James Q. Wilson, *The Marriage Problem: How Our Culture Has Weakened Families* (HarperCollins, 2002), 207.

117 **effective in an urban society:** Peter N. Stearns, *Battleground of Desire: The Struggle for Self-Control in Modern America* (New York University Press, 1999), 43.

CHAPTER 10: LET MY PEOPLE GO

121 **don't even know it:** Quoted in Mark Edmundson, *The Death of Sigmund Freud: The Legacy of His Last Days* (Bloomsbury USA, 2007), 32.

121 **victory over the other:** Carol Tavris, *Anger: The Misunderstood Emotion* (Touchstone, 1989), 41.

122 **it sends an obsession:** Rebecca West, *The Return of the Soldier* (Modern Library, 2004), 70.

122 **steamship for the trip:** Peter Gay, *Freud: A Life for Our Time* (W. W. Norton & Company, 1988), 454.

123 **specialist in the world:** Ibid.

123 **Freud had become a household name:** Ibid.

123 **American medicine and culture:** Eric Caplan, *Mind Games: American Culture and the Birth of Psychotherapy* (University of California Press, 2001), 9.

125 **adherents he found wanting or disloyal:** Gay, *Freud*, 316.

125 **Waldinger's words, 'by the clock':** Ibid., 157.

126 **improvisatory sort of place:** Ibid.

126 **without choking:** Quoted in Evan J. Elkin, "More Than a Cigar," *Cigar Aficionado*, Winter 1994.

127 **facilitation of my self-control:** Quoted in Scott Wilson, "Dying for a Smoke: Freudian Addiction and the Joy of Consumption," *Angelaki: Journal of the Theoretical Humanities* 7, no. 2 (2002): 161–73.

127 **intellectuals committed suicide:** William M. Johnston, *The Austrian Mind: An Intellectual and Social History, 1848–1938* (University of California Press, 1983), 174.

128 **cover under its name:** Sigmund Freud, *The Freud Reader*, ed. Peter Gay (W. W. Norton & Company, 1995), 33.

129 **some acknowledgement of self-control:** Willard Gaylin, "Knowing Good and Doing Good," *Hastings Center Report* 24, no. 3 (June 1994): 37.

130 **too-severe self-discipline:** Robert R. Holt, "Freud's Impact on Modern Morality," *Hastings Center Report* 10, no. 2 (April 1980): 38-45.

130 **acts of judgment:** Freud, *The Freud Reader*, ed. Gay, 18.

131 **there ego shall be:** Sigmund Freud, *New Introductory Lectures on Psychoanalysis*, trans. James Strachey (W. W. Norton & Company, 1965), 100.

CHAPTER 11: THE INTIMATE CONTEST

132 **an equal struggle:** Quoted in A. W. Price, *Mental Conflict* (Routledge, 1995), 183.

134 **who is controlling whom:** Skinner, *Science and Human Behavior*, 229.

137 **from another person:** Quoted in Jon Gertner, "The Futile Pursuit of Happiness," *New York Times Magazine*, September 7, 2003.

137 **managers of a firm:** Richard H. Thaler and H. M. Shefrin, "An Economic Theory of Self-Control," *Journal of Political Economy* 89, no. 2 (April 1981): 392–406.

137 **both master and subject:** Plato, *The Republic*, trans. Desmond Lee, 134–35.

137 **worst of all defeats:** Quoted in Michel Foucault, *The History of Sexuality, Vol. 2: The Use of Pleasure*, trans. Robert Hurley (Vintage, 1986), 68–69.

139 **express volitional deliberation:** William James, *The Principles of Psychology* (Henry Holt and Company, 1890), 122.

140 **yielding to whip and spur:** Plato, *The Dialogues of Plato*, 257.

142 **relies on the prefrontal cortex:** Russell Meares, "The Contribution of Hughlings Jackson to an Understanding of Dissociation," *American Journal of Psychiatry* 156, no. 12 (December 1, 1999): 1850–55.

142 **it's a bargaining process:** George Ainslie, "Précis of Breakdown of Will," *Behavioral and Brain Sciences* 28, no. 5 (2005): 637.

143 **about my further future:** Derek Parfit, *Reasons and Persons* (Clarendon Press, 1987), 313.

CHAPTER 12: THE MIND-BODY PROBLEM

146 **its own decisions:** Quoted in Steve Clark, "'Get Out As Early As You Can': Larkin's Sexual Politics," In *Philip Larkin,* ed. Stephen Regan (Palgrave Macmillan, 1997), 104.

147 **doctors operated yet again:** Jeffrey M. Burns and Russell H. Swerdlow, "Right Orbitofrontal Tumor with Pedophilia Symptom and Constructional Apraxia Sign," *Archives of Neurology* 60, no. 3 (March 1, 2003): 437–40.

147 **neurology of morality here:** Charles Choi, "Brain Tumour Causes Uncontrollable Paedophilia," *New Scientist,* October 21, 2002.

147 **defendant who had prostate cancer:** Nicholas Thompson, "My Brain Made Me Do It," *Legal Affairs,* February 2006.

148 **equipment for the old life:** Quoted in George Loewenstein, Scott Rick, and Jonathan D. Cohen. "Neuroeconomics," *Annual Review of Psychology* 59 (2008).

148 **stone-age mind:** Leda Cosmides and John Tooby. "Evolutionary Psychology: A Primer," Center for Evolutionary Psychology, University of California at Santa Barbara, n.d.; http://www.psych.ucsb.edu/research/cep/primer.html.

149 **people must make every day:** Mark R. Leary, *The Curse of the Self: Self-Awareness, Egotism, and the Quality of Human Life* (Oxford University Press, 2004), 180.

149 **what we need to, and delay gratification:** John Paul Wright and Kevin M. Beaver, "Do Parents Matter in Creating Self-Control in Their Children? A Genetically Informed Test of Gottfredson and Hirschi's Theory of Low Self-Control," *Criminology* 43, no. 4 (November 2005): 1175.

152 **proximate to the reward:** Steven Schultz, "Study: Brain Battles Itself over Short-Term Rewards, Long-Term Goals," Princeton University, October 14, 2004; http://www.princeton.edu/pr/news/04/q4/1014-brain.htm.

152 **talk to one another:** Ibid.

153 **has more dramatic coloring:** This discussion generally follows Deirdre Barrett, *Supernormal Stimuli: How Primal Urges Overran Their Evolutionary Purpose* (W. W. Norton & Company, 2010).

153 **low level of self-control strength:** Leary, *The Curse of the Self,* 180–81.

155 **no longer Gage:** Ibid., 180.

156 **the prod of some environmental demand:** Daniel R. Weinberger, Brita Elvevåg, and Jay N. Giedd, "The Adolescent Brain: A Work in Progress" (The National Campaign to Prevent Teen Pregnancy, June 2005), 2–3; http://www.thenationalcampaign.org/resources/pdf/BRAIN.pdf.

156 **characterized by poor impulse control:** Jane F. Banfield et al., "The Cognitive Neuroscience of Self-Regulation," in Roy F. Baumeister and Kathleen D. Vohs, eds., *Handbook of Self-Regulation: Research, Theory and Applications* (Guilford Press, 2004), 62ff.

158 **good at certain inhibitory tasks:** This whole discussion is indebted to Weinberger, Elvevåg, and Giedd, "The Adolescent Brain," 2–3.

159 **persistence, responsibility, and dependability:** Scott Shane, *Born Entrepreneurs, Born Leaders: How Your Genes Affect Your Work Life* (Oxford University Press, 2010), 26, 157.

160 **spiritual muscle:** J. C. B. Gosling, *Weakness of the Will* (Routledge, 1990), 163.

CHAPTER 13: SELF-CONTROL, FREE, WILL, AND OTHER OXYMORONS

161 **has a mind to do:** Benjamin Franklin, *Autobiography of Benjamin Franklin* (Henry Holt and Company, 1916), 68.

161 **they are determined:** Benedict de Spinoza, *Ethics*, trans. Edwin Curley (Penguin Classics, 2005), 53.

162 **they have little voluntary control:** Quoted in Ibid., 2-3.

164 **physical cleansing:** Chen-Bo Zhong and Katie Liljenquist, "Washing Away Your Sins: Threatened Morality and Physical Cleansing," *Science* 313, no. 5792 (September 8, 2006): 1451–52.

165 **influenced by environmental cues:** Quoted in Foreman, "Environmental Cues Affect How Much You Eat," *Boston Globe*, August 18, 2008.

165 **by example, not by choice:** Michel de Montaigne, *The Complete Essays of Montaigne*, trans. Donald Murdoch Frame (Stanford University Press, 1965), 648.

165 **will automatically eat more calories:** Quoted in Foreman, "Environmental Cues Affect How Much You Eat."

166 **Halloween last night 'cause:** Wegner, *White Bears and Other Unwanted Thoughts*, 3.

167 **does make it implausible:** Quoted in Robert Lee Hotz, "Get Out of Your Own Way," *Wall Street Journal*, June 27, 2008.

170 **hewed closer to its phenotype:** Espen Walderhaug et al., "Interactive Effects of Sex and 5-HTTLPR on Mood and Impulsivity During Tryptophan Depletion in Healthy People," *Biological Psychiatry* 62, no. 6 (September 15, 2007): 593–99.

170 **increased risk was 30 percent:** Emad Salib and Mario Cortina-Borja, "Effect of Month of Birth on the Risk of Suicide," *British Journal of Psychiatry* 188, no. 5 (May 1, 2006): 416–22.

171 **about 60 percent heritable:** Tinca J. C. Polderman et al., "Genetic Analyses of Teacher Ratings of Problem Behavior in 5-Year-Old Twins," *Australian Academic Press*, February 20, 2006; http://www.atypon-link.com/AAP/doi/abs/10.1375/twin.9.1.122.

173 **given neutral texts to read:** Kathleen D. Vohs and Jonathan W. Schooler, "The Value of Believing in Free Will: Encouraging a Belief in Determinism Increases Cheating," *Psychological Science* 19, no. 1 (January 2008): 49–54.

174 **believe in free will:** Theo Anderson,"One Hundred Years of Pragmatism," *Wilson Quarterly* (Summer 2007).

CHAPTER 14: ODYSSEUS AND THE PIGEONS

177 **our case was lost:** B. F. Skinner, "Pigeons in a Pelican," *American Psychologist* 15, no. 1 (January 1960): 28–37.

178 **people we would like to be:** Mary Harrington Hall, "Best of the Century: Interview with B.F. Skinner," *Psychology Today*, September 1967; http://www.psychologytoday.com/print/22682.

178 **of which behavior is a function:** B. F. Skinner, *Science and Human Behavior* (Free Press, 1953), 228.

178 **hard work is actually effortless:** William T. O'Donohue and Kyle E. Ferguson, *The Psychology of B. F. Skinner* (Sage, 2001), 170.

180 **the top and the bottom:** Richard J. Herrnstein, "I.Q.," *Atlantic Monthly*, September 1971.

182 **object of desire in the mind:** The discussion here generally follows the wonderful round-up provided by Shane Frederick, George Loewenstein, and Ted O'Donoghue in "Time Discounting and Time Preference," *Journal of Economic Literature* 40, no. 2 (June 2002): 351–401. John Rae is quoted in this paper.

183 **health is the greater good:** Quoted in George Ainslie, *Picoeconomics: The Interaction of Successive Motivational States within the Person* (Cambridge University Press, 1992), 57.

182 **on a diminished scale:** Frederick, Loewenstein, and O'Donoghue, "Time Discounting and Time Preference," 354.

183 **a single parameter, the discount rate:** Frederick, Loewenstein, and O'Donoghue, "Time Discounting and Time Preference," 351.

184 **more deeply than larger sums:** Stuart Vyse, *Going Broke: Why Americans Can't Hold On to Their Money* (Oxford University Press, 2007), 81.

185 **the local hierarchy of dominance:** Jeffrey R. Stevens and David W. Stephens, "Patience," *Current Biology* 18, no. 1 (January 8, 2008): R11–R12.

186 **had chosen the annual payments:** John T. Warner and Saul Pleeter, "The Personal Discount Rate: Evidence from Military Downsizing Programs," *American Economic Review* 91, no. 1 (March 2001): 33–53.

188 **near and contiguous:** David Hume, *A Treatise of Human Nature* (Oxford University Press, 2000), 343.

191 **chastity and continence, but not yet:** Augustine, *Confessions,* trans. R. S. Pine-Coffin (Penguin, 1961), 169.

CHAPTER 15: CRIMES OF PASSION

192 **throw the fine china:** Quoted in Susan D. Rozelle, "Controlling Passion: Adultery and the Provocation Defense," *Rutgers Law Journal* 37, no. 197 (2005): 221.

194 **offender versatility is overwhelming:** Michael R. Gottfredson and Travis Hirschi, *A General Theory of Crime* (Stanford University Press, 1990), 91.

194 **die at an early age:** Ibid., 92.

194 **likely to engage in them:** Ibid., 14.

195 **personal impulse management:** Holt, "Freud's Impact on Modern Morality."

195 **hospitalized for psychiatric illnesses:** Gottfredson and Hirschi, *A General Theory of Crime,* 93.

195 **low self-control is immense:** Ibid., 91.

195 **predicted crime and similar behaviors:** Travis C. Pratt and Francis T. Cullen, "The Empirical Status of Gottfredson and Hirschi's General Theory of Crime: A Meta-Analysis," *Criminology* 38, no. 3 (August 2000): 931–64.

196 **happen to be male:** Velmer S. Burton et al., "Gender, Self-Control, and Crime," *Journal of Research in Crime and Delinquency* 35, no. 2 (May 1, 1998): 123–47.

196 **increase the chances of victimization:** Christopher Schreck, Eric Stewart, and Bonnie Fisher, "Self-Control, Victimization, and Their Influence on Risky Lifestyles: A Longitudinal Analysis Using Panel Data," *Journal of Quantitative Criminology* 22, no. 4 (December 2006): 319–40.

198 **mistake their instructions:** Aristotle, *The Nicomachean Ethics,* 180–81.

198 **make myself count to ten:** Elster, *Ulysses Unbound,* 13.

198 **confronted with his wife's dishonor:** Cynthia Lee, *Murder and the Reasonable Man: Passion and Fear in the Criminal Courtroom* (New York University Press, 2003), 20–21.

199 **adultery with the wife:** Ibid., 22.

199 **provoked into a heat of passion:** Ibid., 25.

200 **manslaughter instead of murder:** Ibid., 38–39.

200 **the prevailing scholarship assume:** Rozelle, "Controlling Passion," 199.

200 **anger against his servants:** Elster, *Ulysses Unbound,* 14.

200 **lose your temper:** Iggeres Haramban and Avrohom Chaim Feuer, *A Letter for the Ages: The Ramban's Ethical Letter with an Anthology of Contemporary Rabbinic Expositions* (Mesorah Publications, 1989), 28, 31.

201 **Bettelheim believed in it:** Tavris, *Anger, The Misunderstood Emotion* (Touchstone, 1989), 45.

201 **softens our emotions:** Quoted in Tavris, *Anger,* 36.

202 **provocation:** John E. Carr and Eng Kong Tan, "In Search of the True Amok: Amok as Viewed Within the Malay Culture," *American Journal of Psychiatry* 133, no. 11 (November 1, 1976): 1295–99.

202 **outbursts declined dramatically:** John E. Carr and Eng Kong Tan, "In Search of the True Amok: Amok as Viewed Within the Malay Culture," *American Journal of Psychiatry* 133, no. 11 (November 1, 1976): 1295–99.

CHAPTER 16: ADDICTION, COMPULSION, AND CHOICE

203 **What's hard is to decide:** "The Comeback Kid," *The Oprah Winfrey Show,* November 23, 2004. http://www.oprah.com/oprahshow/The-Comeback-Kid/slide_number/3.

204 **and of the public in general:** Gary Greenberg, *The Noble Lie: When Scientists Give the Right Answers for the Wrong Reasons* (Wiley, 2008), 12.

204 **hereditary, family, and contagious diseases:** Gene M. Heyman, "Drug of Choice," *Boston College Magazine,* Fall 2009.

207 **life grew chaotic and brutal:** John C. Burnham, *Bad Habits: Drinking, Smoking, Taking Drugs, Gambling, Sexual Misbehavior, and Swearing in American History* (New York University Press, 1993), 52.

207 **the center of the spiritual order:** Jackson Lears, *Something for Nothing: Luck in America* (Viking, 2003), 60.

207 **have had some success:** Heyman, *Addiction,* 105–6.

209 **function of its consequences:** Ibid., 104.

210 **hypoactivity of the prefrontal cortex:** W. Van Den Brink, "The Role of Impulsivity, Response Inhibition and Delay Discounting in Addictive Behaviors," *European Psychiatry* 22, no. 1 (March 2007): S29.

CHAPTER 17: TOMORROW IS ANOTHER DAY

213 **work before getting a reward:** "Brain's Reward Circuitry Revealed in Procrastinating Primates," National Institute of Mental Health, August 10, 2004, http://www.nimh.nih .gov/science-news/2004/brains-reward-circuitry-revealed-in-procrastinating-primates .shtml.

214 **known to psychologists as conscientiousness:** Dianne M. Tice, Ellen Bratslavsky, and Roy F. Baumeister, "Emotional Distress Regulation Takes Precedence over Impulse Control: If You Feel Bad, Do It!" *Journal of Personality and Social Psychology* 80, no. 1 (2001): 61.

215 **warning voice of conscience:** Rebecca Shannonhouse, ed., *Under the Influence: The Literature of Addiction* (Modern Library, 2003), 41.

216 **their mood could be altered:** Tice, Bratslavsky, and Baumeister, "Emotional Distress Regulation Takes Precedence over Impulse Control," 63.

216 **procrastination is neurotic indeed:** Ibid., 61.

217 **live up to planned schedules:** Quoted in Markus K. Brunnermeier, Filippos Papakonstantinou, and Jonathan A. Parker, "An Economic Model of the Planning Fallacy," National Bureau of Economic Research Working Paper Series No. 14228 (August 2008).

217 **faster than they had predicted:** Ibid.

219 **called a 'procrastination field':** John Sabini and Maury Silver, *Moralities of Everyday Life* (Oxford University Press, 1982), 135–36.

219 **intervals that are irrationally short:** Ibid., 133.

220 **and use birth control:** June P. Tangney and Ronda L. Dearing, *Shame and Guilt* (Guilford Press, 2002), 134–35.

221 **powerful moral emotional factor:** Ibid., 138.

221 **more influenced by environment:** Ibid., 154.

221 **the variance in procrastination is genetic:** Piers Steel, "The Nature of Procrastination: A Meta-Analytic and Theoretical Review of Quintessential Self-Regulatory Failure," *Psychological Bulletin* 133, no. 1 (January 2007): 67.

222 **an input like time invested:** Lisa Belkin, "Time Wasted? Perhaps It's Well Spent," *New York Times,* May 31, 2007.

222 **arrangement of his time:** Thomas Mann, *Buddenbrooks*, trans. H.T. Lowe-Porter (Vintage Books, 1961), 515.

224 **labours of a spasmodic Hercules:** Quoted in Irving Wallace, "Self-Control Techniques of Famous Novelists," *Journal of Applied Behavior Analysis* 10, no. 3 (Fall 1977).

225 **wrestled constantly with his conscience:** McCraw, *Prophet of Innovation*, 221.

225 **free, to quote Sartre:** David Glenn, "Falling Behind? Try Shame, Fear, and Greed," *Chronicle of Higher Education*, March 27, 2009.

225 **when the mood struck them:** Robert Boice, "Contingency Management in Writing and the Appearance of Creative Ideas: Implications for the Treatment of Writing Blocks," *Behaviour Research and Therapy* 21, no. 5 (1983): 537–43.

226 **arrest, Steiner, house arrest:** Schelling, *Strategies of Commitment and Other Essays*, 72.

CHAPTER 18: CUTTING LOOSE

227 **life without self-control:** Quoted in Martin Henley, *Teaching Self-Control: A Curriculum for Responsible Behavior* (National Educational Service, 1997), 1.

228 **Gimme a double scotch:** Don Marquis, *The Lives and Times of Archy and Mehitabel* (Doubleday, 1950), xxiii.

228 **moderation than does folly:** Michel de Montaigne, *Michel de Montaigne: The Complete Essays*, trans. M. A. Screech (Penguin Classics, 1993), 948.

228 **in every time and culture:** Oliver W. Sacks, *An Anthropologist on Mars: Seven Paradoxical Tales* (Knopf, 1995), 64.

231 **on something like groceries:** Ran Kivetz and Itamar Simonson, "Self-Control for the Righteous: Toward a Theory of Precommitment to Indulgence," *Journal of Consumer Research: An Interdisciplinary Quarterly* 29, issue 2, p. 199–217.

232 **hidden director of the experience:** Jessica Benjamin, *The Bonds of Love: Psychoanalysis, Feminism, and the Problem of Domination* (Pantheon, 1988), 262.

233 **many more have such fantasies:** June M. Reinisch and Ruth Beasley, *The Kinsey Institute New Report On Sex* (St. Martin's Press, 1991), 162.

233 **a time when individuality flourished:** Roy F. Baumeister, *Escaping the Self: Alcoholism, Spirituality, Masochism, and Other Flights from the Burden of Selfhood* (Basic Books, 1991), 120ff.

235 **when he unscrewed it:** Anne Tyler, *The Accidental Tourist* (Ballantine Books, 2002), 273.

235 **the indefinitely postponed splurge:** Frederick, Loewenstein, and O'Donoghue, "Time Discounting and Time Preference," 359.

237 **any revolt insipid:** Quoted in Elster, *Ulysses Unbound*, 268.

237 **culture of excess:** Stearns, *Battleground of Desire*, 27.

CHAPTER 19: GOVERNMENT AND SELF-GOVERNMENT

239 **and without assistance:** Quoted in John A. Bargh, Peter M. Gollwitzer, Annette Lee-Chai, Kimberly Barndollar, and Roman Trötschel, "The Automated Will: Nonconscious Activation and Pursuit of Behavioral Goals," *Journal of Personality and Social Psychology* 81, no. 6 (December 2001): 1014–27.

239 **sufficient warrant:** Mill, *On Liberty and the Subjection of Women*, 16.

240 **potentially dangerous, and irreversible:** Quoted in Debra Satz, *Why Some Things Should Not Be for Sale: The Moral Limits of Markets* (Oxford University Press, 2010), 87.

240 **violence of the passions:** Adam Smith, *The Theory of Moral Sentiments* (Cambridge University Press, 2002), 31.

241 **against their own:** Hume, *A Treatise of Human Nature*, 345.

242 **start by refusing:** Alexis de Tocqueville, *Democracy in America* (Penguin Classics, 2003), 262.

243 **in the day of their frenzy:** Frederick, Loewenstein, and O'Donoghue, "Time Discounting and Time Preference."

244 **on camera many times daily:** "Britain Is 'Surveillance Society'," BBC News, November 2, 2006; http://news.bbc.co.uk/1/hi/uk/6108496.stm.

247 **guard against accidents:** Mill, *On Liberty and the Subjection of Women,* 109.

249 **ability to exercise self-control:** Robert Crowe, "Drugs, Surgery May Temper Drive, but Sexual Interest Won't 'Normalize'," *Houston Chronicle,* May 10, 2005.

249 **bogs and precipices:** Ian Carter, "Positive and Negative Liberty," in Edward N. Zalta, ed., *Stanford Encyclopedia of Philosophy,* Winter 2007; http://plato.stanford.edu/archives/win2007/entries/liberty-positive-negative/.

250 **more there must be without:** Quoted in Gertrude Himmelfarb, *The De-Moralization of Society: From Victorian Virtues to Modern Values* (Knopf, 1995), 51.

CHAPTER 20: BE YOUR OWN GODFATHER

251 **I said from her breasts:** Don DeLillo, *White Noise* (Penguin, 1999), 282.

256 **'It's not my money.' It works:** Farah Stockman, "Q and A with Daryl Collins: Financial Secrets of the World's Poorest People," *Boston Globe,* May 17, 2009.

256 **to keep themselves away:** David I. Laibson et al., "Self-Control and Saving for Retirement," *Brookings Papers on Economic Activity* 1998, no. 1 (1998): 91.

258 **and the commitment device:** Stuart Rutherford, *The Poor and Their Money* (Oxford University Press, 2001), 13.

258 **bet it on a number:** Ivan Light, "Numbers Gambling Among Blacks: A Financial Institution," *American Sociological Review* 42, no. 6 (December 1977): 892–904.

259 **a great many employees:** Brigitte C. Madrian and Dennis F. Shea, "The Power of Suggestion: Inertia in 401(k) Participation and Savings Behavior," *Quarterly Journal of Economics* 66, no. 4 (November 2001).

CHAPTER 21: CARPE DIEM

261 **and curb your own:** Homer, *The Odyssey,* trans. Robert Fagles (Penguin, 1999), 253.

263 **it is too continually tense:** Montaigne, *The Complete Essays of Montaigne,* trans. Donald Murdoch Frame (Stanford University Press, 1965), 638.

264 **better selves is biologically costly:** Quoted in Hara Estroff Marano, "Building a Better Self," *Psychology Today,* June 2007.

264 **regions of prefrontal cortex:** Joshua D. Greene and Joseph M. Paxton, "Patterns of Neural Activity Associated with Honest and Dishonest Moral Decisions," Proceedings of the National Academy of Sciences 106, no. 30 (July 28, 2009): 12506-11.

265 **chaff in the blast:** William James, "The Laws of Habit," in *Talks to Teachers on Psychology; and to Students on Some of Life's Ideals* (Henry Holt and Company, 1925).

266 **by more than 70 percent:** Roy F. Baumeister, *Losing Control: How and Why People Fail at Self-Regulation* (Academic Press, 1994), 140.

266 **terrible risk to our self-control:** Howard Rachlin, *The Science of Self-Control* (Harvard University Press, 2000), 67.

267 **be supportive of those changes:** Quoted in Anita Huslin, "Are You Really Ready to Clean Up Your Act?" *Washington Post,* January 2, 2007.

270 **without taking any harmful action:** Jason Zweig, "How to Handle a Market Gone Mad," *Wall Street Journal,* September 16, 2008.

272 **decisive moments:** John A. Bargh and Tanya L. Chartrand, "The Unbearable Automaticity of Being," *American Psychologist* 54, no. 7 (July 1999): 462–79.

272 **obedience to reason becomes habitual:** Quoted in Helen North, *Sophrosyne: Self-Knowledge and Self-Restraint in Greek Literature* (Cornell University Press, 1966), 203.

272 **guard against the plague:** William James, *The Principles of Psychology* (Henry Holt & Co., 1890), 122.

273 **'not that kind of person':** Mark R. Leary, *The Curse of the Self: Self-Awareness, Egotism, and the Quality of Human Life*, 1st ed. (Oxford University Press, 2004), 9.

273 **could not do without them:** Thomas Mann, *Buddenbrooks*, trans. H. T. Lowe-Porter (Vintage Books, 1961), 508.

273 **habits . . . are arts:** John Dewey, *Human Nature and Conduct*: an Introduction to Social Psychology. (Modern Library, 1957), 15.

274 **for a diet to succeed:** Quoted in Charles Duhigg, "Warning: Habits May Be Good for You," *New York Times*, July 13, 2008.

Index

abortion, 11, 47, 73, 247
Accidental Tourist, The (Tyler), 235
accidents, 107, 157, 194
Adam's Rib, 199
addiction, xii, xiii–xiv, 7, 13, 91–92, 151, 184,
    204–11
    as disease, 204–6, 211
    precommitment devices and, 36
    procrastination and, 215, 219
    voluntary aspects of, 209–11
    see also alcohol; drugs; gambling;
      smoking
Adler, Alfred, 216
Adventures of Huckleberry Finn (Twain), 13,
    14
Age of Innocence, The (Wharton), 236
AIDS, 19
Ainslie, George, 138, 142, 143–44, 180, 181,
    186–87, 189–91
akrasia, 86–89, 93–94, 113, 131, 214, 248
alcohol, xiii, 5, 6, 15, 17–19, 75, 77, 92, 107,
    124, 144, 158, 184, 206, 210, 215, 220,
    229, 247, 248, 262
    ancient Greeks and, 92, 93, 94, 95
    Cheever and, 35, 93, 208
    consumption rates of, 207–8
    criminal behavior and, 194, 195
    disease model of alcoholism, 204, 208

    liquor taxes and, 207–8, 248
    precommitment devices and, 36–37, 245
    purchase of, 249
    sobriety minders and, 33
    women and, 169–70
Alger, Horatio, 11
Allende, Isabel, 43
Alpert, Richard, 101
Alzheimer's disease, 6
Ambach, Ferdinand, 192–93
Ambassadors, The (James), 236
Amish, 55–56, 79
Anderson, Dwight, 204
Anderson, Pamela, 43
Andrews, Edmund, 67
anger, 172, 197, 198, 200–201, 206
Anger: The Misunderstood Emotion (Tavris),
    201
Anna Karenina (Tolstoy), 235
anomie, 72
anorexia nervosa, 7, 210
Antabuse, 36, 245
anti-charities, 253–54
anticipation, 144–45
antidepressants, 30, 124
antisocial personality, 195, 197
appearance, physical, 93
Apollo 13, 39

Arendt, Hannah, 94
Ariely, Dan, 38, 42, 136
Aristotle, 4, 10, 65, 72, 82, 84, 87, 89–94, 113,
	131, 141, 173, 198, 237, 248, 267, 272
art, 236–37
Ashley Madison, 45–46
astheneia, 93–94, 214
Athens, 85, 86, 94
Atlantic Monthly, 180
attention management, 268–69
attention problems, 7, 109, 169, 171, 196,
	203–4, 269
Auden, W. H., 77
Augustine, Saint, 141, 191
automobiles, 49–50
	accidents, 107, 157, 194
	seat belt laws, 246
Ayres, Ian, 252, 253, 254

Babbit (Lewis), 236
Babbit, Ellen, 199–200
baby boomers, 65
bankruptcies, 66, 67
banks, 8, 16, 53–54, 67–69, 88, 137
Bargh, John, 162–63, 173–74, 178
bariatric surgery, 1–2, 10
Barnum, P. T., 155
Barrie, J. M., vii
Barth, John, 139
Barthelme, Donald, 71
Bass, Anne, 37
Baumeister, Roy, 195, 215–16, 223, 231, 234,
	264
Bear, John, 253–54
Beaver, Kevin, 196–97
behaviorism, 9, 177–78
Bell Curve, The (Herrnstein and Murray), 180
Benjamin, Jessica, 232
Bennett, William, 11
Bentham, Jeremy, 244–45
Berkeley, William, 116
Bernanke, Ben S., 67
Best Buy, 222
Bettelheim, Bruno, 201
Beyond Freedom and Dignity (Skinner), 180
Biltmore, 62–63
Bing Nursery School, 101–5, 107–8
birth season, 170
Blackmail Diet, The (Bear), 253–54
Blau, Rabbi Yosef, 80
Bodrova, Elena, 108
body mass index (BMI), 24
Böhm-Bawerk, Eugen von, 182

bondage, 231–34
Book of Virtues, The (Bennett), 11
Boone, Angie Luzio, 195
brain, 107–8, 133, 147–52, 157–59, 263
	amygdala in, 133, 149, 170
	basal ganglia in, 272
	crime and, 193, 196, 197
	frontal lobe in, 228, 271
	hot and cool areas of, 103
	injuries or abnormalities in, 146–47,
		154–56, 157, 193, 210
	limbic system in, 133, 149, 151, 152, 156,
		197
	lobotomies and, 157
	lying and, 264
	maturity of, 26, 209
	neocortex in, 149
	neurotransmitters in, *see* neurotransmitters
	obsessive-compulsive disorder and, 170
	orbitofrontal cortex in, 138–39, 147, 156,
		157, 158
	plasticity of, 210
	prefrontal cortex in, 149–50, 197, 210, 264,
		272
	in teenagers, 157–58
Brannigan, Kelly, 43–44
Brunton, Mary, xi
Buddenbrooks (Mann), 78, 222, 273
Buddhism, 78, 112
Buffett, Warren, 54
Buffon, Georges-Louis Leclerc, Comte de, 41
Burke, Edmund, 245, 250

Cacioppo, John, 78
Camus, Albert, 1
cancer, 18, 19
capitalism, 57–59, 113–14, 118, 120, 244, 250
Caplan, Eric, 123
Carter, Jimmy, 65
casinos, 3, 43, 92, 248
	see also gambling
charities, 253–54, 270
chastity belts, 234
cheating, 50, 100, 107, 173
Cheever, John, 35, 93, 208
Cheever, Susan, 208
Cherlin, Andrew J., 74
Chicago Tribune, 122
Chicano, Mark, 199–200
China, 7, 8, 27, 67, 238
choice architecture, 259
cholesterol, 26
Christianity, 4–5, 76, 113

Christmas clubs, 256
Chung, Shin-Ho, 187
Churchland, Patricia, 171
Cicero, 213
city life, 86, 117, 269
Cleland, John, 232–33
climate change, 16, 22, 243, 275
cold-to-hot empathy gap, 136–37
Coleridge, Samuel Taylor, xiii, 32–36, 220
communities, 266–67
Compton-Burnett, Ivy, 132
compulsion, 173, 203, 206, 208–10
conditioning, 178
Confessions, The (Rousseau), 32, 233
Coniff, Richard, 41
conservatives, 11, 61, 247
Constitution, 39, 243
consumer behavior, 186
consumerism, 60–64, 66
contraception, 71, 73, 220
Cook, Philip, 207
"Cookies" (Lobel), 37
Cortez, Hernan, 39
Cosmides, Leda, 148
Courtesans and Fishcakes: The Consuming
    Passions of Classical Athens (Davidson),
    203
Covenant Eyes, 51
Cowen, Tyler, 36, 229
credit, 57, 59, 60, 61
credit cards, 2–3, 8, 35, 38, 52, 57, 68
crime, 107, 192–202, 221
    provocation defense and, 192–93,
    198–200
Crime and Punishment (Dostoevsky), 13–14,
    235
Criminology, 195
crowds, 167–68
cutting loose, 227–38

Daedalus, 110–11
Damasio, Antonio, 138–39
Daniels, Bruce, 115
Darwin, Charles, 117, 120, 201
Daughter of Fortune (Allende), 43
Davidson, James, 86, 94, 203
Davis, Geena, 43
deadlines, 41–42, 218
Dearing, Ronda L., 220, 221
death, 6, 17–19, 134–35
    homicide, 19, 20
    smoking and, 17–21, 31
    suicide, see suicide

debt, 8, 53–54, 56, 59, 66–69, 117, 137, 240,
    241, 275
delay of gratification, 64, 98–106, 108,
    144–45, 149, 168, 238
DeLillo, Don, 251
democracy, 242–46
Demosthenes, 225
Depp, Johnny, 43
depression, 201
Depression, Great, 63, 65
De Quincey, Thomas, 32
Descartes, René, 134, 148
determinism, 161
Dewey, John, 11, 88, 114, 273
Dews, Peter, 187
diabetes, 18, 26, 27, 206
Diagnostic and Statistical Manual of Mental
    Disorders (DSM-IV), 204–5
Diamond, Adele, 108–9
diet and food, 6, 18, 19, 23, 25–27, 46–47, 50,
    93, 107, 136, 151, 249
    addiction to food, 205, 206
    advance decisions about, 48, 270
    choice architecture and, 259
    environment and, 164–65, 271
    exercise and, 240
    fast food, 6, 23, 50
    smoking and, 21
    social isolation and, 77, 78
    weight problems and, 10, 18, 59
Diggins, John Patrick, 66
discounting the future, 182–91
disease, 124, 203–6
    addiction as, 204–6, 211
    alcoholism as, 204, 206, 208
    shame as, 221
divided self, 132–45
divorce, 11, 70, 72, 73–77, 169, 172, 195, 267
domestic violence, 75, 76
Donald Duck, 140–42, 198
dopamine, 30, 151, 158, 159, 213
Dostoyevskaya, Anna Grigorievna, 42
Dostoyevsky, Fyodor, 41–42
    Crime and Punishment, 13–14, 235
Downey, Robert, Jr., 203, 206
drugs, 13, 16, 19, 64, 71, 75, 77, 104, 107,
    124, 136, 158, 194, 205, 206, 209–11,
    215, 220, 247
    Coleridge's use of, xiii, 32–36
    dopamine and, 151
    heroin use in Vietnam veterans, 206
    legalization of, 208
    screening for, 245

drugs (*cont.*)
  sobriety minders and, 32–33, 36
  treatment for addiction to, 206, 207, 209
  war on, 245, 247
dualism, 132–39, 198
Duce, Herbert, 60
Duchovny, David, 11–12
Duckworth, Angela, 105–6
Durant, Will, 89
Durkheim, Emile, 71–72
Durrell, Lawrence, 142
Duty and Character (Smiles), 117
Dworkin, Gerald, 240
Dyer, Geoff, 226

economics, 177, 183
"Economic Theory of Self-Control, An"
  (Thaler and Shefrin), 137
education and school, 6, 61, 74, 75, 104–8, 115,
  116, 141, 144, 169, 180, 194, 220, 248, 249
  cheating and, 50, 100, 107, 173
Edwards, John, 5
ego depletion, 263
Eichmann, Adolf, 94
Eldridge Street Synagogue, 40
Eliot, George, 41
Elliott, Sophie, 192–93
Ellis, Albert, 267–68
Elster, Jon, 200, 237, 262
emotions, 110, 201, 265, 268
  anger, 172, 197, 198, 200–201, 206
employees, 169, 186
End of the Road, The (Barth), 139
energy problems, 242–43
England, 244–45, 250
enkrateia, 82–83, 231
Enlightenment, 113
environment, 164–65, 167, 169, 172, 261,
  268–71
  habits and, 273–74
  priming and, 162–67, 173, 174, 178
Epicurus, 112
Epstein, Robert, 26
estrogen, 168
eudaimonia, 90
Euripides, 85
evangelism, 116
evolution, 16, 23, 25, 120, 142, 148–50, 152,
  153, 172, 188
exercise, 144, 271
  lack of, 17–19, 27, 93
  overeating and, 240
  precommitment devices and, 253, 254

E-ZPass, 52
Ezzati, Majid, 17–18

Fable of the Bees, The (Mandeville), 20
factories, 114, 222
Fadiman, Anne, 224
Faerie Queene, The (Spenser), 88–89
family, 72–75, 77, 128, 241, 261, 267, 269–70
  father in, 72, 74, 98, 129
Fanny Hill (Cleland), 232–33
fast food, 3, 23, 50
Faulkner, William, xiii
federal deposit insurance, 245
Fee, Ronda L., 220, 221
Ferrari, Joseph, 213
Fibonacci, 184
financial crisis of 2007–9, 8, 52–54, 56, 66–69,
  88, 137, 241, 247
Fine, Gary Alan, 5
first-order desires, 12
Flaubert, Gustave, xiv
  Madame Bovary, 8, 235
food, *see* diet and food
football, 237
Ford, Earl S., 27
Foundations of Economic Analysis
  (Samuelson), 20
Fountain Overflows, The (West), 41
401(k) plans, 259, 270
Frank, Robert, 70
Frankfurt, Harry, 12–13, 94, 130, 275
Franklin, Benjamin, 119–20, 161, 179
Frederick, Shane, 144
Freedom for Mac, 51
free will, 9, 161, 167, 170, 171–74
friends, 91, 266–67, 269–70
Freud, Martin, 126
Freud, Sigmund, 5, 7, 30–31, 96, 120, 121–31,
  136, 141–42, 152, 161, 166, 168, 178,
  201, 237, 267
  criminals as viewed by, 194–95
  smoking habit of, 5, 30–31, 124, 126–28
future, 194, 210, 238, 244, 275
  discounting of, 182–91

Gage, Phineas, 154–56, 157
Gambler, The (Dostoyevsky), 42
gambling, 3, 30, 41, 43, 92, 151, 184, 204,
  205, 207, 210, 211, 247, 248
  Internet, 50
  numbers, 257–58
gas heating, 29–30
Gay, Peter, 123, 125–26

Gaylin, Willard, 129
General Theory of Crime, A (Gottfredson and Hirschi), 194–95, 196
genetics, *see* heredity
Gilligan, Carol, 100
global warming, 16, 22, 243, 275
glucose, 263–64
Gnarls Barkley, 9
Goffman, Erving, 221
Goldwater, Barry, 90
Goldwyn, Samuel, 122–23
Gorgias (Plato), 85
Gosling, Justin, 160
Gottfredson, Michael, 194–95, 196
government, 11, 61–62, 77, 239–50
    democracy and, 242–46
Gray, Jeremy, 159
Great Depression, 63, 65
Greeks, ancient, 4, 15, 34, 54, 81–95, 112, 127, 173, 203, 211, 213
    Aristotle, 4, 10, 65, 72, 82, 84, 87, 89–94, 113, 131, 141, 173, 198, 237, 248, 267, 272
    Homer, *see* Homer
    Plato, 4, 9–10, 82, 84–85, 87, 89, 95, 137, 139–40, 142
    Socrates, 15, 83, 84, 87, 89, 92, 134, 139–40, 182
Green, Cee-Lo, 9
Green, Leonard, 191
Greenspan, Alan, 66, 67
guilt, 218–21, 265
gun ownership, 28–29, 33–34, 47, 240
Gunton, George, 62–63

habits, 271–74
Haidt, Jonathan, 72
Hajek, Marcus, 128
Hamlet (Shakespeare), 28, 90–91
Haynes, John-Dylan, 167
Hansen, Julia, 22
Harlow, John Martyn, 155
health insurance, 18, 249
heart disease, 18, 27, 206
Hemingway, Ernest, 218, 224
heredity, 9, 91, 108, 159–60, 170–71, 172, 180
    addiction and, 210
    criminality and, 193, 196–97
    procrastination and, 221
    shame and, 221
Herrnstein, Richard, 180–81, 187, 192
Hesiod, 213
Heyman, Gene M., 209, 210

high blood pressure (hypertension), 17, 26, 206, 248
Hired Power, 33
Hirschi, Travis, 107, 194–95, 196
Hollywood, 206, 237
Holt, Robert R., 130, 195
Holtgrave, David, 267
home ownership, 246, 247
Homer:
    The Iliad, 82
    The Odyssey, 34, 35, 82–83, 89, 136, 189–91, 231–32, 234, 261, 266, 275
homicide, 19, 20
homosexuality, 71, 87, 203
Horace, 112, 198
hormones, 26, 159, 168–69
Hugo, Victor, xiii, 225
Hume, David, 5, 188, 241
Huxley, Aldous, 239
hyperactivity, 169, 196
hyperopia (over-control), 228, 229, 234–38

Icarus, 110–11
ignorance, 240
Iliad, The (Homer), 82
immigrants, 38, 65, 117
Importance of Being Earnest, The (Wilde), 135
impulse disorders, 204
impulsive self, 229
impulsivity, 30, 83, 89, 97, 98, 148, 151, 156, 158, 159, 169, 170, 196
Imus, Don, 5
inactivity, 17–19, 27, 93
incontinence, 87–88, 93
Industrial Revolution, 114, 117, 213–14
inertia, 259, 268
Inglehart, Ronald, 71
inhibition, 265–66
inner voice, 134
Innes, Stephen, 115
Internet, 46, 48, 50–52, 268
    addiction to, 205, 211
    procrastination and, 212, 222, 223
intertemporal choice, 182, 241
IQ, 106, 169
I.Q. in the Meritocracy (Herrnstein), 180
Ishiguro, Kazuo, 236

Jackson, John Hughlings, 142
Jaffa, Scott, 270
James, Henry, 234, 236
James, William, 139, 174, 179, 201, 264–65, 272–73

Javidan, Mansour, 238
Jerome, Saint, 38
Jews, 79–80, 113
  self-control among, 237–38
  suicide among, 127
Johnson, Samuel, 58, 214, 223
Johnson, Scott, 106–7
Johnston, William, 127
Journal of Gambling Studies, 248
Judaism, *yetzer ha-ra* and *yetzer ha-tov*
  concepts in, 138, 139
Judt, Tony, 71
Justine (Durrell), 142

Kahneman, Daniel, 217
Karlan, Dean, 251–53, 254–55
Kay, Alan, 163
Keller, Betsy, 261–62
Kelsey, Frances Oldham, 245–46
Keynes, John Maynard, 63, 188
Kilgore, Greg, 1–2
KIPP (Knowledge Is Power Program), 108
Kivetz, Ran, 230–31
Kligler, Jonathan, 138

Laibson, David, 152
Larkin, Philip, 146
Lawrence, D. H., 110, 119–20
Leach, William, 60
Lears, Jackson, 207
Leary, Mark R., 148–49, 153, 273
Leary, Timothy, 101
Lee, Tommy, 43
Lehman, Mervin, 55
Lemmon, E. J., 87
Leonard, John, 42
Leong, Deborah, 108
Leopold and Loeb, 122
Lewis, Sinclair, 236
Liber Abaci (Fibonacci), 184
liberals, 11, 247
libertarianism, 247
Libet, Benjamin, 166–67, 171
life insurance, 248
life purpose, 72, 78–80
Life in Smoke, A (Hansen), 22
Light, Ivan, 257, 258
Liljenquist, Katie, 163–64
Lindsey, Brink, 64
loans and debt, 8, 53–54, 56, 59, 66–69, 117,
  137, 240, 241, 275
Lobel, Arnold, 37
lobotomies, 157

Locke, John, 13, 21, 113, 249
Loewenstein, George, 92, 136–37
loneliness, 77–78, 266
lotteries, 3, 59, 183, 257
Lukacs, Georg, 225–26
lying, 264

Macbeth effect, 163–64
McClure, Samuel, 150–52
McCormick, Robert, 122
McCraw, Thomas, 225
Mack, John, 69
McMahon, Darrin, 78
McPhee, John, 224
McTeague (Norris), 235, 236
Madame Bovary (Flaubert), 8, 235
Madoff, Bernard, 135
Madrian, Brigitte, 259
Malaysia, 201–2
Maltese Falcon, The, 262
Mandeville, Bernard de, 20, 21
Mann, Thomas, 78, 222, 273
Marcus Aurelius, 105, 112
Marcuse, Herbert, 62
Marquand, David, 3
Marquis, Don, 228
marriage, 6, 35, 43, 70, 73–78, 195, 247
  covenant, 76–77, 248
  divorce and, 11, 70, 72, 73–77, 169, 172,
    195, 267
  infidelity and, 45–46, 78–79
marshmallow test, 99, 101–5, 107, 108
Martell, Daniel, 193
Marty, 268
Marx, Karl, 58, 61, 120
Maslow, Abraham, 62, 64
masochism, 231–34
matching law, 181
Mather, Cotton, 55, 115
Maxa, Rudy, 38
Mayor of Casterbridge, The (Hardy), 235
medications, 26
melioration, 21, 219, 270–71
Melville, Herman, 119
men, 168–70
Mencken, H. L., 17
menstrual cycle, 168
mental illness, 124, 129, 170
metabolic syndrome, 26–27
metabolism, 26
MetroCard, 52
microwave ovens, 23, 25
Middlemarch (Eliot), 41

military, 185–86, 270
Mill, John Stuart, 13, 117, 182, 239, 247
Miller, Jonathan, 161–62
mind-body problem, 146–60
mirrors, 265–66
Mischel, Walter, 96–105, 107–8, 150
moderation, 111, 112–18
money, 37–41, 54, 55–69, 71, 115
  capitalism, 57–59, 113–14, 118, 120, 244, 250
  credit, 57, 59, 60, 61
  credit cards, 2–3, 8, 35, 38, 52, 57, 68
  debt, 8, 53–54, 56, 59, 66–69, 117, 137,
    240, 241, 275
  financial crisis of 2007–9, 8, 52–54, 56,
    66–69, 88, 137, 241, 247, 259
  payment technologies, 52
  precommitment devices for saving, 35,
    254–58
Montaigne, Michel de, 76, 165, 228, 263
morality of taboo, 128–29
Morris, Charles R., 60
Morse, Stephen, 172
mortgages, 53, 56, 67–69, 257
Mosley, Max, 233–34
Muller, Jerry Z., 237
Muraven, Mark, 264
Murray, Charles, 180

Nachman, Rabbi Moshe ben, 200–201
nature, 269
Nazi Germany, 14, 94, 96
Nestle, Marion, 165
neurasthenia, 203
neuroscience, 15–16
neurosis, 216
neurotransmitters, 159, 263
  dopamine, 30, 151, 158, 159, 213
  serotonin, 30, 151, 170, 271
New Yorker, 46, 123, 227
New York Times, 41, 67, 123, 233, 234, 267
Nicomachean Ethics (Aristotle), 89, 91
Nietzsche, Friedrich, 85, 88
Nordgren, Loran, 40
North, Helen, 84, 85, 86

Obama, Barack, 25
obsessive-compulsive disorder, 7, 170, 171,
  210, 215, 218
Odyssey, The (Homer), 34, 35, 82–83, 89, 136,
  189–91, 231–32, 234, 261, 266, 275
Offer, Avner, 250
oil, 242–43
On Bullshit (Frankfurt), 12

On Liberty (Mill), 117, 239
On the Origin of Species (Darwin), 117
Oppenheim, David, 29
Organization Man, The (Whyte), 64
Othello (Shakespeare), 229
over-control (hyperopia), 228, 229, 234–38
overweight and obesity, 1–2, 8, 10, 17, 18,
  22–28, 47, 48–49, 59, 104, 275
  weight-loss contracts and, 251–54

Panopticon, 244–45
Parents and Children (Compton-Burnett), 132
Parfit, Derek, 142–43
Parkinson's disease, 151
passion, crimes of, 192, 198–200
paternalism, 246
  democracy and, 243
  precommitment and, 259–60
  soft, 259
Patten, Simon, 61–62, 63
Paul, Saint, 4, 135, 141
peanuts effect, 211
peer pressure, 267
pengamoks, 201–2
People of Plenty: Economic Abundance
  and the American Character (Potter),
  63–64
Perpetual Orgy, The (Vargas Llosa), 8
Peyre, Henri, 237
Phaedrus (Plato), 139–40, 142
Philadelphia Story, The, 236
Philippines, 255–56
physical appearance, 93
physical inactivity, 17–19, 27, 93
Picoeconomics (Ainslie), 186
pigeons, 175–78, 179–81, 187, 189–91, 269
Pigou, Arthur, 182
planning, 238
planning fallacy, 217
Plath, Sylvia, 29
Plato, 4, 9–10, 82, 84–85, 87, 89, 95, 137,
  139–40, 142
Poe, Edgar Allan, 119
Pogo, 69
poison pills, 40
polis, 86
Pollard, Annie, 40
pornography, 50
Positive Psychology Center, 105
potatoes, 23
Potter, David M., 63–64
poverty, 4, 5, 28, 75, 158, 159
  precommitment and, 254–58

precommitment devices, 32–44, 189, 190–91, 237, 251–60, 262, 270
  alcohol consumption and, 36–37, 245
  government as, 241–42, 243
  Internet use and, 51–52
  paternalism and, 259–60
  saving money and, 35, 254–58
  sex offenders and, 249
  stickK.com, 253–54, 259–60, 266
  tattoos as, 35, 42–44
  taxes as, 250
  weight loss and, 251–54
  writing and, 41–42
preference, revealed, 20, 183
Preventable Causes of Death in the United States, The: Comparative Risk Assessment of Dietary, Lifestyle, and Metabolic Risk Factors, 17–18
priming, 162–67, 173, 174, 178
Principles of Psychology, The (James), 272
privacy, 49–50, 71
procrastination, xiii, 21, 50, 212–26
  as drug, 215–16
  and guilt and shame, 218–21
  as theater, 217–19
  writing and, 42, 223–26
Producers, The, 236
Prohibition, 11, 62, 172, 245, 247
propeteia, 93–94
Protagoras (Socrates), 15, 87, 182
Protestant ethic, 115
Protestantism, 113, 207
psychoanalysis, 121–24, 128, 130, 131, 267
Psychology Today, 178
Puritanism, 114–16, 119, 121, 129
purpose, 72, 78–80
Pygmalion (Shaw), 230

Qatar, 22–23

Rachlin, Howard, 191, 266
radio, 47
Rae, John, 182
Raine, Adrian, 197
Ramban, 200–201
Ram Dass, 101
Rape of Lucrece, The (Shakespeare), 137
Reagan, Ronald, 65, 66, 67
received morality, 128–29
Reformation, 113, 114
release, 111, 118–20
religion, 55, 71, 78–80, 113, 169, 264
  Freud and, 129

Remains of the Day, The (Ishiguro), 236
Republic, The (Plato), 84–85, 137
retirement, 66–67, 256
  401(k) plans for, 259, 270
Return of the Soldier, The (West), 122
revealed preference, 20, 183
rewards, 144–45, 150–52, 168, 172, 211, 215
  and discounting the future, 182–91
  indulgence-promoting, 230
  matching law and, 181
Reynolds, Joshua, 224
Richards, Michael, 5
Richmond, Barry, 213
Rivera, Mariano, 110
Robins, Lee, 195, 206
Robinson, John P., 49
Rodeo Murder, The (Stout), 175
Romalis, John, 251–52
Romans, 112, 213
Romanticism, 110, 118–20
Roosevelt, Eleanor, 70, 73
Roosevelt, Franklin, 70–71, 73, 148
Roth, Philip, 237
Rousseau, Jean-Jacques, 32, 113, 233
Rozelle, Susan, 200
rule-oriented self, 229
running amok, 201–2
Rush, Benjamin, 204
Ryder, Winona, 43

Sabini, John, 218–19
Sacks, Oliver, 228
Sallaz, Jeffrey J., 225
Samuelson, Paul, 20, 183, 186
Sanford, Mark, 78–79
Sartre, Jean-Paul, 225
SAT scores, 104, 107
Scarlet Letter, The (Hawthorne), 235
Schelling, Thomas, 39, 198
school, *see* education and school
Schooler, Jonathan, 173
Schopenhauer, Arthur, 128
Schreck, Christopher J., 196
Schumpeter, Joseph, 46, 224–25
science, 15–16, 246
Science and Human Behavior (Skinner), 178–79
second-order preferences, 12–13, 240, 242, 248, 259, 268, 269
sedentary lifestyle, 17–19, 27, 93
SEED (Save, Earn, Enjoy Deposits), 255–56
self, divided, 132–45
self-concepts, 273

self-control, 161–74
    studies on, 96–109
    see also specific subjects
SelfControl, 51
Self-Control (Brunton), xi
"Self-Control Techniques of Famous
    Novelists" (Wallace), xiii
Self-Help (Smiles), 117
self-talk, 134
Seligman, Martin, 105–6
serotonin, 30, 151, 170, 271
Seven Year Itch, The, 37
sex, 6, 11–12, 45–46, 50, 71, 73, 78, 151, 168,
    220, 221, 247
    addiction to, 205
    brain tumor and, 146–47, 160
    cold and hot states and, 136–37
    Freud and, 124, 125, 128–29
sex offenders, 249
sexually transmitted diseases, 169
sexual masochism, 231–34
Shakespeare, William:
    Hamlet, 28, 90–91
    Othello, 229
    The Rape of Lucrece, 137
shame, 219–21
Shaw, George Bernard, 230
Shea, Dennis, 259
Shefrin, H. M., 137
Shoda, Yuichi, 107
Silver, Maury, 218–19
Simon, Herbert, 39
Simonson, Itamar, 230–31
Simpsons, The, 173–74, 237, 274–75
Sister Carrie (Dreiser), 235, 236
Skinner, B. F., 28, 134, 175–81, 269
Smiles, Samuel, 117
Smith, Adam, 57, 58–59, 62, 113–14, 135, 240
smoking, 6, 17–22, 40, 75, 78, 107, 158, 184,
    206, 209–11, 215, 247
    cigarette purchase requirements, 249
    criminal behavior and, 194
    of Freud, 5, 30–31, 124, 126–28
    genes and, 170
    precommitment devices and, 253, 259–60
    prevalence of, 246
    by women, 168, 169
Sober Champion, 33
social change, 80–80
socialism, 250
social isolation, 77–78, 195, 266
Social Security, 39, 243, 248, 249–50
Sociological Theory of Capital, The (Rae), 182

Socrates, 15, 83, 84, 87, 89, 92, 134, 139–40, 182
soft drinks, 25–26
Solomon, Andrew, 33–34
sophrosyne, 84–86
South Africa, 256
Spanish Civil War, 229
Spenser, Edmund, 88–89
Spinoza, Benedict de, 161
spiritualism, 79
Spitzer, Eliot, 5
SpongeBob SquarePants, 32–33
Stanhope, Philip, 214
Star Trek, 138, 139
Stearns, Peter, 117, 237
Steel, Piers, 214, 222
Steiner, George, 225–26
Stevenson, Betsey, 76
stickK.com, 253–54, 259–60, 266
Stigma: Notes on the Management of Spoiled
    Identity (Goffman), 221
Stockton, John Potter, 243
Stoicism, 112–13, 268
Stout, Rex, 175
Strange Case of Dr. Jekyll and Mr. Hyde, The
    (Stevenson), 118, 135, 235
Strickland, Bonnie R., 98
stroke, 18, 27
Strotz, Robert H., 188–89
Studies in Classic American Literature
    (Lawrence), 119
Sturm, Roland, 24
subconscious, 128–29
sugar, 26
suicide, 19, 28–30, 33–34, 75, 76, 77, 170, 247
    shame and, 220, 221
    among Viennese, 127
Sunstein, Cass, 259
Swerdlow, Russell, 147
Symposium, The (Plato), 87, 95

taboo, 128–29
Taft, William Howard, 25
Talmud, 138, 139, 274
Tangney, June, 195, 220, 221
tattoos, 35, 42–44
Tauchen, George, 207
Tavris, Carol, 201
taxes, 9, 11, 57, 67, 243, 244, 246, 248
    income, withholding of, 257
    on liquor, 207–8, 248
    as precommitment devices, 250
technology, 45–54, 65, 117, 211, 275
    procrastination and, 221–22

teenagers, 157–58, 209
television, 48–49, 237, 250
testosterone, 168
Thaler, Richard, 137, 259
thalidomide, 245–46
Theory of Moral Sentiments, The (Smith),
    135, 240
therapy, 130, 267
    cognitive behavioral therapy, 267–68
    psychoanalysis, 121–24, 128, 130,
        131, 267
Thompson, Paul, 159
Thoreau, Henry David, 119
three-part self, 139–42
Thrift (Smiles), 117
thrift crisis, 245
time inconsistency, 34, 188
Tinbergen, Nikolaas, 153
Tocqueville, Alexis de, 74, 242, 243
Tolstoy, Leo, 165–66, 215, 227
    Anna Karenina, 235
Tooby, John, 148
Tools of the Mind, 108
Torah, 200
Tri-County Land Trust, 56
Trinidad, 97–99, 100, 101
tripartite self, 139–42
Trollope, Anthony, 169, 224, 253
    The Way We Live Now, 14, 169
Trollope, Frances, 224
Tugwell, Rexford, 148
Tversky, Amos, 217
Twain, Mark, 119
    Adventures of Huckleberry Finn, 13, 14
twelve-step programs, 266
"Tying Odysseus to the Mast: Evidence from
    a Commitment Savings Product in the
    Philippines" (Karlan et al.), 255

Ulrich, Laurel Thatcher, 169
Ulysses Unbound (Elster), 237
unconscious, 128–29, 166

values, 72
Vanderbilt, George, 62–63
Vargas Llosa, Mario, 8
Veblen, Thorstein, 61, 62, 63
Victorians, 3, 114, 116–18, 122, 124, 129
violence, 169, 171, 192–202
    domestic, 75, 76
Vohs, Kathleen, 136, 173
Volcker, Paul, 65–66
Vyse, Stuart, 187–88

waiting periods, 47
Walden Two (Skinner), 179
Waldinger, Ernst, 125
Wallace, Irving, xiii, 224
Wall Street Journal, 55, 77
Wansink, Brian, 164–65, 271
war, 39, 40
Watson, Gary, 205
Watson, John B., 177
Way We Live Now, The (Trollope), 14, 169
Weakness of the Will (Gosling), 160
Weatherston, Clayton, 192–93
Weber, Max, 113, 114
Wegner, Daniel, 165–66
weight, 104, 248
    contracts for losing, 251–54
    genes and, 171
    overweight and obesity, 1–2, 8, 10, 17, 18,
        22–28, 47, 48–49, 59, 104, 275
Weininger, Otto, 127
Weinstein, Herbert, 193
Weiss, Nathan, 127, 128
Wells, Max, 151
West, Rebecca, 41, 122
Whitehead, Alfred North, 272
Whitehead, Barbara Dafoe, 68
White Noise (DeLillo), 251
Whitman, Walt, 142
Whyte, William, 64
Wilde, Oscar, 229
    The Importance of Being Earnest, 135
Wilder, Billy, 96
Williams, Edward Higginson, 155
Williams, Robin, 135
willpower, 3, 6–7, 11, 14, 34, 39–40, 88, 93,
    94, 101, 143–44, 147, 160, 171, 228, 244,
    261, 273
    limits of, 247, 262–65
Wilson, James Q., 117
Winslade, Bill, 249
Winthrop, John, 115
Wittgenstein, Ludwig, 37–38, 127
Wolfe, Raymond, 106–7
Wolfers, Justin, 76
women, 168–70
Wood, Wendy, 274
Woods, Tiger, 5, 12
Wordsworth, William, 158
work, 58, 61, 62, 63, 93, 114, 195
    addiction to, 205
    procrastination and, 218, 221–23; *see also*
        procrastination
    Puritans and, 115, 116

workplace safety, 246
World War I, 122
World War II, 6, 63, 65, 229
 Skinner's pigeon experiments during,
 175–78
writing, xi–xiv, 41–42, 223–26, 270–71

Xenophon, 39, 87

yetzer ha-ra and *yetzer ha-tov*, 138, 139
Young Frankenstein, 35–36
youth culture, 47, 64, 72–73, 158

Zaretsky, Eli, 73
Zhong, Chen-Bo, 163–64
Zola, Émile, 224
Zoroaster, 133–34